YEARBOOK IN EARLY CHILDHOOD EDUCATION

W9-DFM-022

Bernard Spodek • Olivia N. Saracho
EDITORS

VOLUME 1
Early Childhood Teacher Preparation
Bernard Spodek and Olivia N. Saracho, Editors

VOLUME 2
Issues in Early Childhood Curriculum
Bernard Spodek and Olivia N. Saracho, Editors

VOLUME 3
Issues in Child Care
Bernard Spodek and Olivia N. Saracho, Editors

VOLUME 4
Language and Literacy in Early Childhood Education
Bernard Spodek and Olivia N. Saracho, Editors

VOLUME 5
Early Childhood Special Education
Philip L. Safford, Editor
with Bernard Spodek and Olivia N. Saracho

VOLUME 6
Meeting the Challenge of Linguistic and Cultural Diversity in Early Childhood Education
Eugene E. Garcia and Barry McLaughlin
with Bernard Spodek and Olivia N. Saracho

YEARBOOK IN EARLY CHILDHOOD EDUCATION

Editorial Advisory Board

The *Yearbook in Early Childhood Education* is a series of annual publications. Each volume addresses a timely topic of major significance in the field of early childhood education, and contains chapters that present and interpret current knowledge of aspects of that topic, written by experts in the field. Key issues—including concerns about educational equity, multiculturalism, the needs of diverse populations of children and families, and the ethical dimensions of the field—are woven into the organization of each of the volumes.

YEARBOOK
IN
EARLY CHILDHOOD EDUCATION
VOLUME 6

MEETING THE CHALLENGE OF LINGUISTIC AND CULTURAL DIVERSITY IN EARLY CHILDHOOD EDUCATION

EDITED BY

Eugene E. García and Barry McLaughlin

WITH

Bernard Spodek and Olivia N. Saracho

TEACHERS COLLEGE PRESS

Teachers College, Columbia University
New York • London

Published by Teachers College Press, 1234 Amsterdam Avenue, New York, NY 10027

Library of Congress Cataloging-in-Publication Data

Meeting the challenge of linguistic and cultural diversity in early
    childhood education / edited by Eugene E. García . . . [et al.].
        p.   cm.—(Yearbook in early childhood education ; v. 6)
    Includes bibliographical references and index.
    ISBN 0-8077-3467-5 (cloth).—ISBN 0-8077-3466-7 (pbk.)
    1. Education, Bilingual—United States. 2. Early childhood
education—United States. 3. Multicultural education—United States.
4. English language—Study and teaching (Early childhood)—Foreign
speakers. I. García, Eugene E., 1946– . II. Series.
LC3731.M44 1995
371.97'00973—dc20   95-4790

Printed on acid-free paper
Manufactured in the United States of America
01 00 99 98 97 96 95   8 7 6 5 4 3 2 1

CONTENTS

v

             and Delivery**   125

             Karen Shu-Minutoli

CHAPTER 9   **Role of Parents in Responding to Issues
             of Linguistic and Cultural Diversity**   141

             *Patricia A. Edwards, Kathleen L. Fear, and
             Margaret A. Gallego*

CHAPTER 10   **Preparing Teachers for Early Childhood
             Programs of Linguistic and Cultural Diversity**   154

             Olivia N. Saracho and Bernard Spodek

CHAPTER 11   **The Future Challenge of Linguistic and Cultural
             Diversity in the Schools**   170

             Olivia N. Saracho and Bernard Spodek

             About the Editors and Contributors   175

             Index   183

Introduction

Eugene E. García and Barry McLaughlin

THE CONTEXT

The main "text" of this volume concerns an increasingly significant number of children in early childhood programs whom we shall refer to as culturally diverse. However, addressing this text requires understanding a broad range of contexts, particularly educational contexts. For instance, the continuing attention to educational reform in this country is a "contextual" marvel (with some 10–20 national reports yearly, ranging from preschool through higher education). These suggested reforms have focused our attention on many variables that today influence our early childhood programs.

Several contextual issues have underlined this ongoing attention to the education of our children.

- Societies—past, present, and future—rest on the fundamental educational capacities of their individual members. In our present, we must prepare our children for the future.
- Our own U.S. society finds itself at a significant competitive disadvantage, which is increasing relative to the "new" global economic context. International trade will be the focus in that developing economy. Presently, between one and ten U.S. jobs are related directly to international trade. In the next 2 decades, it is estimated that over 50% of U.S. jobs will be related to international trade—or the global economy. We will no longer "make and sell" to ourselves.
- Education has become a major activity of noneducational institutions, with only one-third of formal educational endeavors occurring within primary, secondary, and postsecondary educational institutions.
- Although our fathers held one job in one occupation, we have switched jobs various times. Our children will likely change jobs 10 times and change professions between two and three times.
- Only 5–10% of tomorrow's jobs will require less than a high school education, while 30–40% will require at least a high school education, and a whopping

55–65% of tomorrow's jobs will require 3 or more years of postsecondary education.

• About 80% of new jobs will be in the information and service sector of the economy. Employees in these sectors must be flexible, computer literate, creative, highly communicative (preferably in more than one language), and have good people skills.

• We have sustained major value shifts in the past 3 decades. We are being transformed by "new" sexual, recreational, health, environmental, and familial value shifts.

In these new and developing circumstances, what is the role of the early childhood program in the broader context of education and schooling? Early childhood education, and schooling in general, must take on several responsibilities, some similar to and some significantly different from those in the past and present.

1. Education must serve children well with regard to the development of skills—"readin," "ritin," and "rithmetic." We need all individuals to be communicative and literate linguistically, mathematically, and technologically.

2. Education must shift the emphasis to the development of what we call "living" processes that will enhance human relationships, critical thinking, and civic responsibility.

In essence, in the new curriculum of 2000 and beyond, education and schooling must become collaborative, highly social in nature, and process-oriented. Students' lives, even more than our own, will face continuous social, economic, and technological change. As adults, these students will have to be able to react to these changing situations: They will have to act as well-informed individuals, reasonably, with reflection and analysis, no matter what the specific employment, civic, or cultural situation. Of course, this all starts in early childhood.

THE CULTURAL CONTEXT

It is the cultural context that we wish to address in greater detail in this volume. The demographic "facts" have already made California a minority/majority state; in less than 40 years, 70% of California students will be non-Anglo and one-half will speak a language other than English on their first day of school. The same scenario is transforming schools in some 15 other states, including New York, New Jersey, Florida, Michigan, Illinois, and Texas, to name a few. Such transformed states will hold over 50% of the U.S. population.

In short, we are a country of incredible cultural and linguistic diversity. Yet we are singularly nationalistic—"American" to the core and, as of yet, unaccepting of the diversity among us. Recent sociological perception data suggest that over the past 3 decades, "majority" Anglo adults have not changed their view of minority populations—those populations continue to be perceived as lazy, less intelligent, and of lower moral character (Gonzalez, 1990). This is absolutely frustrating, considering that within these 3 decades we have witnessed a civil rights movement, a women's movement, and an equal educational opportunity initiative. Millions of dollars and, more significant, millions of person hours have been dedicated to addressing the inequalities and human injustices of our age.

Many "minorities" have been asked to leave their language and culture at the preschool schoolroom door. In a nationwide survey of families, Wong-Fillmore (1991) found evidence of serious disruptions of family relations when young children learn English in their early childhood years and lose the use of the home language. The study revealed that while language-minority parents recognize the importance of English and want their children to learn it at school, they do not want it to be at the expense of the home language. Many of the parents expressed a concern that their children would lose their language and become estranged from their families and cultural heritage. Other reported that their children had already lost or were losing the language.

An interviewer told the story of a Korean immigrant family in which the young children had all but lost the ability to speak their native language after just a few years in American schools (Wong-Fillmore, 1991). The parents could speak English only with difficulty, and the grandmother, who lived with the family, could neither speak nor understand it. She felt isolated and unappreciated by her grandchildren. The adults spoke to the children exclusively in Korean. They refused to believe that the children could not understand them. They interpreted the children's unresponsiveness as disrespect and rejection. It was only when the interviewer, a bilingual Korean-English speaker, tried to question the children in both languages that the parents finally realized that the children were no longer able to speak or understand Korean. The father wept as he spoke of not being able to talk to his children. One of the children commented that she did not understand why her parents always seemed to be angry.

It may take years before the harm done to families can be fully assessed. One interviewed family that has been in the United States for nearly 20 years told how breakdowns in family communication can lead to the alienation of children from their parents. The four children, now teenagers, had completely lost their ability to speak or understand Spanish as very young children. The children were ashamed of Spanish, it was reported. They did not acknowledge it when their parents spoke it, even though it was the only language the parents knew. The mother indicated that her 17-year-old son was having problems in school. He was often truant and was in danger of dropping out. She had tried to influence him but couldn't because he didn't understand her. Attempts at discussion ended in physical violence, with mother and son "coming to blows" when words failed them (Wong-Fillmore, 1991). It is this marriage of culture and early childhood education that concerns early childhood educators in a diverse cultural society.

DEFINING THE CULTURAL CONTEXT

When we speak of "culture" to which an individual belongs, our reference is generally to the system of understandings (values, prescriptions, proscriptions, beliefs, and other constructs) characteristic of that individual's society, or some subgroup within his or her society—that is, ethnic minorities, social classes, countercultures, generations, genders, and occupational groups. This is the traditional notion of culture employed by functionalist anthropologists in their analyses of the behavioral patterns and normative customs of groups.

The Group-Culture Concept

The culture concept, with its technical anthropological meaning, was first defined by Edward Tylor in 1871 as "that complex whole which includes knowledge, belief, art, law, morals, custom, and other capabilities and habits acquired by man as a member of society" (Kroeber & Kluckhohn, 1963, p. 81). Since Tylor's time a great variety of definitions of culture have been advanced by anthropologists. These definitions commonly attempt to encompass, as did Tylor's, the totality (or some subset of the totality) of humanity's achievements, dispositions, and capabilities. And virtually every anthropologist considers culture to be something that is learned, as it is transmitted from generation to generation.

Most definitions of culture include another social dimension, the notion that culture is something that members of a group share in common. A recently published anthropology textbook states, for example, that behaviors and ideas may be considered cultural only insofar as they are shared among members of a social group (Nanda, 1990). This formulation is useful for anthropological comparisons between societies or subgroups within societies. Its basic assumption, however, is that of uniformity in the cultural equipment of individual members of societies and their subgroupings. In this formulation, the ontological locus of culture is some kind of group.

At the same time, all anthropologists acknowledge that members of all sorts and sizes of societies display differences in their behaviors and ways of thinking and valuing. That is to say, societies are characterized to some extent by intercultural heterogeneity. But such discussions remain most often at the

level of the group, as in statements about the "looseness" or "tightness" of societies' cultural systems. When these researchers proceed to write their ethnographies, their deep descriptions and analysis of a group, they tend to ignore
interindividual variations as they abstract what they apparently consider to be
"an essential homogeneity from the background noise of insignificant diversity"
(Schwartz, 1978, p. 419).

Along these lines, anthropologist Ralph Linton defined culture as "the sum
total of ideas, conditioned emotional responses, and patterns of habitual behavior which the members of [a] society have acquired through instruction or imitation and which they share to a greater or less degree" (quoted in Kroeber &
Kluckhohn, 1963, p. 82). Although acknowledging that cultural items (ideas or
learned behavioral habits) need not be totally shared by everyone in a group,
in this concept it is nevertheless the property of sharing that defines the domain
of culture.

This emphasis on shared traits is relevant to any consideration of the conceptual requirements of understanding the role of culture with respect to education. This emphasis on shared traits leaves little, if any, room for the conceptual recognition of each student's individuality within the framework of the
culture concept. Individuality becomes the domain of psychology, relevant only
to discussions of personality, while the culture concept is reserved for behavioral and ideational features of the individual's group. The latter might be appropriate to the goal of educating (or re-educating) a group, as in modernization
programs applied by developing countries to their peasant populations. But the
focus of education is the education of the individual student, not the education
of his or her ethnic group.

The relevance of this problem lies in the possible consequences of the
group-oriented culture concept for the perceptions and expectations of teachers in their interactions with culturally diverse children. It is our contention
that a group-oriented notion of culture may serve to distract the teacher's attention from important culture-generating processes, in and outside of schooling.
The connection between teacher–student interaction and the culture concept
derives from the fact that assumptions about the student's "culture"—whether
right or wrong—may serve to stereotype the student and thus preclude the
flexible, realistic, and open-minded quality of teacher–student interaction
needed for effective instruction. This possibility becomes more apparent when
one realizes that the educational process is fundamentally a process of social
interaction, with socialization as a primary goal, especially in early childhood.

Picture, if you will, a situation where a teacher is perplexed by some action
or response on the part of a minority child. If the teacher has studied some of
the anthropological ethnographies of the child's ethnic culture, he or she may
leap to an interpretation of the child's behavior in terms of idealized or modal
characteristics attributed to that culture. To construe an individual's behavior

solely on the basis of generalization about group traits is to stereotype the individual, no matter how valid the generalizations or how disinterested one's intentions may be. It would be better for the teacher to pursue the meaning of the child's behavior in the way anthropologists most often come to understand the people they study. Even though they write about cultures in collective terms, they come to know about them through observations of individuals. Of course, the teacher's efforts to understand the individual child could (and should) benefit from knowledge of cultural orientations that are widely, or typically, held in the child's ethnic community. But this fund of knowledge should be viewed only as background information. The question of its applicability to the particular child should be treated as inherently problematical. Many studies (e.g., Rodriguez, 1989; Tharp & Gallimore, 1989) also caution educational personnel against hasty "ethnographic/cultural" generations on the grounds that all linguistic-cultural groups continuously undergo significant cultural changes.

Thomas Carter's (1968) research into the effects of teachers' expectations on student learning and classroom behavior—namely, that Chicano students may sometimes actualize in their behavior the negative expectations held for them by teachers—confirms the concerns expressed here. It may be expected, of course, that this pattern would be less likely among teachers who have elected to teach in Spanish/English, bilingual/bicultural settings. It should be noted, however, that many teachers teach in bilingual/bicultural settings even though they may not be formally designated as such. And even minority teachers may be considered to be in some ways "culturally different"—in terms of generational and acculturational differences—from children of their own ethnic group. This observation is not recent. Guerra (1979) points to linguistic and other cultural variations both within (student–student) and between (student–teacher) generations of bilingual populations. And Cuellar (1980) argues that one's understanding of the meaning and value of culture and language must account for the fact that "a community's characteristics reflect the composition of the different generational cohorts in the different age strata" (p. 198).

The Individual-Oriented Culture Theory

Fortunately, anthropological theory contains a parallel individual-oriented conception of culture developed and used by a number of psychologically oriented anthropologists. As Ted Schwartz (1978) notes, these theorists "invoked the individual in critical response to the superorganic view of culture, which often chose metaphors which would lead one to imagine culture as floating somehow disembodied in the noosphere or, at best, carried by human beings as a conductor might carry an electric current containing information" (p. 434).

An early expression of the individual-oriented concept of culture is seen in the work of another anthropologist, J. O. Dorsey in the 1920s. Sapir (quoted in Pelto & Pelto, 1975) wrote the following about Dorsey's orientation:

> Living as he did in close touch with the Omaha Indians, [Dorsey] knew that he was dealing, not with a society nor with a specimen of primitive man . . . but with a finite though indefinite, number of human beings who gave themselves the privilege of differing from each other not only in matters generally considered as "one's own business" but even on questions which clearly transcended the private individual's concerns. (p. 1)

Advocates of the individual-oriented approach to culture frequently describe a society's culture as a "pool" of constructs (rules, beliefs, values) by which a society's members conceptually order the objects and events of their lives. The participation of individuals in this pool is seen as variable. Spiro (1951), for example, has distinguished between the cultural "heritage" of all members of a society (that which has been made available to them by their predecessors) and each individual's particular cultural "inheritance" (that portion of the group's heritage that he or she has effectively received, or "internalized," from the past). Schwartz (1978) has stressed that the individual also manipulates, recombines, and otherwise transforms inherited constructs. This, together with the outright creation of new constructs, is a major source of cultural change. The individual's own portion of a society's culture is termed by Wallace (1970) as a "mazeway," by Schwartz (1978) as a "idioverse," and by Goodenough (1981) as a "propriocept." This constitutes for these anthropologists the ontological locus of culture.

For some of the anthropologists employing an individual-oriented concept of culture, "the private system of ideas of individuals is culture" (Pelto & Pelto, 1975, pp. 12–13). Other individual-oriented anthropologists, however, reject the implication in such a notion of "individual cultures." As they see it, the contents of one subjective system cannot be considered a culture. Like Schwartz, these theorists consider a cultural system to consist of all the constructs available to a society's members. Nevertheless, the society itself is not the locus of culture; its individual members are. The culture is a distributive phenomenon in that its elements are widely distributed among the individual members of a society. A major implication of this distributive model of culture is a rejection of the traditional assumption of cultural homogeneity; it implies that each individual's portion of the culture differs in some ways from those of the other members of society.

According to Schwartz (1978), Wallace's antidote to the homogeneous view of culture is an overdose in that it leads to the opposite malady of ignoring the degree of cultural sharing that in fact does occur between individuals. Schwartz's own model of culture takes into account both the sharing and non-sharing of cultural constructs between members of a society, and he argues that both are functionally essential to the viability of any society. Diversity, he argues, increases a society's cultural inventory—what any individual could contain within his or her head would make up a very small culture pool—and commonality permits communication and coordination in social life. In Schwartz's words, "it makes as little sense to depict the distribution of a culture among the members of a society as totally heterogeneous and unique in each individual as it did to argue for complete homogeneity. We must dispense with the a priori assumption of homogeneity" (p. 438).

We view Schwartz's formulation as the most appropriate model of culture for addressing issues of culture: simultaneous recognition of a child's "ethnic" culture (children share with their ethnic peers constructs that are not shared with out-group members) and those characteristics that define each person as a relatively unique individual (all individuals are in some ways different from their ethnic peers). It also permits recognition of traits shared with members of the larger culture, such as those acquired through acculturation, of which schooling is a major variable.

Acculturation is a crucial variable in the analysis of ethnic minorities in plural societies, and its processes contribute significantly to the heterogeneity of ethnic cultures. Writing about U.S. "Hispanic" culture, Bell, Kasschau, and Zellman (1976) note, for example, that among Chicanos "many have ancestors who came to North America several centuries ago, but others are themselves recent immigrants. Hence, a simple cultural characterization of [this] ethnic group should be avoided" (p. 7). These authors also caution against a simplistic view of the process of acculturation, noting that it "may not be linear, in the sense that one simply loses certain Mexican attributes and replaces them with Anglo attributes" (pp. 31–32). The process may be characterized more by complex patterns of combination and by ongoing recombination than by simple substitution. Therefore, the degrees of acculturation among individuals contribute to the cultural heterogeneity of any ethnic population, that is, the relative uniqueness of its members.

We might add, parenthetically, that some people are likely to respond to the individual-oriented conception of culture with the question, "What about customs?" Chicanos, for example, might point out that they recognize certain *costumbres* that distinguish them as a group from the larger society. This points to a realm of culture that is highly shared and more likely to belong to the public sphere than to the individual's subjective orientation. Referring to the "layered" nature of culture, anthropologist Benjamin Paul (1965) has observed that:

> what we call customs rest on top and are most apparent. Deepest and least apparent are the cultural values that give meaning and direction to life. Values influence people's perceptions of needs and their choice between perceived alternative courses of action. (p. 200)

What we are emphasizing here is the problematical nature of the variability and sharing of values and other constructs as internalized by individuals. The individual's participation in culture reflects his or her unique set of life experiences. This variable participation and the relative uniqueness of the individual that it engenders is, we believe, no less important for the education of culturally diverse students than the "real" cultural differences between ethnic groups. Education must deal with both.

At the same time we hasten to add that teachers who work with young children from linguistic and/or culturally diverse populations must not only be keenly aware of the instructional objectives of education but must also be knowledgeable about and sensitive to the impact that culture and language have on the children. These affect a child both as an individual and as a member of an ethnic group. Again, education must deal with both.

MEETING THE CHALLENGE

If by understanding diversity and respecting individuality educators can better serve culturally diverse students, is that all that is required? We believe it is not enough. Our culturally diverse populations have been and continue to be highly vulnerable in today's society and in our schools. It is in the best interests of all of us for them to succeed educationally, economically, and socially. They will carry us all to either a bright or a beleaguered future.

Recognizing the present circumstances and the magnitude of this challenge, what is called for? What must early childhood education do? We can suggest several ingredients that might provide answers to these questions.

1. Personal commitment
2. Knowledge of what makes a difference
3. Educational leadership

Personal Commitment

We need not be fooled by any liberal or conservative rhetoric. We have not achieved educational equality for our culturally diverse populations. If we are to make any substantive progress, we will need further resolve. It often is said that with Head Start, school choice, restructuring, site-based management, cooperative learning, whole language, educational technology (computer-assisted instruction), and so forth, we have solved or soon will solve the underachievement of linguistically and culturally diverse populations. Although these new contributions may be important, our own U.S. educational past suggests that we should be doubtful about any miracle cures. No new methodologies, reorganizations, or curriculum will satisfactorily address this problem unless the individuals who implement these initiatives are deeply committed to the enterprise. The change that is necessary must be fueled by the type of social energy that sends us forward with vigorous and consistent resolve. As in the "New Frontier" or "War on Poverty" eras, we must grasp the spiritual importance of this new educational challenge.

More than a decade after Jimmy Carter warned of a crisis of spirit in America, a warning that proved politically disastrous for him and a boon to his rival, Ronald Reagan, a broad spectrum of the nation's social and intellectual leadership is concluding that Carter was right. In fact, they say, the crisis has deepened. It was heresy when Carter declared, "We've always had a faith that the days of our children would be better than our own. We are losing that faith."

A consensus has emerged that a lack of confidence in the future, and in one another, among Americans lies at the heart of the nation's ills. A nation that passed much of the 1970s, in the aftermath of Vietnam, in search of its soul and self spent the 1980s in what many see as a self-consuming materialism and entered the 1990s in a cynical, dispirited mood. "There is disturbing evidence to suggest that most forms of responsibility toward others have eroded in recent decades," Derek Bok, former president of Harvard, asserts in his book, *Universities and the Future of America* (1990). The percentage of people who feel that most individuals in power try to take advantage of others has doubled over the past 2 decades and now exceeds 60 percent.

One source for this analysis is the book *The Cynical Americans* by Donald L. Kanter and Philip H. Mirvis (1989). Based on a national survey of attitudes, Kanter concludes:

> The tendency to behave cynically is being reinforced to an unprecedented degree by a social environment that seems to have abandoned idealism and increasingly celebrates the virtue of being "realistic" in an impersonal, acquisitive, tough-guy world. In citizen and country alike, there seems to be a loss of faith in people and in the very concept of community. A recent national survey found that 43 percent of Americans—and more than half of those under age 24—believe selfishness and fakery are at the core of human nature. (p. 61)

Big majorities of those sampled say they feel most people lie if they can gain by it, sacrifice ethical standards when money is at stake, and pretend to care about others more than they really do.

Some have argued that we have lost the ability to inspire our children. Others go so far as to say we have lost the ability to inspire ourselves. Inspiration is the mother and father of resolve. We cannot afford to be without it. We will need inspiration, resolve, commitment, and passion. Borrowing from Jaime Escalante, the noted educator in the popular film, *Stand and Deliver,* we will need *Ganas*—the *will* to overcome great challenges.

Early childhood educators must commit themselves to bridging their students' familial culture with their own developmentally appropriate culture in their programs. Such commitment often may be difficult. These children and families may seem strange, unaccommodating, and difficult to understand. Many early childhood educators may not have been trained in or have personally experienced this diversity. Yet, these children and families must feel welcomed, nurtured, and valued.

Knowledge

We will also need a new knowledge base. Recent research has redefined the nature of our culturally diverse students' educational vulnerability. It has destroyed both stereotypes and myths and laid a foundation upon which to re-conceptualize present educational practices and launch new initiatives. This foundation recognizes the homogeneity/heterogeneity within and between such populations. Educationally effective practices with linguistically and culturally diverse students have been documented in selected sites throughout the United States (Carter & Chatfield, 1986; García, 1991; Villegas, 1991). The case study approach adopted in these studies included examination of preschool, elementary, and high school classrooms. Teachers, principals, parents, and students were interviewed, and specific classroom observations were conducted that assessed the "dynamics" of the instructional process.

The results of these studies for early childhood provide important insights with regard to general instructional organization, literacy development, academic achievement in content areas like math and science, and the perspectives of students, teachers, administrators, and parents. Interviews with classroom teachers revealed an interesting set of perspectives regarding the education of the students in these schools. Classroom teachers were highly committed to the educational success of their students; perceived themselves as instructional innovators utilizing "new" learning theories and instructional philosophies to guide their practice; continue to be involved in professional development activities, including participation in small-group support networks; had a strong, demonstrated commitment to student–home communication (several teachers were utilizing a weekly parent interaction format); and felt that they had the autonomy to create or change district guidelines. They had high academic expectations for all their students ("everyone will learn to read in my classroom") and also served as an advocate for their students. They rejected any conclusion that their students were intellectually or academically disadvantaged.

In summary, effective early childhood educators recognize that academic development has its roots in sharing "expertise" and experiences through multiple processes of communication. Effective early childhood curricula provide abundant and diverse opportunities for speaking and listening, along with scaffolding to help guide children through the learning process. However, effective programs for diverse children encourage them to take risks, construct meaning, and seek reinterpretations of knowledge within compatible social contexts. Within this knowledge-driven curriculum, skills are tools for acquiring knowledge, not a fundamental target of teaching events. It is this new knowledge that will assist us also in meeting the challenge of our diverse groups of children.

Educational Leadership

Unfortunately, a new knowledge base and commitment/passion/spirit are not enough. We will need leadership, particularly leadership that recognizes the following interlocking domains:

1. *Knowledge transmission.* We will need to disseminate new knowledge to those who can utilize it. This requires training, retraining, and more retraining. Individually and institutionally, new knowledge must be appropriated by those in the field. It is of no use for researchers to share their knowledge only with themselves. New avenues for knowledge dissemination and appropriation are required, as is leadership in this domain.
2. *Skill development.* New knowledge alone does not automatically lead to a new set of pedagogical or curricular skills by practitioners. New knowledge must be transferred/translated to specific instructional contexts. Time and energy must be devoted to the collaboration required to develop new skills. Moreover, these skills must be evaluated "in the field"—they must prove themselves effective. We will need to hold ourselves and others "automatically" accountable. This requires leadership in skill development.
3. *Dispositions for leadership.* "Many are called, but few will self-select." Needed to meet this challenge is a generation of educational leaders who are willing to sacrifice, work very hard and long, take risks, learn from failure, rise above frustration, shift paradigms, and collaborate with and support their colleagues. Also needed is for those who do not possess these dispositions to step aside, minimize obstruction, and otherwise admit that if they cannot be part of the solution, they will not be part of the problem.
4. *Effective engagement.* We will need leadership that embraces our culturally diverse children, adopts them, nurtures them, celebrates them, and challenges them. "They" must become "us." Anything short of raw advocacy every minute, hour, and day will not suffice. We must not give up hope— too many of these students have given up hope in themselves.

Mostly educators need to act. Presidents and governors "proclaim" and set national educational goals; educators need to move beyond such proclamations.

The task at hand is not just to see the future for our culturally diverse children and our present and future culturally diverse society but also to act in ways that enhance that future. The chapters in this volume offer suggestions on how educators are meeting the challenge presented by linguistically and culturally diverse students.

OVERVIEW OF THE TEXT

We were very selective in requesting contributions to the volume. We felt it was important to attempt a comprehensive treatment of this domain of early childhood, while emphasizing a concern for in-depth treatment of significant issues. The first five chapters deal directly with early childhood educational challenges: Second language acquisition, bilingual development, bilingual education, and related programmatic issues. The last five chapters cover broader early childhood and developmental issues that need to be addressed by early childhood educators and child and family support professionals engaged in serving highly diverse populations. Contributors address socialization issues, disability circumstances and the broader role of parental involvement, and professional early childhood teacher preparation. In providing this overview, the volume is an important formulation foundation of critical knowledge related to issues of serving culturally diverse children and families. There are both "do's" and "don'ts," and the conceptual frameworks and related empirical evidence related to them.

Early Childhood Education Program Issues

Rachel Grant in Chapter 1 addresses the specific instructional and program features relevant to effective second language learning in early childhood. This chapter might be used by early childhood instructors and administrators to assess their educational environment as it relates to second language learners.

Chapter 2 by Fred Genesee and Elena Nicoladis addresses the acquisition of two languages by children who live with bilingual parents. Using historical and common trends, the authors examine how the acquisition and development of a second language occurs with children who are bilingual during preschool years. Issues such as language confusion, differentiation, acquisition, and performance are summarized and presented within a cultural and social environment. The authors' treatment of this growing phenomenon sheds light on the developmental attributes that characterize children raised in multilingual environments.

Chapter 3 reports on a follow-up study of a 10-year project initiated in 1980 with a group of kindergarten students. The author, Jim Campos, conducted a series of tests to examine the academic development of students who attended the bilingual preschool program. Standardized data were analyzed to determine the academic and social growth of the students, who at one point were monolingual (non-English) speakers. The results showed that the students' use of their first language was not hampered by the acquisition of English; instead, students seem to have been aided in learning English by first learning their dominate language. This longitudinal study destroys the myth that bilingual education in early childhood is "bad medicine." It is studies like this that allow early childhood educators to support their own efforts to enhance bilingual development while ensuring themselves and parents that children are not placed at academic risk.

In Chapter 4, Celia Genishi and Margaret Borrego Brainard engage the significant challenge of assessment of linguistically and culturally diverse students. In their discussion, there are more "don'ts" than "do's." Treating diverse children in ways that reliably and validly assess their abilities and potentials has not yet achieved the status of sound psycho-educational practice. Nevertheless, the authors' treatment of this important area is clear and comprehensive.

Chapter 5 adds more to the "don't" column. Howard Smith and Paul Heckman, in a highly articulate case study, address the omnipresent tension in schooling endeavors that attempt to selectively meet the needs of English speakers and non-English speakers. Schools, as products of the communities they serve, can perpetuate these divisions or diminish the differences. Using longitudinal and qualitative data, the authors discuss a playground incident that vividly illustrates how perceptions of language and culture can segregate and alienate students. The chapter seems to suggest that such social stratification is neither inevitable nor impossible to change. Teachers in this school construct new beliefs as new actions are undertaken in response to linguistic and cultural differences found within the institution. As members of the school community reflect upon and redefine schooling practices, they also confront new issues and tensions that require more effective ways to organize children and adults. This work begins to address a central issue in early childhood and school reform, How can conditions be created in a school setting that foster a critical examination of existing practices and the development of positive alternatives that respond to ever-evolving issues and tensions?

Developmental, Family, and Service Provider Issues

The remaining chapters in this volume address broader familial and service issues that go beyond the critical issues of development, learning, and teaching in early childhood education contexts. Chapter 6 by George Knight, Martha Bernal, and Gustavo Carlo provides a theoretical framework based on recent conceptual and empirical advances. The model focuses on the development of cooperative, competitive, and individualistic behaviors. Particularly, references center on how socialization affects ethnic groups and how value systems encourage or discourage the distribution of reward. The argument is that socialization and the development of a value system are directly affected by social forces in an individual's environment. In essence, the child's experiences in the "culture" of the family cannot be ignored in the educational/service environment that we construct. Bridges between those experiences and early childhood support programs are critical.

Francisco Villarruel, David Imig, and Marjorie Kostelnik in Chapter 7 expand on this theme. Cultural diversity is explored in its varying intricacies. Human development occurs in cultural contexts. To view human development as independent from the social context in which it unfolds, both affected by and affecting that context, is not new. But conceptually and in practice, diversity in those contexts, embodied in the diversity in our nation's families, must concern early childhood educators throughout the functions we perform. Moreover, if our children are our future, the diversity must be considered a resource, not a problem.

Karen Shu-Minutoli authors Chapter 8, which details the way services and support are delivered to families and in particular to families with severely developmentally disabled young children. In her discussion, Shu-Minutoli provides a detailed definition of family diversity and its relation to the Individualized Family Services Plan and the Education of the Handicapped Act Amendments of 1986 (Public Law 94–457). The chapter centers around family support and its implications. The chapter concludes by offering constructive and practical suggestions to support diverse families.

Chapter 9 by Patricia Edwards, Kathleen Fear, and Margaret Gallego offers a detailed historical account of major legal cases that allowed parents to become more active in their children's education. The writers provide insightful case studies related to the struggles of African American and Hispanic families to make their educational systems reflect their values and way of life. The chapter centers around the theme of how parents of "minority" children are expanding the definition of parental involvement. Culturally diverse parents not only provide academic support but also maintain cultural ties, promote language development, and hold high academic expectations. Overall, the chapter reminds us about the great and dynamic influence parents can bring to schools and institutions, particularly parents that are usually written off as nonparticipants.

Olivia Saracho and Bernard Spodek in Chapter 10 address the most critical aspect of our present and future challenge to enhance early childhood programs' responsiveness and efficacy for our diverse populations. We know of no early childhood educator or service provider who is performing her or his responsibilities without a deep personal and professional commitment to children and families. Yet, many of them do not have the knowledge base and related skills to address the challenges of diversity. Commitment is a critical ingredient, but, without substantive training, that commitment is not enough. This chapter provides an overview of professional preparation issues. It is a useful guide for those already in the profession, for those preparing to enter the profession, and for those engaged in providing that preparation.

CONCLUSION

In this Introduction, we have tried to set the "context" for a more thorough discussion of the educational challenges facing this country's early childhood educators, for all children and specifically for our culturally diverse children. This country's educational future will be very different from our educational past. We will need to respond to a variety of structural, global, and value transformations. Moreover, we will do this with a highly diverse set of students who will provide a particularly challenging set of agendas. Historically, our schools' efforts have been flawed conceptually and have not produced academic success for all students. However, new conceptual insights, new research, and new educational practices suggest that we can meet this challenge successfully.

In the chapters of this volume, our colleagues will more clearly define the notions of culture introduced here and the related social, cultural, linguistic, and related knowledge bases that are relevant to meeting this challenge. This volume must be understood as a forum through which knowledge about children, families, communities, and schools can be transmitted. That knowledge must be combined with action on the part of educators if the challenges we have articulated are to be met head on and successfully overcome.

REFERENCES

Bell, D., Kasschau, P., & Zellman, G. (1976). *Delivering services to elderly members of minority groups: A critical review of the literature.* Santa Monica, CA: Rand Corporation.

Bok, D. (1990). *Universities and the future of America.* Durham, NC: Duke University Press.

Carter, T. P. (1968). The negative self-concept of Mexican-American students. *School and Society, 96,* 217–219.

Carter, T. P., & Chatfield, M. L. (1986). Effective bilingual schools: Implications for policy and practices. *American Journal of Education, 95*(1), 200–234.

Cuellar, J. B. (1980). A model of Chicano culture for bilingual education. In R. Padilla (Ed.), *Ethnoperspectives in bilingual education research: Vol. II. Theory in bilingual education* (pp. 179–204). Ypsilanti: Eastern Michigan University, Department of Foreign Languages and Bilingual Studies.

García, E. (1991). Bilingualism, second language acquisition in academic contexts. In A. M. Ambert (Ed.), *Bilingual education and English as a second language: A research annual* (pp. 181–217). New York: Garland.

Gonzalez, G. (1990). *Chicano education in the segregation era: 1915–1945.* Philadelphia: Balch Institute.

Goodenough, W. H. (1981). *Culture, language, and society* (2nd ed.). Menlo Park, CA: Benjamin/Cummings.

Guerra, M. H. (1979). Bilingualism and biculturalism: Assets for Chicanos. In A. Trejo (Ed.), *The Chicanos: As we see ourselves* (pp. 129–136). Tucson: University of Arizona Press.

Kanter, D. L., & Mirvis, P. H. (1989). *The cynical Americans: Living and working in an age of discontent and disillusion.* San Francisco, CA: Jossey-Bass.

Kroeber, A. L., & Kluckhohn, D. (1963). *Culture: A critical review of concepts and definitions.* New York: Vintage Books.

Nanda, S. (1990). *Cultural anthropology.* New York: D. Van Nostrand.

Paul, B. (1965). Anthropological perspectives on medicine and public health. In J. K. Skipper, Jr., & R. C. Leonard (Eds.), *Social interaction and patient care* (pp. 195–206). Philadelphia: J. B. Lippincott.

Pelto P., & Pelto, G. H. (1975). Intra-cultural variation: Some theoretical issues. *American Ethnologist, 2*(1), 1–45.

Rodriguez, C. E. (1989). *Puerto Ricans born in the U.S.A.* Winchester, MA: Unwin Hyman.

Schwartz, T. (1978). Where is the culture? Personality as the distributive locus of culture. In G. Spindler (Ed.), *The making of psychological anthropology* (pp. 137–156). Berkeley: University of California Press.

Spiro, M. E. (1951). Culture and personality: The natural history of a false dichotomy. *Psychiatry, 14,* 19–46.

Tharp, R. G., & Gallimore, R. (1989). *Challenging cultural minds.* London: Cambridge University Press.

Villegas, A. M. (1991). *Culturally responsive pedagogy for the 1990s and beyond.* Princeton, NJ: Educational Testing Service.

Wallace, A. F. C. (1970). *Culture and personality* (2nd ed.). New York: Random House.

Wong-Fillmore, L. (1991). When learning a second language means losing the first. *Early Childhood Research Quarterly, 6*(3), 323–347.

CHAPTER 1

Meeting the Needs of Young Second Language Learners

Rachel Grant

In recent years, demographic shifts in population have offered opportunities for teachers at all levels to teach students who come from increasingly more diverse backgrounds. Statistics from the United States Census Bureau confirm that immigrants to the United States during the 1980s represented greater ethnic, racial, and socioeconomic diversity than at any time earlier in this century. In a stark contrast to immigration patterns at the turn of the century, three out of four immigrants who now enter this country each year come from non-Western European countries. Many recent immigrants have left their homes—in Southeast Asia, Central America, and Eastern Europe—to escape war, political turmoil, and poverty. Statistics indicate that the nonwhite population reached 25% of the total population in the 1980s, a 20% increase from the previous decade. Current U.S. immigration laws ensure that the diversification of the population will continue (Lewis, 1991).

Classrooms throughout the United States now represent a variety of ethnic, racial, and cultural groups as well as the languages and dialects of many countries. The shift toward greater linguistic and cultural heterogeneity in our nation's schools has been widely covered by the popular press. Recently, one newspaper reported on the impact of immigration trends on the schools of several counties. According to the article, in one county the number of foreign-born students was increasing nearly 20% annually. In another county the international student population was 16,000 and included students from 150 countries who spoke 101 different languages. A third county reported more than 17,000 foreign-born students from 150 countries, speaking 75 languages (Odum, 1993). Clearly, the education of nonnative speakers of English has become an important issue for our schools. This chapter sorts out some of the issues that surround language diversification and examines its implications for the education of young children. Mainstream educators of young children who

1

have not had special training in teaching young second language learners may wish to use this chapter as a springboard for finding out more about how they can better serve the needs of young language-minority learners in their classrooms. The first section begins with a definition of second language learners. Next, some dimensions of second language proficiency are presented that help to shape a framework for determining how our schools might deal with language-minority learners. In the third section, the issues of culture that affect second language learners in school environments are explored. The final section discusses some instructional practices that have been used successfully with young second language learners.

WHO ARE SECOND LANGUAGE LEARNERS?

Second language often refers to the chronology of language acquisition (Bernhardt, 1991). In educational settings, young learners who speak no or very little English fall into two general categories. The first includes those children who come to this country at a very young age or are born here to immigrants who have lived in areas of the world where the language as well as the culture, systems of government, and social structures are quite unlike those of the United States. The second category comprises learners who are native born, such as Native Americans or Alaskan natives, yet enjoy different languages, personal histories, and cultures. The terms "bilingual learner," "English as a second language (ESL) student," "students who have limited English proficiency" (LEP), "language-minority learner," "second language learner" (SLL), "English language learner" (ELL), "linguistically and culturally diverse" (LCD), and "linguistically diverse student" refer to students whose first language is not English and whose cultural backgrounds differ from those of middle-class white children (Reyes, 1992). Although there may be similar concerns for students who speak dialects of English, such as black English or Appalachian English, the discussion in this chapter is limited to students whose first languages contain a linguistic base that is syntactically, phonetically, semantically, and rhetorically distinct from English.

IMPORTANT DIMENSIONS OF SECOND
LANGUAGE PROFICIENCY

Students may vary considerably in language proficiency skills in both their native language (L1) and a target language (L2). Young second language students in particular are less likely to possess highly developed literacy skills in reading or writing. Teachers who have not received special training may mistake a lack of language skill for low intellectual capacity. As a consequence, SLLs may be placed in the lowest groups, where they encounter inadequate role models and receive instruction that is based on a watered-down version of the curriculum (Reyes & Molner, 1991; Ryder & Graves, 1994). The first part of this section discusses indicators that have been used by school personnel to judge whether a second language student is ready to receive subject matter instruction in a mainstream setting. Definitions of some of the terms that have been used to characterize the levels of language proficiency for second language learners are presented. The second part of this section is devoted to a discussion of the elements of surface fluency and conceptual-linguistic knowledge, and linguistic interdependence. The latter has helped to shape the theoretical framework of language proficiency and the approaches to instruction for second language learners. Experts in the fields of education, linguistics, and psychology continue to formulate theories about the best means by which children can acquire second language proficiency. In this discussion, two important dimensions of language proficiency—basic communicative skills and academic achievement skills—are covered. However, explanations or resolutions of the issues regarding language acquisition and academically related aspects of second language learning are beyond the scope of this work.

Determining Language Proficiency

How do schools determine when a student is proficient enough in a language to receive English only instruction in content areas? Over time, a number of somewhat arbitrary factors have been used including age on arrival, that is, the age at which an individual entered the country in which the second language is spoken, and length of residence or number of months or years of second language exposure, both inside and outside of the formal classroom (Collier, 1989). Two other factors have been used somewhat consistently to judge whether a child has attained enough English language development to be mainstreamed into a regular classroom: the student's reading level and the amount of language instruction the child has received (Grant & Wong, 1994).

The goal of teaching a child to read a language is paramount in education. According to Saville-Troike (1984), "academic achievement in reading and in content areas—not just the learning of English—has a clear priority in our curriculum" (p. 199). Indeed for many educators, reading English is the only measure used to determine literacy. In some cases reading performance levels on standardized tests are used to indicate whether second language learners are ready to be mainstreamed. Tests such as the Comprehensive Test of Basic Skills (CTBS), a standardized group-administered instrument, and the Woodcock Reading Test (WRT), a standardized individual reading assessment measure, have been used to compare the reading achievement of SLL and native speakers. Gunderson (1984) compared the test scores of native and nonnative speakers in grades 3, 4, and 5 on the CTBS and WRT. The comparisons of students' scores yielded several interesting findings about how young native English speakers and second language speakers performed on the measures. Most notably, Gunderson pointed out that when compared with native speakers, the scores of SLLs varied more, depending on the instrument used. Gunderson cautioned teachers to be aware that group-administered standardized measures of reading ability may tend to overestimate the reading level of language-minority learners, and individually administered standardized measures of reading ability may tend to underestimate the reading level of these learners. Importantly, although a second language student's reading level may be identical with a native speaker's or may vary somewhat, teachers should be aware that students come to the classroom with skills in reading and overall literacy development that may not be adequately represented by a standardized test score.

A second factor that schools often use to determine if a student is ready to be mainstreamed for all or part of the school day is the amount of special English instruction the child has received. Several types of programs have been used to deliver English instruction to second language learners. Bilingual and ESL programs are available to most students. According to García (1992), ESL and bilingual education program initiatives in public school did not surface until the mid-1960s. Title VI of the 1964 Civil Rights Act was the major piece of legislation that made possible a mechanism for addressing the educational needs of language-minority learners. In 1968 the Bilingual Education Act (Title VII) became law. Title VII was enacted to support programs for language-minority children; however, support was limited to families having low incomes. In 1974 the low-income criterion was eliminated and in 1978 Title VII was expanded to include all language-minority students, even those whose speaking/listening abilities were adequate, but who still needed considerable help in reading and writing English (Crawford, 1989).

Presently, a wide variety of school programs are available to second language learners. However, great disparities exist among programs in terms of the theory-based approaches used to frame instruction, the personnel responsible for program delivery, and the quality of programs. Peregoy and Boyle (1993) pointed out that the range of programs extends from those carefully tailored to meet students' specific linguistic and cultural needs to programs in which very little is done differently to accommodate them. In an effort to distinguish among the many programs offered to SLLs, it is best to note that programs generally are either bilingual, offering literacy instruction in both the native language and English, or monolingual, in which literacy instruction is offered only in English. Many special language programs may last 2–3 years. However, longitudinal studies indicate that it may take between 5 and 7 years for second language students to approximate native speakers' norms (Collier, 1989). As a rule, the students remain in a special language class until they acquire at least the "minimal oral language skills" necessary to enter the regular classroom.

Language programs offered to SLLs vary in fundamental ways. Frequently, there are differences in the amount of time per day or number of times a week devoted to instruction. Also, the method of language instruction, audiolingual or interactive approaches, differs. Generally, school districts that have larger populations of immigrant learners tend to devote more resources to language instruction for second language students. For example, in the Washington, D.C. metropolitan area during the 1992–1993 school year, the enrollment for students with limited English skills was approximately 38,000. Schools located in counties with larger SLL enrollments had fairly comprehensive programs that provided students with an average of 2 hours of daily ESOL (English for speakers of other languages) instruction. In schools where fewer SLLs were enrolled, students received no more than 35–45 minutes a week of ESOL. In one second-grade ESOL class, the following account was given to depict the teacher's frustration:

> On a recent Wednesday, [the teacher] used play money in a lesson for the fidgeting youngsters, who included a girl from Vietnam, one from Hong Kong, one from Russia, and a Cambodian-Hispanic boy. "What would you do with $20 of birthday money?" [the teacher] asked, instructing her pupils to write their answers in a sentence. Two students appeared confused, while two others immediately seized their pencils. . . . By the time they wrote and read their sentences aloud, class was over. (Sevilla, 1994, p. 5)

A second way in which programs can differ is the type of English instruction they provide. Young children who are mainstreamed into English-only classrooms for subject matter instruction may emerge from special language classes where any number of pedagogical decisions have influenced the type of English instruction they have received, as well as whether their language instruction has included the basic rudiments of reading and writing in their native language or English. Gunderson (1991) noted that some researchers maintain that second language learners should not be taught to read or engage in content-specific instruction (e.g., social studies and science) until they have become orally proficient in English, while others suggest students should be involved regardless. Even when students receive language instruction over extended periods of time, it may be that "audiolingualism"—which involves mimicry, memorization, and pattern drills—was the dominant paradigm for teaching nonnative speakers. Students who are taught to speak with audiolingual methods may have flawless English. However, they may not possess an understanding of language that increases their cognitive academic proficiency in the classroom (Cummins, 1984).

Even those SLLs who receive language instruction that includes English reading may be taught to read English using skills-based or phonics approaches which often utilize short-term literacy tasks. Often, "breaking the code" or correct pronunciation is the major goal. In recent years, much of the reading instruction for native speakers has utilized literature-based approaches, but this may not always be so when language-minority learners are involved. (For more information about approaches to curricular design in reading for SLLs, see Dubin, Eskey, & Grabe, 1986; Gunderson, 1991; Peregoy & Boyle, 1993.)

As the result of the different special language instruction offered to students, mainstream teachers encounter language-minority learners who have attained different levels of bilingualism. Terms such as "additive bilingualism," "dominant bilingualism," and "semilingualism" have been used to distinguish the ways in which learners have achieved proficiency in their native languages and English. According to Cummins (1979) and Skutnabb-Kangas and Toukomaa (1976), those students who are additive bilingual have high levels of language development in both languages, L1 and L2. Dominant bilingual learners have attained native-like language skills in one language, L1 or L2. Semilingual learners may have low levels of language proficiency in both languages. In this case, the development in both languages may be fairly balanced, or one of the languages may slightly dominant over the other.

Understanding Levels of Attainment

To more fully understand how the level of language development might affect a student's performance in the classroom, it is important to note that levels of language attainment also reflect the amount of surface fluency and conceptual-linguistic knowledge that a learner possesses. Skutnabb-Kangas and Toukomaa (1976) were among the first to make the distinction between surface fluency in a language and academically related aspects of language proficiency. In a body of work that examined the schooling of Finnish students in Sweden, these researchers noted the basic communicative skills and cognitive academic development of children at different ages and different levels of language proficiency in their native language (Skutnabb-Kangas, 1979; Skutnabb-Kangas & Toukomaa, 1976). Skutnabb-Kangas and Toukomaa found that relatively young children, preschoolers, and children ages 6 to 8 were able to communicate in peer-appropriate ways. That is, within less formal contexts (e.g., play situations) the Finnish children used verbal and nonverbal skills to communicate with their peers. However, in formal classroom situations that required the children to use the target language to demonstrate cognitive/academic skills, these children were not as successful. Skutnabb-Kangas (1979) found that slightly older, 9- to 11-year-old Finnish school children who had recently arrived in Sweden after several years of schooling in Finland demonstrated significantly higher levels of cognitive academic skills in the Swedish language than did younger, 6- to 8-year-old Finnish students who had received almost all of their schooling in

Sweden. Even after accounting for developmental differences due to age, the competence in their native language that the older students had already developed at the time of intensive exposure to the Swedish language was cognitively and academically beneficial in L1. This early work pointed out the differences between the development of language skills for basic communicative survival and academically related communication. Additionally, the results of this work later would provide the impetus for examining the linguistic interdependence of first and second language development.

The distinction between basic communicative language and language development for academic purposes can be applied to a broad range of theoretical and educational situations. Included among these is the hypothesis that the level of language development in a first language can facilitate linguistic proficiency in another language, depending on the language skills a student possesses in a native language. In an explanation of linguistic interdependence and the educational development of bilingual children, Cummins (1979) proposed a model of bilingual education in which educational outcomes are explained as a function of the interaction between sociocultural, linguistic, and school program factors. Cummins argued that only a model of bilingual education that considered the complex interactions of several variables could be used to explain or evaluate the outcomes of bilingual education. In this seminal work Cummins formulated and combined two hypotheses, developmental interdependence and threshold, to support the central thesis that "a cognitively and academically beneficial form of bilingualism can be achieved only on the basis of adequately developed first language skills" (p. 222). The threshold hypothesis is concerned with the cognitive and academic consequences of different patterns of bilingual skills. (For more information about linguistic interdependence and threshold, see Cummins, 1979; Collier, 1989.)

Building on the work of Skutnabb-Kangas, Cummins (1988) formalized the terms "basic interpersonal communicative skills" (BICS) and "cognitive/academic language proficiency" (CALP) in an effort to explain why language-minority learners appeared to have little trouble communicating in a target language within certain contexts of the school. According to Cummins, BICS refers to the "manifestation of language proficiency in everyday communicative contexts, whereas CALP indicates the manipulation of language in decontextualized academic situations" (p. 382).

Cummins later extended the application of BICS and CALP to educational settings by applying the concepts to Bloom's taxonomy of educational objectives (Bloom & Krathwohl, 1977). Cummins proposed that BICS represented

Knowledge—remembering something previously encountered or learned
Comprehension—grasping basic meaning, without necessarily relating it to other material
Application—using abstractions in particular and concrete situations

On the other hand, CALP involves

Analysis—breaking down a whole into its parts so that the organization of elements is clear
Synthesis—putting elements into a coherent whole
Evaluation—judging the adequacy of ideas or material for a given purpose

Saville-Troike (1984) examined several of the background, child input, and educational treatment factors proposed by Cummins, to explain why a group of children who had been matched for English proficiency and socioeconomic status (SES) when they started a school year, and who were subsequently taught and tested through the medium of English, differed in their school achievement at the end of that year. Saville-Troike considered variables that included relative productive competence in English morphology, syntax, and vocabulary; verbosity; patterns of social interaction; first language performance; and personality.

The subjects in this study were children in grades 2–6 and ranging in age from 6 years, 11 months to 12 years. Criteria for subject selection were (1) very little or no prior exposure to English, (2) well-educated families (at least one parent possessing a graduate degree), and (3) initial literacy in their native language. Several generalizations are drawn that examine further the linguistic interdependence hypothesis. The findings have relevance for ESL curriculum organization and instructional practice. Saville-Troike concluded that vocabulary knowledge is the single most important area of second language competency when learning content through that language is the dependent variable; grammatical accuracy is of little importance to students' immediate academic needs; communicative competence in social interaction does not guarantee communicative competence in academic situations; and the use of the first language enhances conceptual development, even when it is tested through the second language.

Although the theories framed by Cummins do not exhaust all possible explanations for the differences between language acquisition and academically related aspects of second language proficiency, the notion of BICS and CALP does offer important implications for classroom practices. First, the framework used by Cummins is informative in terms of providing an explanation for how language-minority learners might acquire peer-appropriate second language conversational proficiency sooner than they acquire peer-appropriate academic proficiency. This factor suggests that SLLs may need more time in bilingual programs in order to narrow the gap between their basic interpersonal language skills and academic language skills. Second, teachers need to carefully plan activities, so that SLLs will develop cognitive academic competence through the medium of the target language. Finally, school personnel and classroom teachers need to consider social, personality, and motivational factors as well as economic and other background variables when planning curricula for young second language learners.

CULTURAL INFLUENCES IN THE CLASSROOM

Peregoy and Boyle (1993) define culture as "the shared beliefs, values, and rule-governed patterns of behavior that define a group and require group membership" (p. 8). Peregoy and Boyle proposed that culture comprises three essential aspects: what people know and believe, what people do, and what people make and use. In the classroom SLLs face many situations that may question or disregard the acquired knowledge they use to both interpret experience and generate behavior. For example, how are children disciplined and by whom, how do girls interact with boys, and how are individual effort and group effort perceived. SLL children often have a history and culture that are distinctly different from those who use the language for wider communication (Grant & Wong, 1994). Often a second culture contains a unique set of cultural assumptions and behavioral norms. Bernhardt (1991) stated that "while a second culture may share a value system that overlaps to an extent with another culture, it does not share exactly the same sociopolitical history" (p. 3). In other words, the classroom adjustment that SLLs experience is influenced by the degree of social, political, and psychological distance between the learner and the majority language culture.

Recognizing the Importance of Culture

Many teachers often fail to consider the extent to which SLLs are influenced by the beliefs and practices of their native culture (Grant & Wong, 1994). The language-minority learner is a product of a culture that may have very different ideas about how students behave in educational settings (Dubin, Eskey, & Grabe, 1986). In the case of very young learners, García (1991) emphasized that preserving their cultural heritage is important to the identity and sense of well-being for the children and their families: "Culture and linguistic identity provides a strong and important sense of self and family belonging, which in turn supports a wide range of learning capabilities, not the least of which is learning a second language" (p. 2). For young children, language development and learning about one's culture are closely linked. García suggests that caregivers and teachers (1) be well-trained, sensitive providers who speak the same language as the child and represent the child's cultural group, or (2) regardless of their own language background and cultural heritage, become educated about and sensitive to issues of language and culture.

Cummins (1986) argued forcefully for considering the interplay between power relations and the language-culture of schools. Cummins contended that the intergroup power relations that exist within classrooms determine the extent to which students' language and culture are incorporated into the school program and constitute a significant predictor of academic success. He noted that considerable research data suggest that "students' school success appears to reflect both the more solid cognitive/academic foundation developed through intensive target language instruction and the reinforcement of their cultural identity" (p. 376). Further, Cummins pointed out that when language-minority learners are not alienated from their own cultural values, they do not experience widespread school failure. Moreover, when SLLs are positively oriented toward both their own and the dominant culture they do not perceive themselves as inferior and thus school performance improves (Cummins, 1984; Heath, 1983; Ogbu, 1978; Troike, 1978). There are several examples of the positive results that occur when culture is used to help SLLs succeed in the classroom. The Kamehameha Early Education Program (KEEP) in Hawaii is an example of the important role that culture can play in children's academic success. KEEP was established as a research and development center to meet the educational needs of native Hawaiian children. These ethnic language-minority children were not achieving well in school, especially in reading (Au & Jordan, 1981). To address the concern for student academic achievement, a communication feature that incorporated the children's home culture into reading lessons was introduced into primary classrooms. Instead of traditional classroom discussions of stories, discussion was adjusted to incorporate the Hawaiian storytelling tradition of conarration to which children were accustomed. The major differences between Hawaiian talk story and mainstream classroom speech events are that talk story entails a high proportion of taking turns involving joint performance, and cooperative production of a response by two or more children. The tradition of joint narration in Hawaiian storytelling is more than just a means for conveying information; it also serves to affirm the relationship between the conarrators.

In addition to incorporating features of the culture, the KEEP program used a system of instruction that challenged students but provided support, assistance, and encouragement. The KEEP program borrowed largely from a concept about learning and development introduced by Russian psychologist Lev Vygotsky (1896–1934). Teaching, Vygotsky (1962) urged, must aim not at today's, but at tomorrow's, development. Vygotsky used this concept, the "zone of proximal development," to advocate that children need to be challenged, but with support and encouragement so that they can exercise their next level of development. An important result of KEEP has been that, over time, reading achievement scores increased and have remained at national-norm levels for over a decade. (For more information about the KEEP program, see Au & Jordan, 1981; Peregoy & Boyle, 1993.)

Using Culture to Enhance Learning

Cazden (1986) contended that differences in culture as well as language can pose barriers to excellence for language-minority children in our schools. Further, she noted that when teachers fail to fight against these barriers to educational achievement, children are placed at very high risk—risk of failure and risk of dropping out of school. To help eradicate the barriers to excellence that culture may pose for SLLs, Cazden offered several practical suggestions to teachers, which included

1. Using children's own words as beginning reading texts, instead of imported basal readers. This might be accomplished by creating illustrated books out of children's "key words" such as ball, car, and chair.
2. Including peer collaboration in learning centers organized for practice of academic skills. Teachers might allow children to practice following and giving directions for basic literacy tasks such as turning pages during reading, using pictures to tell a story, telling a story in sequence, and noting the names of main characters in a story.
3. Allowing for voluntary participation instead of strictly enforced turn-taking, teacher-led reading lessons.
4. Creating new reading texts. Teachers might have students dictate stories about special personal events.
5. Reorganizing the classroom social structure. Teachers should try different grouping techniques so that SLL as well as native speakers have opportunities to serve as authorities and participants in group activities.

Cazden encourages teachers to become sociolinguistically knowledgeable so that they will be more empathetic and at least give culturally different children the benefit of the doubt.

Given the variety and mobility among second language groups, it is likely that most teachers will at some time encounter students whose language and culture they know little about (Peregoy & Boyle, 1993). Interestingly, although half of all public school teachers in the United States in 1980 had language-minority students in their classes, only 1 in 17 had any preservice or inservice training in teaching second language learners (Hamayan, 1990). This fact may be due in part to teaching certification practices. Surprisingly, only 33 states and the District of Columbia offer teaching certification in ESL. Regardless of certification practices, all teachers will need to establish procedures for implementing frameworks of culture into their classrooms. The remainder of this section presents some factors teachers of young children might consider for using second language culture in their classrooms.

Saville-Troike (1978) proposed a guide to culture in the classroom by outlining the content of culture. The component parts of culture were categorized as: (1) family structure; (2) definitions of stages, periods, or transitions during a person's life; (3) roles of children and adults and corresponding behavior in terms of power and politeness; (4) discipline; (5) time and space; (6) religion; (7) food; (8) health and hygiene; and (9) history, traditions, holidays, and celebrations.

Peregoy and Boyle (1993) extended the guide to culture in the classroom by adding a number of questions that teachers should ask about their own culture and the cultures of the students, including

1. *Family structure:* What constitutes a family? Who among these or others live in one house? What is the hierarchy of authority?
2. *Life cycle:* What are the criteria for defining stages, periods, or transitions in life? What rites of passage are there?
3. *Roles and interpersonal relationships:* What roles are available to whom, and how are they acquired? Is education relevant to learning these roles?
4. *Discipline:* What is discipline? What counts as discipline and what does not?
5. *Time and space:* How important is punctuality? Speed in completing a task?
6. *Religion:* What restrictions are there concerning topics that should not be discussed in school?
7. *Food:* What is eaten? In what order? How often?
8. *Health and hygiene:* How are illnesses treated and by whom? What is considered to be the cause?
9. *History, traditions, holidays:* Which events and people are a source of pride for the group? To what extent does the group in the United States identify with the history and traditions of the country of origin? What holidays and celebrations are considered appropriate for observing in school? (For a more complete description of the guide to culture and the questions for teachers, see Peregoy & Boyle, 1993, pp. 8–10.)

Answers to these and other questions about cultures will help teachers to analyze the level of cultural congruence in the patterning of teacher–pupil interaction, identify cross-cultural similarities and differences, and utilize aspects of culture to help children achieve.

INSTRUCTIONAL PRACTICES

Teachers need to be thoughtful about the instructional approaches, materials, strategies, and tasks they use in their classrooms with language-minority learners. Many of the instructional programs that are used with native speakers require adaptation of instructional strategies and techniques for SLLs (Maldonado-Colon, 1991). As educators begin to direct more attention to meeting the needs of SLLs, teachers will be able to use more effective approaches to help students. Although much research is needed, many of the methodologies and practices that have been used with first language learners also may be of benefit to language-minority students. This section presents the salient features of several instructional approaches that have been used with second language learners.

Cooperative Learning

Cooperative learning approaches are widely used in classrooms with young children. Although classroom formats and applications vary considerably, cooperative learning models are usually described as those in which there is positive interdependence among a group of students in the learning process, and each student is both individually accountable for his or her own learning and responsible for other group members' learning as well (Sapon-Shevin & Schniedewind, 1992).

In many situations working in cooperative groups can benefit both native speakers and second language speakers because they receive equal attention from teachers and equal opportunities to learn from each other (Reyes & Molner, 1991). According to Johns (1992), cooperative grouping helps language-minority students by: (1) allowing the students to hear and produce English in a nonthreatening, secure environment; (2) creating an atmosphere where children can better understand assignments and adjust to the culture of the school; (3) creating a supportive climate for children to develop friendships with other children who speak different languages; and (4) helping students to raise their self-esteem because teachers create opportunities for them to assume authority in group situations and learn to be active participants who learn from their peers.

When developing cooperative groups, teachers may either assign members randomly or set up membership to ensure that each group includes a variety of students in terms of gender, ethnicity, language proficiency, and academic achievement. Teachers also may wish to balance groups in terms of personality characteristics: shy/outgoing, quiet/talkative, and so forth. In addition to heterogeneous grouping, procedural roles are assigned to students in each group: recorder, observer, encourager, and reporter. These roles are rotated so that all students have opportunities to assume leadership responsibility and participate as supportive group members (Peregoy & Boyle, 1993). Cooperative/collaborative techniques that have been used successfully with young language-minority learners include the following:

- *Jigsaw.* Jigsaw is one cooperative technique in which one segment of a learning task is assigned to each group member, who works to become an "expert" in that area. After researching their special areas, the experts from each group meet to compare notes and extend their learning. Finally, the original groups meet again, and the experts report back to their original groups. The jigsaw technique might be used with young SLLs to help them become experts on a favorite animal, a month of the year, or a special holiday.
- *Buddy system.* The buddy system helps second language learners become members of the classroom society and more comfortable in the school. To implement the buddy system, teachers pair students in terms of more capable/less capable, younger/older, shy/outgoing, newly arrived immigrant/long-term second language resident, English proficient/less proficient. The buddy helps students in and out of the class and school routines.
- *Writing response groups.* Writing response groups can assist SLLs in becoming more independent, improve their writing, give them an audience for their writing, and provide immediate response to their writing. In the groups students share their writing with one another, concentrate on the good elements of their writing, and help one another improve their writing. To begin this procedure, the teacher models good response comments and gives students specific strategies for improving their papers.
- *Literature response groups.* Literature response groups help students to use their background knowledge to respond to literature, and to become independent readers of literature. Teachers begin this technique by modeling responses to literature and emphasizing the variety of acceptable comments. According to Peregoy and Boyle (1993), these groups help students learn to value individual responses and to support responses with what they have read. Students focus first on individual feelings and later on structure and form. All students, regardless of their ability levels, will be able to respond to narrative stories or share in writing their ideas with one another. However, teachers will need to adjust for individual differences. For example, less capable writers can dictate their ideas to more able students. Students may respond to stories that they read as well as stories that are read aloud to them.

Language Experience Approaches

The Language Experience Approach (LEA) is one of the most frequently recommended approaches for beginning second language readers (Peregoy & Boyle, 1993). The LEA builds on the linguistic, social, and cultural strengths and experiences that the student brings to school. As a result, this approach is tailored to the learner's own interests, background knowledge, and language proficiency. The core of the language experience approach is stories based on real-life experience that are dictated to the teacher by individual children, small groups, or the whole class. As a rule, the children's stories are written down verbatim, after which students read them back. Even less proficient children usually are able to read their own stories with minimal decoding skills because they understand what they mean. According to Peregoy and Boyle, through the LEA students learn to see reading and writing as purposeful communication about their own interests and concerns. Building on the LEA stories, the teacher is able to extend the children's literacy development by helping them create word banks that contain new and challenging words they wish to remember, construct sentence strips for each sentence in their story so that they can practice story sequencing, and practice editing techniques for spelling development.

Several other methods and strategies have proven effective in fostering the linguistic and cognitive development of young second language students. Among these are storytelling (Tiedt, 1983), shared literature (Barrett, 1982), story webbing and semantic mapping (Perhsson & Robinson, 1985), and learning frames (Flores, Rueda, & Porter, 1986). However, before using these or any learning approach with students, educators should be reminded that "a given strategy will not work for all students every time under all conditions, and the success of a strategy depends on its adequacy for the population involved and its implementation by the practitioner" (Maldonado-Colon, 1991, p. 38).

SUMMARY

Today, the linguistic and cultural heritage of our school population reflects a rapidly changing American society. The extent to which educators prepare language-minority learners for the future will determine America's role as a world leader in the next century. By the year 2000, 15% of Americans will have a language other than English as their first language; one in every three Americans will be nonwhite; and four out of every five persons entering the work force will be women, minorities, or immigrants (Mid-Atlantic Equity Center, 1989).

The major demographic shifts caused by the changes in our nation's immigration practices will create a student population whose ethnic composition and cultural heritage will be dramatically different from the past. To ensure that all children will be prepared to face the challenges of a rapidly changing society, our schools will need to become better informed about the linguistic and cultural diversity of students, be willing to modify old approaches, and explore new techniques to educate our nation's children. In this discussion of some of the issues surrounding language diversification and the implications for the education of young language-minority children were presented. We invite educators to (1) embrace the linguistic and cultural diversity that children bring with them into the classroom, (2) examine the theories that drive our instruction, and (3) adopt programs and practices that promote academic success for all students.

REFERENCES

Au, K. H., & Jordan, C. (1981). Teaching reading to Hawaiian children: Finding culturally appropriate solutions. In H. T. Trueba, G. P. Guthrie, & K. H. Au (Eds.), *Culture and the bilingual classroom: Studies in classroom ethnography* (pp. 139–152). Boston: Newbury House.

Barrett, F. L. (1982). *Cognitive psychology and its implications* (2nd ed.). New York: W. H. Freeman.

Bernhardt, E. B. (1991). *Reading development in a second language: Theoretical, empirical, and classroom perspectives.* Norwood, NJ: Ablex.

Bloom, B., & Krathwohl, D. (1977). *Taxonomy of educational objectives: Handbook I. Cognitive domain.* New York: Longman.

Cazden, C. (1986). ESL teachers as language advocates for children. In P. Rigg & D. S. Enright (Eds.), *Children and ESL: Integrating perspectives* (pp. 9–21). Washington, DC: TESOL.

Collier, V. (1989). How long? A synthesis of research on academic achievement in second language. *TESOL Quarterly, 23,* 509–531.

Crawford, J. (1989). *Bilingual education: History, politics, theory, and practice.* Trenton, NJ: Crane.

Cummins, J. (1979). Linguistic interdependence and the educational development of bilingual children. *Review of Educational Research, 49,* 222–251.

Cummins, J. (1984). *Bilingual and special education: Issues in assessment and pedagogy.* San Diego, CA: College-Hill.

Cummins, J. (1986). Empowering minority students: A framework for intervention. *Harvard Educational Review, 56,* 372–390.

Cummins, J. (1988). Language proficiency, bilingualism, and academic achievement. In P. A. Richard-Amato (Ed.), *Making it happen: Interaction in the second language classroom* (pp. 372–390). White Plains, NY: Longman.

Dubin, F., Eskey, D. E., & Grabe, W. (1986). *Teaching second language reading for academic purposes.* Reading, MA: Addison-Wesley.

Flores, B., Rueda, R., & Porter, B. (1986). Examining assumptions and instructional practices related to the acquisition of literacy with bilingual special education students. In A. C. Willig & H. F. Greenberg (Eds.), *Bilingualism and learning disabilities* (pp. 149–165). New York: American Publishing.

García, E. E. (1991). Caring for infants in a bilingual child care setting. *The Journal of Educational Issues of Language Minority Students, 9,* 1–10.

García, E. E. (1992). Linguistically and culturally diverse children: Effective instructional practices and related policy issues. In H. C. Waxman, J. Walker de Fleix, J. E. Anderson, & H. P. Baptiste, Jr. (Eds.), *Students at risk in at-risk schools: Improving environments for learning* (pp. 65–86). Newbury Park, CA: Corwin.

Grant, R., & Wong, S. (1994). Teaching second language learners: Special considerations for content teachers. *Literacy Issues and Practices, 11,* 23–29.

Gunderson, L. (1984). Reading achievement of L1 and L2 students in regular classrooms. *TEAL Occasional Papers, 8,* 31–40.

Gunderson, L. (1991). *ESL literacy instruction: A guidebook to theory and practice.* Englewood Cliffs, NJ: Prentice-Hall.

Hamayan, E. (1990). Preparing mainstream teachers for teaching potentially English proficient students. In *Proceedings of the first research symposium on limited English proficiency students issues* (pp. 1–22). Washington, DC: United States Department of Education, Office of Bilingual Education and Minority Languages Affairs.

Heath, S. B. (1983). *Ways with words: Language, life, and work in communities and classrooms.* Cambridge: Cambridge University Press.

Johns, K. M. (1992). Mainstreaming language minority students through cooperative grouping. *The Journal of Educational Issues of Language Minority Students, 11,* 221–231.

Lewis, A. C. (1991). Washington news. *Educational Digest, 56,* 51–53.

Maldonado-Colon, E. (1991). Development of second language learners' linguistic and cognitive abilities. *The Journal of Educational Issues of Language Minority Students, 9,* 37–60.

Mid-Atlantic Equity Center. (1989). *Equity assistance brochure.* Washington, DC: American University.

Odum, M. E. (1993, September 20). Guiding teachers through a sea of diversity. *The Washington Post,* pp. 1, 6.

Ogbu, J. U. (1978). *Minority education and caste.* New York: Academic Press.

Peregoy, S. F., & Boyle, O. F. (1993). *Reading, writing, and learning in ESL.* New York: Academic Press.

Perhsson, R., & Robinson, H. A. (1985). *The semantic organizers approach to writing and reading instruction.* Rockville, MD: Aspen.

Reyes, M. (1992). Challenging venerable assumptions: Literacy instruction for linguistically different students. *Harvard Educational Review, 62,* 427–446.

Reyes, M., & Molner, L. A. (1991). Instructional strategies for second-language learners in content areas. *Journal of Reading, 35,* 96–103.

Ryder, R. J., & Graves, M. F. (1994). *Reading and learning in content areas.* New York: Merrill.

Sapon-Shevin, M., & Schniedewind, N. (1992). If cooperative learning's the answer, what are the questions? *Journal of Education, 174,* 11–33.

Saville-Troike, M. (1978). *A guide to culture in the classroom.* Rosslyn, VA: National Clearinghouse for Bilingual Education.

Saville-Troike, M. (1984). What really matters in second language learning for academic achievement. *TESOL Quarterly, 18,* 199–219.

Sevilla, G. (1994, June 5). Immigrant students shorted, activists say. *The Washington Post,* pp. 1, 5.

Skutnabb-Kangas, T. (1979). *Language in the process of cultural assimilation and structural incorporation of linguistic minorities.* Rosslyn, VA: National Clearinghouse for Bilingual Education.

Skutnabb-Kangas, T., & Toukomaa, P. (1976). *Teaching migrant children's mother tongue and learning of the host country in the context of the socio-cultural situation of the migrant family.* Helsinki: Finnish National Commission for UNESCO.

Tiedt, I. (1983). *The language arts handbook.* Englewood Cliffs, NJ: Prentice-Hall.

Troike, R. (1978). Research evidence for the effectiveness of bilingual education. *NABE Journal, 3,* 13–24.

Vygotsky, L. S. (1962). *Thought and language.* Cambridge, MA: MIT Press.

CHAPTER 2

Language Development in Bilingual Preschool Children

Fred Genesee and Elena Nicoladis

Second language acquisition during early childhood is often viewed with suspicion and is the subject of much controversy among the population at large and among educators. This can be particularly true in monolingual communities and among speakers of dominant international languages, such as English, French, and Spanish, where the populace comes to regard monolingualism as the norm and therefore "normal." In such situations, early bilingualism is sometimes viewed as undesirable because it is believed to threaten children's language development and even their intellectual skills. For example, some English-speaking educators in North America argue that English should be used in the homes of immigrant children as much as possible, to the exclusion of the home language, in order to prepare the children for all-English education. Such views often reflect sociopolitical attitudes—for example, the desire to assimilate newcomers to the dominant culture, rather than a knowledge of the true course of second language acquisition in young children.

It is important that educators working with children who come to school knowing more than one language or who are in the process of mastering a second language understand these children's language development so that their work with the children is not based on false assumptions and misunderstandings. In this chapter, we discuss the linguistic development of children who are raised bilingually during the preschool years. This can result from parents who use two languages in the home or from exposure to parental use of one language in the home and the use of another language or languages outside the home by relatives, childcare workers, or playmates. We consider only children who learn two languages more or less simultaneously. We do not consider children who have acquired a second language after age 3, that is, after their first language is well established. The reader is referred to McLaughlin (1978) and Hakuta (1986) for useful summaries of research on these children.

We start by looking at the issue of language confusion, that is, whether bilingual children can differentiate between the languages they are learning. We then describe general patterns and milestones in bilingual development. Next, we examine whether language acquisition and the resulting language performance of children raised bilingually are different from those of monolingual children. We then examine some sociocultural aspects of bilingual development. We concluded by suggesting classroom implications of all this.

LINGUISTIC CONFUSION OR BILINGUAL COMPETENCE?

Young bilingual children often use elements from both languages in the same utterance or stretch of conversation when they start speaking; this has been noted by many researchers and is often referred to as code mixing (see Genesee, 1989 and Meisel, 1994 for reviews of this research). It has been reported for different aspects of language, including sounds, words, and grammatical structures (see Genesee, 1989). Let us look at a couple of examples. Using a word from one language while using the other language is the most common form of mixing. For example, a young Spanish-German bilingual boy talking to his Spanish-speaking mother said, *"Das no juegan." Das* is the German word for "that" and *no juegan* is Spanish for "do not play" (Redlinger & Park, 1980, p. 341). Using the syntactic (grammatical) patterns of one language while speaking another language is another form of mixing. Saunders (1982) reported that his 5-year-old German- /English-speaking son said to his English-speaking mother, "Mum, I had my school jumper all day on" (p. 178). While German requires this word order, this construction is not grammatical in English.

Bilingual children's use of elements from both languages in the same utterance or conversation often has been interpreted to mean that they confuse their two languages and treat both as if they were part of a single linguistic system (Redlinger & Park, 1980; Swain, 1977; Volterra & Taeschner, 1978; see also Oksaar, 1971). According to this view, code mixing reflects a lack of differentiation of the two languages. Separation of the two languages has been reported to occur by about age 3 (Leopold, 1949). At this age, bilingual children appear to be especially sensitive to the language spoken by their addressee. They recognize the language their addressee speaks most fluently and they use that language exclusively with them (Volterra & Taeschner, 1978).

It is important to note here that adult bilinguals in some communities also code mix a lot (Sridhar & Sridhar, 1980). Research in these communities has shown that code mixing is a sophisticated, systematic, and rule-governed form of communication that is used to achieve a variety of goals, such as conveying emphasis, role playing, or establishing sociocultural identity. Moreover, it also has been shown that code mixing is used most by linguistically competent bilinguals (Poplack & Sankoff, 1988). The precise forms and functions of code switching can differ depending on the community (Poplack, 1987). In any case, code switching is a legitimate, useful, and sophisticated feature of language use in many bilingual communities. Thus, in contrast to the interpretation of bilingual mixing by young children, mixing by adults is interpreted as a sign of competence and proficiency.

Not all the evidence supports the confusion interpretation of children's code mixing. In fact, it has been suggested that bilingual children do not go through a stage of confusion at all (Bergman, 1976; DeHouwer, 1992; Genesee, 1989; Goodz, 1994; Meisel, 1994; Padilla & Liebman, 1975). In a study of four English-French bilingual children in Montreal, we found that their code mixing was not associated with a lack of differentiation between the languages (Genesee, Nicoladis, & Paradis, 1995). We recorded the children's language use in their homes three times: once with their mothers alone; once with their fathers alone; and once with both parents. The children were between 22 and 26 months old. Even at this young age, these children were able to use their two languages in a context-sensitive manner—they used substantially more French than English with their French-speaking parent and substantially more English than French with their English-speaking parent, even when the parents were in the same room.

If it is indeed the case that bilingual children can separate their languages from the beginning, we still have a puzzle on our hands: Why do bilingual children mix their languages? One explanation may be that they learn to code mix from their parents, who, as we just noted, might code switch extensively themselves. In a 3-year study of the language development of 13 French-English bilingual children in Montreal, Goodz (1989) found that even parents who reported using only their dominant language with their child code mixed. Of particular interest, she also found that parental code mixing correlated with individual children's rates of mixing. It stands to reason that children who hear extensive code mixing by parents and other adults in their environment will mix extensively themselves. If parental mixing is part of a community-wide style of communication, then it is to be expected that children growing up in such communities also will learn this style. It will become an integral part of their repertoire of communication skills as adults. Indeed, acquisition of this style of language is essential if they are to communicate with other members of the community.

Parental code mixing may not be the only explanation. Another may be that bilingual children simply know one language better than the other. When they find they do not know the words or syntactic devices for expressing themselves in their weaker language, they simply might switch to their stronger language. We have noted this frequently in our own research. We also have found that parents sometimes use what they suppose to be the child's stronger language, even though it may mean switching languages in the same utterance. For example, one English-speaking father said that he commonly used the word *dodo* (a French word used with young children to mean "nap," "sleep," or "sleeping") in his English utterances because this is what his son knew.

Yet another possible explanation comes from Lanza (1992) and Goodz (1994), who suggest that code mixing is a strategy used in bilingual families to facilitate communication between parent and child at a stage when the child's linguistic resources are limited. These researchers have found that code mixing by bilingual children does not cause a breakdown in communication. Nor do parents tend to reprimand the children for using both languages or request them to use only one. To the contrary, it is usually observed that parents generally understand their children's code mixed utterances and often respond by repeating or paraphrasing the child's mixed utterance in a single language or, in some cases, by code mixing themselves. Such partial or complete repetitions of children's utterances are also frequent in the language of parents in monolingual families and are generally thought to represent confirmation checks on the part of parents (Demetras, Post, & Snow, 1986; Newport, Gleitman, & Gleitman, 1977).

It is not uncommon for parents to provide a child with complete or corrected paraphrases of the child's incomplete or incorrect forms. Goodz (1989) reports a particularly interesting example of lexical correction by a parent in a bilingual family that resulted in the parent code mixing. Pointing to a pineapple, the child referred to it as a "pinetree." In response, the French-speaking mother corrected his lexical usage by saying, "*Non, ce n'est pas un* pinetree, *c'est un* pineapple; *c'est un* pineapple. *Dis* pineapple" (p. 42). Such patterns of parental communication with children in bilingual families not only may maintain communication with their children, but may also sanction code mixing by the children.

To summarize, while it often has been suggested that bilingual children pass through a stage of language confusion when they are unable to differentiate between their two languages, we now understand that code mixing does not mean that bilingual children are confused. To the contrary, our own findings suggest that even very young children are able to use their developing languages in context-sensitive ways. More plausible explanations of mixing are that it is due to code mixing by parents themselves, communication strategies that serve to maintain conversations between parents and their children, and language dominance. Overall, it seems that parents in bilingual families use the same interaction strategies as parents in monolingual families.

DEVELOPMENTAL MILESTONES

We now have detailed information about the language development of monolingual children, especially children who learn English (see, for example, Bloom, 1991). Such information is useful for at least two reasons. It is useful theoretically because it provides clues about the cognitive processes and acquisitional strategies that underlie normal language development. It is useful practically because it provides language specialists and educational professionals with a general profile of the developmental milestones that children normally exhibit as they move from no to full competence in language. This information can be used to identify children with language-related problems and to provide remedial services for them. In this section, we examine some important milestones in the language development of children raised bilingually.

It is not possible to describe the developmental patterns of bilingual children in precise detail as has been done for monolingual children because there are so few comprehensive longitudinal studies of bilingual children. Nevertheless, the evidence that is available indicates that children who are raised bilingually exhibit the same basic milestones as monolingual children. Children raised bilingually, on average, utter their first words at the same age as monolinguals, namely, about 11.2 months of age (Doyle, Champagne, & Segalowitz, 1978). It is important to note that this is *on average*. There is a great deal of variability among individual children in the age of appearance of their first words. Although monolingual children have been found to utter their first words at approximately 11 months of age, the range is from about 9 months to about 16 months (Bloom, 1973). The same variability also characterizes bilingual children.

Bilingual and monolingual children also use similar kinds of linguistic units to communicate in the early stages of language acquisition. In addition to units that correspond to adult words, monolingual children sometimes use unanalyzed segments (or chunks) of language as single word-like units to express meaning. An unanalyzed segment of language refers to what would be more than a single word in adult language. Bilingual children do the same thing. Fantini (1974) reported that his Spanish-English bilingual son said, "Don't touch" in English and "*Donde esta?*" ("Where is it?") in Spanish while he was in the one-word stage and before he used inflected verbs spontaneously; the child was never observed using each of the component words separately. We have seen similar phenomena in the French-English children we are studying.

Bilingual and monolingual children also demonstrate the same general progression with respect to the development of linguistic complexity. Monolingual children pass through a one-word stage, during which most of their utterances consist of one word, and then a two-word stage, during which most of their utterances consist of two words. After the two-word stage, they begin to express themselves in multiword utterances and to use grammatical inflections and more complex syntactic constructions. Goodz's longitudinal study of French-English children indicates that they progress through the same basic stages (see also Arnberg, 1981). Our own data are also consistent with these findings.

When it comes to rate of acquisition, there is some evidence that the rate of vocabulary development in bilingual preschool children is slower, at least when each language is considered separately, than in children learning the same languages monolingually (see Ben-Zeev, 1977; Bialystok, 1988; Doyle, Champagne, & Segalowitz, 1978; and Nicoladis, 1992). It is important to point out here that researchers have found that bilingual children acquire vocabularies in each language that are equivalent to those of monolingual children sometime during the primary school grades (Fantini, 1974; Saunders, 1982) so that the slower vocabulary development that we have discussed here is not long-term.

That bilingual children initially might have smaller vocabularies when each language is considered separately should not be surprising when one considers a couple of facts. The memory capacity of young children is limited and presumably restricts their rate of vocabulary acquisition, even if only one language is involved. Bilingual children have equally limited memory capacities but two sets of vocabularies to learn. Thus, at any particular point during development, one would expect them to know fewer vocabulary items in each language but approximately the same number when both languages are taken together. In fact, if the vocabulary scores for both languages of bilingual children are combined, their vocabulary equals or exceeds that of monolingual children (Bialystok, 1988; Nicoladis, 1992). The delay that has been observed in vocabulary acquisition has not been observed in other domains of language development. In our study of bilingual English-French children, we have found that they display the same syntactic patterns in each language as monolingual children and that these patterns emerge at the same time in bilingual children as in monolingual children (Paradis & Genesee, 1994).

Language experience also may play a role in the vocabulary development of bilingual children. It is common for bilingual children to learn each of their languages from different adults—the mother and father or grandparents and other relatives—and therefore in somewhat different social contexts. As a result, their vocabulary skills in each language may be limited to specific domains. Assessing bilingual children's vocabulary skills in each language separately taps only half their resources and could give the appearance of retarded or deficient development since only domains that are relevant to one language are being tapped. To obtain valid indications of bilingual children's overall vocabulary development, it is necessary to examine their vocabulary skills in both languages.

Language experience plays an important role in bilingual children's overall rate of development in each language. Bilingual children generally exhibit more rapid progress and more ability in whichever language predominates in their social environment. They can undergo dramatic fluctuations in language proficiency, from dominance to subordinance in the same language, if there are fluctuations in their exposure to the language. This can happen if they move from one language community to another or if there are changes in the composition of their families that result in changes in the languages being used. For example, Leopold (1949) reported that his daughter Hildegaard had much difficulty expressing herself in English upon returning to the United States after a visit of some 7 months in Germany; she was, however, apparently able to understand English well. These effects are usually short-lived so that the children soon adjust to the linguistic demands of their current environment.

A further indication of the importance of the language environment is evident in some children's insistence on using a particular language in certain situations or with certain people, even though use of the other language is appropriate or encouraged and even though the child obviously knows the language well. An example of this is reported by Volterra and Taeschner (1978). The German-Italian girl they were observing insisted on using the Italian word *occhiali* to refer to her Italian-speaking father's glasses when speaking with her German-speaking mother. The mother made repeated attempts to get the child to refer to her father's glasses using the German word *Brillen*. Not all bilingual children respond in this fashion; rather it appears to be a highly individualized response pattern. While such situation-specific language preferences are not well understood, we believe that they may be the result of personality and attitudinal factors—they may reflect individual children's views of how language works and their feelings about which languages they prefer to use, where, and with whom.

In summary, the developmental milestones of children raised bilingually are the same as those of children raised monolingually in most important respects (see also DeHouwer, 1992). At the same time, bilingual children's rate of development and their level of proficiency in each language are sensitive to experiential factors. It is important to recognize that general or situation-specific experiential factors can influence bilingual children's rate and level of language development in noticeable ways. It is also important to understand that these effects are not the result of some constitutional disability or an inherent deficiency associated with bilingualism. Rather, in most cases, they are by-products of complex experiential factors that often characterize bilingual children's language learning environments.

UNDERSTANDING BILINGUAL LANGUAGE PERFORMANCE

Naturally, the linguistic performance of children who have not yet acquired full proficiency in language differs from that of adults—for example, in the early one- and two-word stages, children usually drop word endings and important function words, such as prepositions, articles, and auxiliary verbs. These features of child language performance sometimes have been conceptualized as *errors*. Viewing children's language performance in this way, however, is to view their developing abilities in language in terms of incompetence. An alternative conceptualization is to view the special characteristics of children's linguistic performance as a reflection of their current organization of language and of their strategies for acquiring and using language at particular points during their development. Thus, for example, rather than viewing the use of "goed" instead of "went" as an error, it can be seen as children's formulation of a general rule for forming the past tense of verbs that they apply to all verbs, even irregular ones that have idiosyncratic past tense forms. Such an interpretation identifies what children have accomplished, rather than what they have not accomplished, and therefore is truer to a developmental perspective.

Such a perspective is doubly important in understanding the language performance of children raised bilingually. Because they are learning two languages simultaneously, it is to be expected that their language will differ from that of children raised monolingually. Bilingual children have the possibility of making so-called "interference" or "transfer errors" of the code mixing type referred to in the previous section, as well as developmental errors that characterize all children's language acquisition (Romaine, 1989). To view children's code mixing simply as error runs the risk of missing important and interesting insights about the processes that underlie children's acquisition of two languages because it focuses only on surface linguistic features.

Let us explore this further by re-examining bilingual children's code mixing. Code mixing by children can be interpreted in terms of acquisitional strategies that have been identified in the language development of monolingual children. Thus, code mixing in the form of lexical borrowing can be viewed as *overextensions* or overgeneralizations that are commonly reported in monolingual children (Ingram, 1989). The most famous (and embarrassing) example of overextension by monolingual children is the use of "daddy" to refer to all adult males. Children stop overextending the use of particular words once they learn more appropriate labels. Thus, monolingual children make use of whatever vocabulary they have acquired to meet their communication needs; as their vocabulary expands, they use more appropriate, less overextended words. This is equally true of bilingual children, the only difference being that bilingual children overextend interlingually as well as intralingually, whereas monolingual children overextend intralingually only.

Overly restricted use of particular words (as in the eye glasses example) has been observed in monolingual children in the form of *underextensions;* that is, use of a particular word with a particular referent even though it could be used more widely with other referents. Anglin (1977), in fact, has suggested that underextensions are more frequent than overextensions but they often go unnoticed because they do not violate adult usage. Bilingual children may underextend more and longer than monolingual children because they hear more instances of particular words being used in specific contexts (e.g., the German word for "glasses" being used in German contexts or by German speakers), whereas monolingual children are more likely to hear the same words used in different situations (e.g., the word "glasses" used in all contexts and by all speakers when eye glasses are referred to). Using words in specific situations is at the heart of bilingual proficiency. Indeed, bilingual children's use of specific words, expressions, and so forth, in specific language or social contexts is accepted and encouraged by bilingual parents.

Finally, some aspects of language are harder to learn and are, in fact, acquired later than others because they require cognitive, motor, or perceptual skills that young children acquire only later in development. To give a simple example, certain sounds in English ("ba," "da") are acquired early because they are easy to produce, while other sounds ("el," "ar") are acquired late because they require sophisticated articulatory control (e.g., see Smith, 1973). This can be true of grammatical rules as well. Children learning two languages simultaneously might mix elements because of the relative difficulty of certain aspects of the two languages being learned. To be more specific, the sounds or grammatical rules needed to express a certain meaning in one language may be more complex than the child can manage at a given point in his or her development, while an equivalent and much easier form or rule exists in the other language. Thus, on a given occasion bilingual children may use a linguistic element or structure from one language to express a certain meaning, while using the other language simply because it is easier than the corresponding device or element in the target language. Thus, bilingual children, like monolingual children, use whatever linguistic resources they are able to manage at each point in their development.

What is important about these explanations of bilingual language performance is that they indicate that, despite some superficial differences in language performance, bilingual and monolingual children probably go about the task of learning language in the same way. Indeed, on theoretical grounds as well, one would not expect differences in the processes and strategies young children use to learn two versus one language (see Genesee, 1988, for more details).

LANGUAGE SOCIALIZATION OF BILINGUAL CHILDREN

In the preceding sections, we focused on the strictly linguistic aspects of learning two languages at the same time. It is important to keep in mind that learning language, one or two, entails more than learning a set of linguistic structures and rules. It also entails learning how to use the linguistic code to communicate and interact appropriately and effectively with others. This is the topic of this section.

It is now well understood that there are different ways of using language depending on the nature of the social situation, event, or interaction: Face-to-face conversations are different from telephone conversations; talk between children is different from talk between children and adults; talk between close friends is different from talk between strangers; and so on (John-Steiner, Panofsky, & Smith, 1994). When they learn language, children learn the ways of expressing themselves and communicating with others that are characteristic of the social situations that are typical and important in their families and communities.

The ways in which language is used in different situations vary from one culture to another—people from different cultural groups transact business in different ways; converse with one another in different ways; praise, criticize, and greet one another in different ways; and so on. Variations in the ways cultures organize the use of language reflect differences in cultural beliefs, values, and goals concerning social roles and relationships in their group (Crago, 1992a; Schieffelin & Ochs, 1986). Most relevant to our concerns here is the following: The way parents and other caregivers use language with infants and children is closely related to their cultural beliefs about the status and role of children in society, to the social organization of caregiving, and to conceptions of how children learn language (Schieffelin & Eisenberg, 1984). This has important implications for what it means to learn a language and can be illustrated more clearly by looking at some differences that characterize the social context for language learning in different cultures.

In some cultures, it is believed that children are not appropriate conversational partners for adults and that the ability to learn language is not associated with the child's active use of language. In these cultures, young children are usually not expected or encouraged to initiate topics of conversation that are self-focused, and they are not encouraged to talk before a certain age (see Schieffelin & Eisenberg, 1984, for a useful review of research on cultural variations on conversations with children). Often, these beliefs about language learning also parallel views about learning in general, so that children in such cultures are often expected to learn by listening to and observing competent adults model the behavior or skill to be learned (Crago, 1992a). Much valuable learning goes on as well among the children themselves.

In comparison, in most European and majority North American cultural groups, it generally is believed that children are appropriate conversational partners for adults and that language learning is related to the child's active use of language. In these cultures, children are encouraged to talk with adults and to talk about themselves. Moreover, much adult talk is child-centered. North American parents even engage preverbal infants in pseudo-conversations by construing their nonlinguistic vocalizations and physical gestures as conversational turns worthy of response. Adults also accommodate their topics of conversation and their speech styles to children. So-called baby talk or caregiver speech, as this modified form of language is called, is highly simplified and repetitive, and it has a number of distinct acoustic properties (Snow & Ferguson, 1977). Modified language input to child language learners and conversations with verbal and even preverbal infants are not typical of cultures that do not view the child as a legitimate conversational partner or do not believe that the child's active use of language is important for language learning (Schieffelin & Ochs, 1986).

The important point here is that infants and children in different cultures are exposed to different patterns of language use and through these experiences are exposed to different belief systems about their status and role in relationship to adults and to the world at large. Thus, the way in which children construct a model of the world and discover their place and power of control within it is strongly influenced by the sociocultural values and orientations that are encoded and transmitted in the everyday conversations they have with parents and other adults in their community (Wells, 1986). It is through the process of learning language that is embedded in systems of cultural beliefs and values that children learn the sociocultural values and ways of the group into which they are being socialized. And it is through language learning that children become members in good standing in their own cultural group. As Heath (1983) has so aptly stated, "Language learning is cultural learning" (p. 145).

All children learn the sociolinguistic rules and sociocultural values that characterize life in their community; bilingual children are no different in this regard. What is different in the case of children raised bilingually is that they must learn the rules and values that are associated with two languages and communities, and they must learn when they are appropriate. There also can be rules of language usage and ways of behaving that are particular to the social situations that characterize life in bilingual communities. These also must be learned and used appropriately. Taken together, then, children learning two languages simultaneously learn patterns of language use, cultural values, and social behaviors that are characteristic of monolingual contexts as well as those that are specific to bilingual contexts. This means that children raised bilingually develop rich and complex patterns of communication and interaction (Pease-Alvarez & Vasquez, 1994).

There are times, however, when bilingual children might appear less than competent. This can occur if they are called upon to use one or both of their languages in social situations that have not been part of their experiences learning those languages. If, for example, Spanish-English bilingual children have not had the opportunity to play with monolingual English-speaking children of the same age, then they may lack the linguistic and social competence necessary to interact effectively with these children. In such cases, it is not unusual for children either to use whatever communication and general social skills they have, in admittedly inappropriate ways, or simply to withdraw and not communicate or interact with others at all. Such behavior might be interpreted as delayed or, worse, impaired development. This would be a false evaluation since in most cases it is a lack of social experience that underlies the child's language performance, not an underlying deficit. Given sufficient time and experience, most bilingual children will acquire the skills needed to communicate and interact in new situations.

Learning new language skills in school can be a challenging task for bilingual children if the social behaviors and cultural values associated with the new language skills they need conflict with existing values and behaviors (Crago, 1992b; Genesee, 1992). For example, children from some cultures learn that it is inappropriate to initiate conversations with adults, to participate publicly in competitive ways with others, and to look directly at adults. In comparison, in mainstream North American schools it is appropriate for children to initiate communication, to compete verbally with others, and to make eye contact during interactions with others. Indeed, it is through the use of these and other forms of communication that school children are expected to display what they have learned. Moreover, teachers in most North American schools evaluate and grade students by their ability to participate in classroom activities in these ways. Delay or apparent hesitancy in learning new language skills actually may reflect the difficulties bilingual children face in reconciling new cultural values and orientations with existing ones. It is important that professionals working with bilingual children understand this. At the same time, it is important that they not overlook the extensive linguistic resources that bilingual children have already acquired.

CLASSROOM IMPLICATIONS AND CONCLUSIONS

In the preceding sections, we have sought to describe and understand some of the salient features of language development in children raised bilingually. Here we identify some implications of these research findings for classroom teachers.

- Appreciate that when bilingual children start school they must learn new ways of using language that are unrelated to their previous language experiences.
- Be aware that in school bilingual children must learn more than new language skills; they also must learn new social and cultural values and skills that are associated with schooling.
- Assume that the language skills you observe in bilingual students are the tip of the iceberg; there is much more below the surface that they are capable of.
- In order to arrive at a valid assessment of bilingual students' language abilities, observe them using both languages; for example, observe them in inter-

action with peers who speak both languages or talk with their parents and others who can describe their use of both languages outside school.

- Learn about the sociocultural habits and values of the families and communities of your bilingual students so that you can understand the challenges they face in adapting to school.
- Be sensitive to the challenges that bilingual students face as they learn communication skills and social values that are appropriate for schooling but may conflict with norms in their homes and communities.
- Give bilingual students time to learn new communication skills and to become integrated into the new culture that is part of schooling.
- To facilitate the social integration of bilingual students into the life of the school and the classroom, twin new students with fully integrated students, preferably students who speak one of their languages.
- Be sensitive to individual differences in bilingual students that might reflect differences in their prior educational, social, and cultural experiences.
- Avoid attributions of incompetence or resistance if bilingual students do not fit in right away; look for explanations in their backgrounds or the organization of the classroom.
- Provide multiple learning opportunities so that children with different styles and preferences can find those that suit them.
- Draw on the linguistic, cultural, and personal experiences of bilingual students when planning instructional activities so that you provide them with opportunities to learn that are familiar to them.
- Create a supportive learning environment that respects and includes the linguistic and cultural resources that bilingual students bring to the classroom.

In conclusion, teachers should adopt a procompetence attitude toward children who grow up bilingually. They should focus on what children can do, not on what they cannot do. Prior to coming to school, bilingual children have grown up in rich and complex social environments and have learned to function effectively in these environments. The linguistic and cultural differences that they present in comparison with mainstream monolingual students are evidence of this richness. Their competence in learning the linguistic and cultural skills needed to adapt to bilingual homes or communities attests to their ability to learn the skills they need to adapt to and succeed in school.

REFERENCES

Anglin, J. M. (1977). *Word, object and conceptual development.* New York: Norton.
Arnberg, L. (1981). *A longitudinal study of language development in four young children exposed to English and Swedish in the home.* Linkping, Sweden: Linkping University, Department of Education.

Ben-Zeev, S. (1977). The influence of bilingualism on cognitive development and cognitive strategy. *Child Development, 48,* 1009–1018.

Bergman, C. R. (1976). Interference vs. independent development in infant bilingualism. In G. D. Keller, R. V. Taeschner, & S. Viera (Eds.), *Bilingualism in the bicentennial and beyond* (pp. 86–96). New York: Bilingual Press/Editorial Bilingue.

Bialystok, E. (1988). Levels of bilingualism and levels of linguistic awareness. *Development Psychology, 24,* 560–567.

Bloom, L. (1973). *One word at a time.* The Hague: Mouton.

Bloom, L. (1991). *Language development from two to three.* New York: Cambridge University Press.

Crago, M. (1992a). Ethnography and language socialization: A cross-cultural perspective. *Topics in Language Disorders, 12,* 28–39.

Crago, M. (1992b). The sociocultural interface of communicative interaction and second language acquisition: An Inuit example. *TESOL Quarterly, 23,* 487–506.

DeHouwer, A. (1992). *The acquisition of two languages from birth: A case study.* Cambridge: Cambridge University Press.

Demetras, M. J., Post, K. N., & Snow, C. E. (1986). Feedback to first language learners: The role of repetitions and clarification questions. *Journal of Child Language, 13,* 275–292.

Doyle, A-B., Champagne, M., & Segalowitz, N. (1978). Some issues in the assessment of linguistic consequences of early bilingualism. In M. Paradis (Ed.), *Aspects of bilingualism* (pp. 13–20). Columbia, SC: Hornbeam Press.

Fantini, A. E. (1974). *Language acquisition of a bilingual child: A sociolinguistic perspective.* Brattleboro, VT: Experiment Press.

Genesee, F. (1988). Bilingual development in preschool children. In D. Bishop & K. Mogford (Eds.), *Language development in exceptional circumstances* (pp. 62–79). Edinburgh: Churchill Livingstone.

Genesee, F. (1989). Early bilingual development: One language or two? *Journal of Child Language, 16,* 161–179.

Genesee, F. (1992). *Language and cultural diversity in education.* Unpublished manuscript, McGill University, Psychology Department, Montreal.

Genesee, F., Nicoladis, E., & Paradis, J. (1995). Language differentiation in preschool bilingual children. *Journal of Child Language,* in press.

Goodz, N. (1989). Parental language mixing in bilingual families. *Infant Mental Health Journal, 10,* 25–44.

Goodz, N. (1994). Interactions between parents and children in bilingual families. In F. Genesee (Ed.), *Educating second language children* (pp. 61–81). New York: Cambridge University Press.

Hakuta, K. (1986). *Mirror of language.* New York: Basic Books.

Heath, S. B. (1983). *Ways with words: Language, life, and work in communities and classrooms.* Cambridge: Cambridge University Press.

Ingram, D. (1989). *First language acquisition.* Cambridge: Cambridge University Press.

John-Steiner, V., Panofsky, C. P., & Smith, L. W. (1994). *Sociocultural approaches to language and literacy.* Cambridge, MA: Cambridge University Press.

Lanza, E. (1992). Can bilingual two-year olds code-switch? *Journal of Child Language, 19,* 633–658.

Leopold, W. (1949). *Speech development of a bilingual child: A linguist's record.* Evanston, IL: Northwestern University Press.

McLaughlin, B. (1978). *Second language acquisition in childhood.* Hillsdale, NJ: Erlbaum.

Meisel, J. M. (1994). Code-switching in yong bilingual children. *Studies in second language acquisition, 16,* 413–440.

Newport, E. L., Gleitman, H., & Gleitman, L. R. (1977). Mother, I'd rather do it myself: Some effects and non-effects of maternal speech style. In C. Snow & C. Ferguson (Eds.), *Talking to children* (pp. 109–150). New York: Cambridge University Press.

Nicoladis, E. (1992). *Phonological and word awareness in preschool children: The effect of a second language.* Unpublished M.A. thesis, McGill University, Montreal.

Oksaar, E. (1971). Code switching as an interactional strategy for developing bilingual competence. *Word, 27,* 377–385.

Padilla, A. M., & Liebman, E. (1975). Language acquisition in the bilingual child. *Bilingual Review, 2,* 34–55.

Paradis, J., & Genesee, F. (1994, November). *Language differentiation in bilingual children: Evidence for the acquisition of functional categories.* Paper presented at the Boston University Conference on Language Development, Boston.

Pease-Alvarez, C., & Vasquez, O. (1994). Language socialization in ethnic minority communities. In F. Genesee (Ed.), *Educating second language children* (pp. 82–102). New York: Cambridge University Press.

Poplack, S. (1987). Language status and language accommodation along a linguistic border. In P. Lowenberg (Ed.), *1987 Georgetown University round table on language and linguistics* (pp. 90–118). Washington, DC: Georgetown University Press.

Poplack, S., & Sankoff, D. (1988). Code switching. In H. von Ulrich Ammon, N. Dittmar, & K. Mattheier (Eds.), *Sociolinguistics: An international handbook of the science of language and society* (pp. 1174–1180). Berlin: de Gruyter.

Redlinger, W. E., & Park, T. (1980). Language mixing in young bilinguals. *Journal of Child Language, 7,* 337–352.

Romaine, S. (1989). *Bilingualism.* Oxford: Basil Blackwell.

Saunders, G. (1982). *Bilingual children: Guidance for the family.* Clevedon, UK: Multilingual Matters.

Schieffelin, B., & Eisenberg, A. R. (1984). Cultural variation in children's conversations. In R. Schiefelbusch & J. Rickar (Eds.), *The acquisition of communicative competence* (pp. 379–418). Baltimore, MD: University Park Press.

Schieffelin, B., & Ochs, E. (1986). Language socialization. *Annual Review of Anthropology, 15,* 163–246.

Smith, N. V. (1973). *The acquisition of phonology: A case study.* Cambridge: The University Press.

Snow, C., & Ferguson, C. (Eds.). (1977). *Talking to children.* New York: Cambridge University Press.

Sridhar, S. N., & Sridhar, K. K. (1980). The syntax and psycholinguistics of bilingual code switching. *Canadian Journal of Psychology, 34,* 407–416.

Swain, M. (1977). Bilingualism, monolingualism, and code acquisition. In W. Mackey & T. Andersson (Eds.), *Bilingualism in early childhood* (pp. 28–35). Rowley, MA: Newbury House.

Volterra, V., & Taeschner, T. (1978). The acquisition and development of language by bilingual children. *Journal of Child Language, 5,* 311–326.

Wells, G. (1986). The language experience of five-year-old children at home and at school. In J. Cook-Gumperz (Ed.), *The social construction of literacy* (pp. 69–93). New York: Cambridge University Press.

CHAPTER 3

The Carpinteria Preschool Program: A Long-Term Effects Study

S. Jim Campos

Educating language-minority Latino students is a challenge that school districts increasingly face in the United States. Recent waves of Latino immigrants have caused their numbers to swell as high as 887,757 in California's schools alone (Language Census Report, 1993). They do not speak English, presenting a challenge to our schools. Because Latino children in general have a long history of poor performance in U.S. schools, it is imperative that our schools educate them effectively or there could be significant negative national repercussions.

The effectiveness and quality of bilingual education programs have been the focus of much debate over the past 2 decades. The major studies addressing these issues, however, have failed to produce conclusive results (Baker & de Kanter, 1983; Danoff, Coles, McLaughlin, & Reynolds, 1977; Willig, 1985). The debate remains high, and Latino educational attainment and achievement remain low. In the early 1990s, Latinos were lagging on every school level; from preschool to college, they were underrepresented and losing ground nationally (Anderson, 1990; Kantrowitz & Rosado, 1991; Merl, 1991).

The evaluation of bilingual education has been plagued by the preponderance of ineffective bilingual programs in ineffective schools (Carter & Chatfield, 1986). There is a need to study quality programs within quality settings to ascertain the effectiveness and implications of bilingual education.

Bilingual program effectiveness has been stymied by intervention efforts that focus singularly on transitioning language-minority children to English without attending to the social and cultural context of learning (Cummins, 1986). The result is that bilingual programs tend to support conditions that are harmful to children's cognitive and psychological development. The list includes loss of a child's cultural identity; loss of the positive effects of first language maintenance on second language development; loss of the cognitive benefits of bilingualness; loss of family participation in school matters because of a school–home language difference; the breakdown of the family unit and psychosocial support structures as the child becomes fluent in English and loses the ability to communicate with caregivers in the home language; inferior status conveyed to minority cultures; loss of self-esteem from all of the above, and more. In the case of the language-minority Latino child who is of low social status—characterized by caregivers who are youthful, poor, vocationally unskilled, and of low educational attainment—and whose cultural heritage in the United States historically has not been valued, it is not surprising that one-dimensional linguistic interventions are ineffective.

Recently, a number of scholars have developed the view that to be effective, schools must alter significantly the relationships between educators and minority students, and between schools and minority communities (Cummins, 1986; Tharp, 1993; Trueba, 1989). Uppermost in models proposed is the notion of "empowering" language-minority children to learn through the social and cultural context.

In Carpinteria, California, a bilingual education preschool program was developed in 1980 under an Elementary Secondary Education Act (ESEA) Title VII grant, with the goal of empowering language-minority Latino children and their families cognitively and psychologically through the social and cultural context. Key to the program was an all-Spanish format. The role of Spanish was perceived as critical to the enhancement of learning opportunities within the peer group, between teacher and child, and in the home. Although success in an English language environment was the long-term goal of the program, English was not used and was viewed as a deterrent to participation, communication, and the development of thought processes.

The Carpinteria Preschool implemented a highly cognitive-academic program within a developmentally appropriate environment for its students. The teachers set up experiences daily that provided students with the opportunity to think and problem solve, both individually and as a group. The emphasis of experiences was on exploration and discovery, with students making sense out of their experiences and then talking about them. Teachers assisted in the process by probing students to talk about the "what" and "why" of their actions and modeling language for them, expanding, extending, and refining its use. The result is that language and cognitive growth went hand in hand, each assisting the other's development.

Parents were made an integral part of the program. Their role as the child's first and "other" teacher was strongly emphasized. Teachers spoke with parents on the telephone several times a month regarding their child's school progress; monthly parent meetings were held to discuss issues related to the program and parenting in general; a central parent advisory committee was formed to train parents in how the school system functioned; a subscription to the preschool magazine *Sesame Street* (with English sections translated, usually orally, into

Spanish by preschool staff) was given to each family; and song sheets, riddles, and rhymes were distributed to parents throughout the year. Parent contributions to the classroom were also accentuated. Regional songs, oral stories, rhymes, and tongue-twisters from Mexico were solicited from the parents and put on tape and into print for classroom use; parents were strongly encouraged to volunteer in the classroom at least once a month and to follow up on homework assignments through a "contract" agreement that they signed; subcommittees from the central parent advisory committee were formed to keep the facility looking beautiful, raise funds for special student events, organize fiestas, teach the children folkloric dances, and so on.

In sum, the major components of the Carpinteria Preschool program were as follows:

1. Development of a strong conceptual foundation in Spanish by the children.
2. Promotion of increased learning opportunities in the home by making parents an integral part of the program.
3. Implementation of an interactional approach to language/concept development through constantly integrating language with the children's preschool experiences.

Short-term results demonstrated that Carpinteria Preschool students entered the Carpinteria Unified School District's (CUSD) kindergarten program recording high levels of developmental skills and cognitive achievement in Spanish (Campos, 1985; Campos & Keatinge, 1988). Kindergarten teachers reported that the students were highly motivated, independent learners and that their parents were active in supporting the school. The Carpinteria Preschool thus represents a high quality, effective intervention in bilingual education. The ultimate test of the effectiveness of this bilingual education program, however, is its efficacy in enhancing the participating students' success in school over the long term. The purpose of the study reported in this chapter, therefore, was to investigate the long-term progress of the Carpinteria Preschool children.

To determine whether the Carpinteria Preschool participants continued demonstrating success in school, I did a quantitative study of these children's achievement in school, from kindergarten to junior high school, comparing their archival records with those of three groups of children in the CUSD. I selected comparison groups that controlled for the initial language of school instruction and level of socioeconomic status (SES). These groups were (1) the language-minority comparison preschool group, children whose home language was Spanish and who participated in community preschool programs other than the Carpinteria Preschool; (2) the entitlement group, English-speaking students who had participated in an entitlement program; and (3) the nonentitlement group, English-speaking children who did not participate in an entitlement program. This is the question I sought to answer: Would the Carpinteria Preschool participants differ from the three groups on scores, ratings, and frequencies from selected measures of standardized achievement tests, nonstandardized report card assessments, and other documents in the archival record?

NATURE OF THE STUDY

Site

The site of the investigation, Carpinteria, is a rural, predominantly middle-class community of about 13,000 people. About 40% of the population is of Latino origin, consisting mostly of long-time Carpinterian Mexican American families and an ever-increasing number of new arrivals from Mexico. The new arrivals are minimum-wage earners who supply the labor force for the large agricultural industry and the factories of the city. They speak Spanish and are generally not fluent in English. Their children make up the Spanish-dominant subjects who attend the Carpinteria Unified School District.

The K–12 CUSD student population of about 2,500 children reflects the same ethnic ratio as the community, about 40% Latino, with the majority of Latino students coming from homes where Spanish is the primary language. Those students who enter school with Spanish as their dominant language are placed in a program of bilingual education. During the years that this investigation covered, the program was of the transitional bilingual education (TBE) variety.

The CUSD's general education program went from kindergarten through grade 12. The kindergarten program was exploratory, hands-on, thinking- and meaning-centered. Grades 1–6 shifted to a more didactic, textbook-driven approach. Entering junior high, students left the self-contained elementary classroom and went to a modular schedule where they received instruction, usually in lecture format, from as many as six different teachers a day, and from some teachers no more than twice a week.

The Carpinteria Unified School District's TBE program went from kindergarten to sixth grade. There was no bilingual program at the secondary grade level, and bilingual services were limited to an instructional aide serving only those students with the greatest language needs. In the TBE program, language-minority students were taught core subjects—for example, reading, language, and math—in the dominant language, Spanish, while English was developed. The program was designed so that language-minority children could use their first language to keep up with instruction until a transfer to English was possible. When students met CUSD exit criteria guidelines, they were transferred to English-only classrooms.

The CUSD teaching staff of about 120 teachers was ethnically disproportionate to the student population, with only 10% being Latino. This was different from the Carpinteria Preschool staff, which was predominantly Latino.
CUSD Latino staff members were concentrated at the primary grades, with the
majority teaching in bilingual education classrooms.

Students of the Study

The subjects of the investigation were the Carpinteria Preschool children
who entered the kindergarten program in the CUSD in the fall of either 1982 or
1983. They were the sons and daughters of the migrating Mexican families in
Carpinteria. The Carpinteria Preschool children were compared with three
groups of children entering the kindergarten program in the CUSD in the fall of
either 1982 or 1983. A description of the Carpinteria Preschool group and the
three groups follows.

The Carpinteria Preschool Group. The Carpinteria Preschool group of
children were Spanish dominant and of low-SES family background. All were of
Mexican descent. Seventy-three percent were born in the United States, and
27% were born in Mexico. The ratio of boys to girls was 52% to 48%. The group
at kindergarten consisted of 50 students in the CUSD. They were placed in the
District's TBE program. The group attritioned to 35 students by junior high
school.

The Language-Minority Comparison Preschool Group. The
language-minority comparison preschool group differed from the Carpinteria
Preschool group in their preschool experience, having participated in community programs that emphasized English language development. Their preschool
program is best described as based on "concurrent bilingual education" practices, where the dominant language, Spanish in this case, is used primarily to
promote English acquisition, rather than primary language development. Otherwise, the language-minority comparison preschool group was similar in language, cultural, and socioeconomic characteristics to the Carpinteria Preschool
group. They were dominant Spanish-speaking children, of Mexican descent,
and from low-SES homes. Seventy-two percent were born in the United States,
and 28% were born in Mexico. The ratio of boys to girls was 35% to 65%. The
group size at kindergarten was 34 students in the CUSD. They were placed in
the District's TBE program. The group attritioned to 24 students by junior
high school.

The Entitlement Group. The entitlement group was made up of
English-speaking children who participated in an entitlement program, that is,

Head Start or Community Action Center, and/or qualified for the CUSD free lunch program. Thus, they fell within low eligibility income guidelines similar to those of the Title VII and language-minority comparison preschool groups. The occupations of the parents of these children, however, were different from those of the Spanish-speaking children's. Whereas Spanish-dominant children's parents worked almost exclusively in agricultural or factory benchmark positions, the parents of the entitlement group children were spread across a variety of job classifications, with the exception of professional ones. Also, at the time the children in this group entered school at kindergarten, almost half came from a single-parent home. None of the other groups had more than a 15% rate of single-parent families upon entry into kindergarten. Thus, inclusion in the entitlement group may have been more a result of a temporary setback in economic fortune, that is, the result of a broken marriage, than actual low-SES condition. Ethnically, only 24% of this group was white, and the majority, 65%, were Latino. All but one subject from this group were born in the United States. The ratio of boys to girls was 70% to 30%. The group size at kindergarten was 37 students in the CUSD and attritioned to 32 by junior high school.

The Nonentitlement Group. The nonentitlement group was made up of English-speaking children who had never participated in an entitlement program. Because the subjects in this group numbered over 100, the group was reduced in size to approximate the sizes of the other groups. Thirty-six subjects were randomly selected. Almost half of the parents in the nonentitlement group had professional occupations, and there was clearly a middle- to upper-SES feel to the occupations of the parents in this group. All but one subject was born in the United States. Ethnically, only 22% were Latino, and the majority, 75%, were white. The ratio of boys to girls was 56% to 44%. With two exceptions, none of the children in this group experienced interruptions in his or her CUSD program. As a result, there was little missing data for the subjects in this group, unlike for the subjects in the other groups, where the group sizes eroded with each succeeding year.

Instruments

Data from the archival records of the subjects were collected for analysis. The outcome measures were taken from three basic categories: (1) school competency assessment data, (2) nonstandardized assessment data, and (3) standardized assessment data.

School Competency Assessment Data. Data related to competency in school and the completion of school requirements were collected for grade retention, special education placement, attendance, and suspensions. Specific to the language-minority subjects was the collection of data that gave the time of transfer from a bilingual classroom to an English-only classroom and the time at which language--minority subjects were designated as proficient in English by the CUSD on a language proficiency test (usually the Language Assessment Scales [LAS] test by De Avila and Duncan, 1985, and in some cases the Bilingual Syntax Measure [BSM] test by Burt, Dulay, and Hernandez, 1973).

Nonstandardized Assessment Data. Data from student report cards were collected on academic achievement, and on evaluations of conduct, from kindergarten to junior high school. Academic achievement data were in basic skills, that is, reading, language, and math. Data on conduct were in effort, achievement work study habits, social work study habits, social skills, and behavior skills. Teacher assessments of students' academic achievement and conduct on report cards were usually in the form of descriptive ratings. These were converted into numerical scores—excellent = 3, average = 2, poor = 1—for analysis.

Standardized Assessment Data. California Achievement Test (CAT; Educational Testing Service, 1985) scores, featuring reading, language, and math subtests, plus a total battery score, were collected at fifth grade. Fifth grade was a key year in the CUSD's testing program. At fifth grade, all subjects in the Carpinteria Preschool group and in the language-minority comparison preschool group were required to present their end-of-year tests in English. Prior to this grade, the majority of language-minority Latino students from these groups had tested in Spanish on the Spanish Assessment Battery Examination (SABE; Educational Testing Service, 1988) instead of the CAT. Also at fifth grade, all students in the CUSD were evaluated on proficiency in basic skills. The fifth-grade District Proficiency Test consisted of selected test items (key items) taken from the fifth-grade CAT. On the proficiency test, each student was assessed a "pass or fail" rating in the areas of reading, spelling, language, and math.

Data Analysis

Analysis of variance (ANOVA) was employed to analyze data on standardized and nonstandardized assessment outcome measures. Using the Systat statistical software program, the ANOVA was performed to check for overall significance ($p < .05$), and a post hoc Tukey test was used to determine significance among the groups. All data collected that were not in the form of a test or rating score, that is, the pass/fail assessment of the fifth-grade District Proficiency Test, and all of the school competency assessment outcome measures were analyzed as frequencies.

OVERALL ANALYSIS

Outcome measure results answered the question of the study—how the Carpinteria Preschool group differed from the language-minority comparison preschool group, the entitlement group, and the nonentitlement group.

The Carpinteria Preschool Group Compared with the Language-Minority Comparison Preschool Group

The Carpinteria Preschool group was superior in performance to the language-minority comparison preschool group on most scores, ratings, and frequencies from the selected measures of school competency assessments, nonstandardized report card assessments, and standardized achievement tests in the archival record. The difference between the two groups was most pronounced at kindergarten, and on standardized outcome measures of cognitive achievement and measures of English acquisition.

School Competency Assessment Data. In school competency assessment areas, 26% of the Carpinteria Preschool group was retained (repeated a grade) compared with 63% of the language-minority comparison preschool group. Most of the retentions for the Carpinteria Preschool group, 77%, occurred *after* the kindergarten year, whereas most of the retentions for the language-minority comparison preschool group, 75%, occurred at kindergarten. Sixteen percent were placed in a program of special education, compared with 21%. Eleven percent demonstrated an irregular attendance pattern, compared with 13%. Eighteen percent were suspended from school, compared with 17%—student suspensions were specific to the junior high school years for both groups.

The Carpinteria Preschool group demonstrated superior performance over the language-minority comparison preschool group in outcome measures of English acquisition. Ten years after preschool, 95% of the Carpinteria Preschool group was rated fully fluent on proficiency tests of English, compared with 84% of the language-minority comparison preschool group. The Carpinteria Preschool group also demonstrated a greater facility for transferring out of the bilingual education classroom and into the regular English-only classroom than did the language-minority comparison preschool group. By fourth grade 76% of the Carpinteria Preschool group had transferred to a mainstream English-only class, compared with 32% of the language-minority comparison preschool group.

Nonstandardized Assessment Data. On K–6 report card evaluations of reading, language, and math, the Carpinteria Preschool group achieved higher ratings than the language-minority comparison preschool group in virtually every basic skill area, at every grade, although a significant difference of means usually was not found. Only on math at second grade did the language-minority comparison preschool group achieve a higher overall rating than the Carpinteria Preschool group. The greatest difference in ratings between the two groups occurred at kindergarten, where the Carpinteria Preschool group demonstrated a significant difference of means in all three basic skill areas over the language-minority comparison preschool group.

On outcome measures of conduct, usually no significant difference of means was found between the Carpinteria Preschool group and the language-minority comparison preschool group. The Carpinteria Preschool group, however, showed a steady pattern of improvement from kindergarten to junior high. There was no apparent pattern on outcome measures of conduct for the language-minority comparison preschool group. The greatest difference between means of these two groups occurred at kindergarten, where the Carpinteria Preschool group received its worst evaluations on conduct and the language-minority comparison preschool group received its best ones.

On the results of overall GPA (grade point average) at junior high, no significant difference was found between the Carpinteria Preschool group and the language-minority comparison preschool group. The Carpinteria Preschool group achieved at a C− average, and the language-minority comparison preschool group at a D+ average.

Standardized Assessment Data. A significant difference of means favoring the Carpinteria Preschool group over the language-minority comparison preschool group was found in the reading and math subtests of the fifth-grade CAT and on the total battery of the test. The language subtest group mean scores came very close to demonstrating a significant difference in favor of the Carpinteria Preschool group. Perhaps a more important finding than the group mean score results on the CAT was that only one-half of the language-minority comparison preschool group were administered the regular version of the fifth-grade CAT. The other half of this group was administered a scaled-down version of the fifth-grade CAT. In contrast, only two children from the Carpinteria Preschool group were administered a scaled-down version of the fifth-grade CAT.

On the fifth-grade District Proficiency Test, the Carpinteria Preschool group's passing rate on proficiency outcome measures was superior to that of the language-minority comparison preschool group. On the average, 80% of the Carpinteria Preschool group passed the proficiency tests per subtest category of reading, spelling, language, and math, compared with an average of 30% for the language-minority comparison preschool group.

The Carpinteria Preschool Group Compared with the Entitlement Group

The Carpinteria Preschool group usually mirrored the achievement of the entitlement group, and sometimes demonstrated superior performance on scores, ratings, and frequencies from the selected measures of school competency assessments, nonstandardized report card assessments, and standardized achievement tests in the archival record. The difference between the two groups was most pronounced at kindergarten.

School Competency Assessment Data. In school competency assessment areas, 26% of the Carpinteria Preschool group was retained, compared with 38% of the entitlement group. Most of the retentions for the Carpinteria Preschool group, 77%, occurred *after* kindergarten, whereas most of the retentions for the entitlement group, 62%, occurred at kindergarten. Sixteen percent were placed in a program of special education, compared with 34%. Eleven percent demonstrated an irregular attendance pattern, compared with 13%. Eighteen percent were suspended from school, compared with 13%—student suspensions were specific to the junior high school years for both groups.

Nonstandardized Assessment Data. On K–6 report card evaluations of basic skills, the Carpinteria Preschool group usually achieved higher ratings than the entitlement group in language and math. The entitlement group usually achieved higher ratings in reading. Outside of kindergarten, only in a single instance was a significant difference of means found between the two groups. The greatest difference in ratings between the two groups occurred at kindergarten, where the Carpinteria Preschool group demonstrated a significant difference of means in all three basic skill areas over the entitlement group.

On outcome measures of conduct, there were no significant differences of means between the Carpinteria Preschool group and the entitlement group. As previously stated, the Carpinteria Preschool group showed a steady pattern of improvement from kindergarten to junior high. By fifth and sixth grade, the conduct evaluation mean scores were better for the Carpinteria Preschool group than for the entitlement group.

On the results of overall GPA at junior high, no significant difference was found between the Carpinteria Preschool group and the entitlement group. Each group achieved at a C− average.

Standardized Assessment Data. No significant difference was found between the Carpinteria Preschool group and the entitlement group on any subtest of the fifth-grade CAT. Demonstrating how similarly these groups achieved, on the total battery of achievement of the fifth-grade CAT, the group mean scores of the Carpinteria Preschool and entitlement groups were only a single point apart, 226.77 to 225.30, in favor of the Carpinteria Preschool group.

On the fifth-grade District Proficiency Test, the Carpinteria Preschool group's passing rate on proficiency outcome measures was superior to that of the entitlement group. On the average, 80% of the Carpinteria Preschool group passed its proficiency tests per subtest category of reading, spelling, language, and math, compared with an average of 70% for the entitlement group.

The Carpinteria Preschool Group Compared with the Nonentitlement Group

The Carpinteria Preschool group usually performed at a lower level than the nonentitlement group on scores, ratings, and frequencies from the selected measures of school competency assessments, nonstandardized report card assessments, and standardized achievement tests in the archival record. Lower achievement differences between the two groups were most pronounced in assessments of reading, and much less so in assessments of language and math. The two groups performed most similarly at kindergarten. On conduct, teachers almost always rated the nonentitlement group best of all groups.

School Competency Assessment Data. On school competency assessment areas, 26% of the Carpinteria Preschool group was retained, compared with 11% of the nonentitlement group. Most of the retentions for the Carpinteria Preschool group, 77%, occurred *after* kindergarten, whereas 100% of the retentions for the nonentitlement group occurred at kindergarten. Sixteen percent were placed in a program of special education, compared with 17%. Eleven percent demonstrated an irregular attendance pattern, compared with 8%. Eighteen percent were suspended from school, compared with 3%—student suspensions were specific to the junior high school years for both groups.

Nonstandardized Assessment Data. On report card evaluations of basic skills, the Carpinteria Preschool group achieved lower ratings than the nonentitlement group at every grade except kindergarten. The difference in group mean ratings was most pronounced in reading, where a significant difference of means was usually found. This was not the case for language and math, where usually no significant difference of means was found. Ratings at kindergarten, however, were radically different from ratings at the rest of the grade levels. At kindergarten, the Carpinteria Preschool group achieved slightly higher group mean ratings than the nonentitlement group on basic skills, and there was no significant difference between the two groups in any of the basic skill areas.

On outcome measures of conduct, mean scores for the Carpinteria Preschool group were worse than those for the nonentitlement group, and usually a significant difference of means was found. While the Carpinteria Preschool group demonstrated steady improvement on outcome measures of conduct, the nonentitlement group proceeded from kindergarten to junior high with consistently superior mean ratings. Almost without exception, they were rated best among all groups on measures of conduct.

On the results of GPA outcome measures at junior high, there was an entire grade difference between the B− average achieved by the nonentitlement group and the C− average of the Carpinteria Preschool group. The nonentitlement group was found to be significantly different from the Carpinteria Preschool group, and the other groups as well.

Standardized Assessment Data. The Carpinteria Preschool group did not achieve to the same high levels on the fifth-grade CAT as the nonentitlement group. (The scores of the nonentitlement group on the fifth-grade CAT were representative of the upper quartile rank, while the Carpinteria Preschool Group's were representative of the fiftieth percentile level.) A significant difference of means, however, was found only on the reading subtest and the total battery of the fifth-grade CAT. No significant difference of means between the Carpinteria Preschool group and the nonentitlement group was found on the language and math subtests of the fifth-grade CAT.

On the fifth-grade District Proficiency Test, the Carpinteria Preschool group's passing rate on proficiency outcome measures was lower than that of the nonentitlement group. On the average, 80% of the Carpinteria Preschool group passed the proficiency tests per subtest category of reading, spelling, language, and math, compared with an average of 95% for the nonentitlement group.

IMPLICATIONS

The results suggest that the Carpinteria Preschool program had beneficial long-term effects for its language-minority students. The scores, ratings, and frequencies from the selected measures of school competency assessments, nonstandardized report card assessments, and standardized achievement tests in their archival record show the students to be literate in English and competent in school. Most important, the evidence demonstrates that attending to the social and cultural context of learning, specifically in the use of the first language to empower students and their families cognitively and psychologically, did not delay English acquisition or detract from the subsequent learning of skills in an English language environment.

The results of the study demonstrate a direct correlation between progress in school and attending to the social and cultural context of learning for language-minority Latino students. To illustrate, the best period of achievement occurs when the students are only a year removed from the all-Spanish preschool program, and at a grade, kindergarten, that is similar in program philosophy to that of the preschool. The students continue to progress in the subsequent years to sixth grade, although less robustly than at kindergarten, under a change in philosophy to more traditional educational practices, but with a program of bilingual education and bilingual personnel maintained. In junior high, where there are virtually no bilingual education services or personnel available, there is a decline in achievement. Rather than a "fading" of effects, reduced attention to the social and cultural context of learning explains the Carpinteria Preschool students' progress through school.

The importance of the social and cultural context of learning is also demonstrated by the results of outcome measures in social behavior. The evidence suggests that the Carpinteria Preschool students had more trouble adjusting to the school social environment than the academic one. Of the groups in the study, only the nonentitlement group achieved consistently acceptable behavior in school on teachers' ratings. This probably occurred because for this group the sociocultural context of the home most closely matched that of the schools. The ethnically disproportionate CUSD teacher–student ratio and/or the lack of training in bilingual education on the part of the majority of the staff may have created misunderstandings between the school and its language-minority Latino students.

As stated above, there was no evident delay in the rate of English acquisition by the Carpinteria Preschool students, and they demonstrated competency in applying their English language skills. When compared with the language-minority comparison preschool group, they acquired English language fluency faster, transitioned out of bilingual education classrooms sooner, and achieved in English language classrooms and on English language standardized tests better. Clearly, first language development in their preschool program did not interfere or delay their second language learning. Instead, the results suggest that they were better prepared to understand and utilize opportunities in their learning environment. In contrast, the results for the language-minority comparison preschool group suggest that a lack of substantial amounts of first language development decreased their chances for success in school.

Although information about family participation was not part of the archival record of the students in the study, it should be noted that parents from the Carpinteria Preschool program were highly active in the CUSD. They organized committees that they named the "comite de padres latinos" (COPLA) at each elementary school site in the CUSD. At the time of the study, each COPLA committee was led by a parent trained by the Carpinteria Preschool program, and the majority of committee members were also the parents of students who had participated in the program. The home–school link established by the Carpinteria Preschool program thus was maintained and should augur well for the ultimate success of these students.

CONCLUSION

Schools challenged by student populations that do not speak English must look to the social and cultural context of learning to educate them effectively. To do otherwise is to perpetuate the failures of the past within certain minority populations in this country. A school or district-wide program that attends to the social and cultural context of learning will empower language-minority students and their families to be successful in school as they acquire English. Furthermore, school staffs must be trained in sociocultural issues, and must proportionately represent the community they serve, to ensure that cultural differences are respected and learning opportunities made meaningful to all students.

For their part, students who participated in the Carpinteria Preschool program, despite an apparent interruption of positive growth at junior high, appear poised and prepared for ultimate success. An update of this investigation provides evidence of perseverance and resiliency on their part. A current check of their progress in high school demonstrates improved grades from the junior high program (up to a C+ average); retention of bilingual skills, which should serve them well in the emerging global economy; almost all of them on-line to graduate (one has been accepted at Harvard University, another the University of California, Berkeley); and a lack of involvement in gang-related activity, which is a growing phenomenon in the Carpinteria community. Weikart (1989) notes that the continuity of effects from a "quality" early learning intervention are manifested best for minority children on "real-world" indicators, like job status, income, and good citizenship, *after* they have left school. In the long run, I believe the students who participated in the Carpinteria Preschool will prove to be positive and productive contributors to society in the United States.

REFERENCES

Anderson, P. (1990, July 17). Study: Latinos lag in education. *Santa Barbara News–Press*, p. A–9.

Baker, K. A., & de Kanter, A. (1983). *Bilingual education.* Lexington, MA: D.C. Heath.

Burt, M. K., Dulay, H. C., & Hernandez, E. (1973). *Bilingual syntax measure.* New York: Harcourt, Brace, Jovanovich.

Carter, T. P., & Chatfield, M. L. (1986). Effective bilingual schools: Implications for policy and practice. *American Journal of Education, 95*(1), 200–232.

Campos, S. J. (1985). A Spanish-language preschool program. *Second language learning by young children* (pp. 82–94). Sacramento: California State Department of Education.

Campos, S. J., & Keatinge, H. R. (1988). The Carpinteria language minority student experience: From theory, to practice, to success. In T. Skutnabb-Kangas & J. Cummins (Eds.), *Minority education: From shame to struggle* (pp. 299–307). Clevedon, UK: Multilingual Matters.

Cummins, J. (1986). Empowering minority students: A framework for intervention. *Harvard Educational Review, 56*(1), 18–36.

Danoff, M. N., Coles, G. J., McLaughlin, D. H., & Reynolds, D. J. (1977). *Evaluation of the impact of ESEA Title VII Spanish/English bilingual education programs: Vol. 1. Study design and interim findings.* Palo Alto, CA: American Institutes for Research.

De Avila, E., & Duncan, S. E. (1985). *Language Assessment Scales.* Monterey, CA: CTB/McGraw-Hill.

Educational Testing Service. (1985). *California Achievement Test.* Monterey, CA: CTB/McGraw-Hill.

Educational Testing Service. (1988). *Spanish Assessment Battery Examination.* Monterey, CA: CTB/McGraw-Hill.

Kantrowitz, B., & Rosado, L. (1991). Falling further behind: A generation of Hispanics isn't making the grade. *Newsweek, 118*(8), 60.

Language Census Report for California Public Schools. (1993). Educational Demographics Unit Research, Evaluation and Technology Division. California Department of Education, Sacramento.

Merl, J. (1991, January 25). Latinos lagging on every school level, study finds. *The Los Angeles Times,* pp. 1, 30.

Tharp, R. (1993). *Cultural specifics and universals.* Presentation to the Bilingual Research Group, University of California, Santa Cruz.

Trueba, H. (1989). *Raising silent voices: Educating the linguistic minorities for the 21st century.* New York: Newbury House.

Weikart, D. P. (1989). *Quality preschool programs: A long-term social investment* (Occasional Paper No. 5). New York: Ford Foundation.

Willig, A. C. (1985). A meta-analysis of selected studies on the effectiveness of bilingual education. *Review of Education Research, 55,* 269–317.

CHAPTER 4

Assessment of Bilingual Children: A Dilemma Seeking Solutions

Celia Genishi and Margaret Borrego Brainard

Of the numerous dilemmas in early childhood education, assessment is one of the thorniest. Position statements from professional organizations such as the National Association for the Education of Young Children (NAEYC) urge practitioners *not* to use standardized tests, unless children and their teachers clearly benefit from knowledge of test results (NAEYC & National Association of Early Childhood Specialists in State Departments of Education, 1991). Moreover, policy makers and educators view fundamental changes in assessment practices as key to school reform (LaCelle-Peterson & Rivera, 1994). Thus a range of alternatives to standardized tests are currently being developed. These include teacher-created ways of assessing (Genishi, 1992), portfolios (Grace & Shores, 1992), and performance-based assessment systems (Meisels, Dichtelmiller, Dorfman, Jablon, & Marsden, 1993).

Ideally, these efforts at reform, aimed at broadening educators' definition of assessment to include both standardized tests and their alternatives, extend to programs for children who are bilingual or who are learning English in early childhood settings. However, because of federal and state funding patterns that support bilingual programs apart from "regular" classrooms, the challenge of assessing non-English speakers is seldom integrated into general efforts to reform assessment. Moreover, the assessment of young children learning English, or English language learners (ELLs),[1] carries with it the social, political, and linguistic issues attached to bilingual education, as well as the dilemmas inherent in the assessment of all young children.

The purpose of this chapter is to provide an overview of the issues that need to be understood as early childhood educators make decisions about assessment of ELLs. The ELLs of greatest interest here are those who are learning English in a school or center setting. These may be immigrants, children of immigrants, or U.S.-born children whose first language is not English. Because they begin their schooling as non-English speakers, they are often seen—appropriately or not—as a population that will find school learning difficult. We include a discussion of standardized measures, along with school district and teacher-based means of assessing what and how these children learn. In the Appendix is a list of some of the standardized measures currently used with ELLs.

WHAT IS VALUED IS ASSESSED

One of the truths of current educational practice is that a teacher's, center's, or school's assessment measures tell much about the curriculum and the values of teachers and administrators. So in a school district in which kindergartners all take a reading readiness test at the beginning of the year, we can infer that reading instruction is valued. If instead there is no testing of children in any subject matter until the fourth grade, we can infer that there is not great emphasis on the basics of reading and math and/or there is no pressure to test children in order to qualify for funds for special programs. In a school district where there are many ELLs and tests for bilingual or potentially bilingual children are given in English only, we can infer that even in "bilingual" programs the valued language is English, and not the learner's first/home language. We also can infer that tests are not available in many of the children's home languages.

This set of inferences shows that the kinds of programs and assessment that adults choose for children are never without a social and political context. Further, as authors of a chapter like this we do not take a neutral stance. Our position is compatible with that of the NAEYC and other professional organizations such as the Association for Childhood Education International (ACEI). We think that standardized tests are generally inappropriate for young children (birth through age 8) unless they are necessary to demonstrate the need for special facilities or services. We also think that the people who are closest to children—family members and teachers—are often the most reliable sources of information about young children's abilities, including their linguistic abilities. With respect to ELLs, we think that a learner's home language is a *resource* that should be maintained or at least not discouraged in educational settings, to enhance learners' opportunities to communicate freely. Finally, the decision about whether a program is bilingual, that is, aimed at the facilitation of learning English as a second language (L2) *and* maintaining the home language (L1), should be made by staff *and* parents and not by school district or staff alone. Like the authors, school and community members have beliefs and values that guide such a decision.

Despite the position taken by professional organizations and individual educators against widespread testing, many young children are still required to take a range of standardized tests (Charlesworth, Fleege, & Weitman, 1994). In the next section, we discuss the development of standardized measures that are used primarily with bilingual or ELL children, and include a commentary on their strengths and inadequacies and issues associated with their use.

STANDARDIZED TESTS FOR BILINGUAL CHILDREN

Standardized tests to measure the language proficiency of bilingual children have been developed largely because legislation requires that children be placed in programs that meet their particular needs. Every state handles assessment for placement differently. California, for example, measures whether a student's language is "English superior" or "primary language superior" (Merino & Spencer, 1983). Other states may have no provision for languages other than English.

Challenges of Testing Language

Categories for placement of children grow out of a tradition of test development that roughly coincides with researchers' understanding of children's language acquisition (Rivera & Simich, 1981). For example, language tests based on behaviorist theory measure "discrete-point" elements such as pronunciation, vocabulary, and grammar (Henning, 1987). These tests often require children to identify objects, repeat sentences, or respond to specific oral directions, and score responses as simply right or wrong. These tests have been criticized over the years, however, as linguists have come to understand that language skills are rarely acquired or used in isolation.

An increasing number of tests include more integrated tasks that show that language is used in context, that is, that speakers always draw upon *pragmatic rules* or rules of language use. Such tasks include close procedures, sentence completion, dictation, and story re-telling (Rivera & Simich, 1981). These measures take into account relationships between isolated units of language.

Most recently, sociolinguists have begun to design measures that attempt to "utilize the richness of linguistic production of children in naturalistic contexts and to avoid the rigid atmosphere sometimes associated with traditional testing" (Powers, Johnson, Slaughter, Crowder, & Jones, 1985, p. 960). These tests include the analysis of informal discussions among children or conversations between examiners and children concerning stories or pictures.

One of the difficulties of measuring competence in more than one language is to determine how the sequence of skills, from simple to complex, can be compared across languages. The development of syntax in English, for example, does not neatly match that of the syntax of Spanish because the two languages are structured differently. Various tests have attempted to take this into account, with mixed results (Graham, 1978; Haber, 1985). The Bilingual Syntax Measure (BSM), described later, comes closest to taking this important feature into account (Merino & Spencer, 1983).

Persistent Issues of Testing

In evaluating any standardized test, it is important to be aware of what test developers refer to as "content validity," which is the ability of a test to measure what is actually taught in the classroom or, in the case of young ELLs, actually used in daily conversation. It is therefore necessary to examine the items on a test to see how they might match with a student's actual language (Ligon, 1985). This is further complicated in bilingual evaluations, since it is likely that students may have different proficiency in the languages that they use at home, at school, or in their neighborhood (Merino & Spencer, 1983).

Another issue affecting a student's placement in a bilingual program is the test developer's definition of *language proficiency*. The process of defining and justifying the concepts underlying a test is often referred to as finding the "construct validity" of a test, and different instruments define the basic construct of "proficiency" in different ways. The Language Assessment Battery (LAB), for example, speaks of finding the "language effectiveness" (Barrows-Chesterfield, 1985) of a student; the BSM purports to determine the "syntactic ability" (Graham, 1978) of a student; while the Language Assessment Scales (LAS) measure language proficiency according to how a student compares with a monolingual speaker who has been given tasks similar to those on the test (Haber, 1985).

Similarly, administration and scoring procedures vary depending on the test developers' definition of language proficiency. While discrete-point tests are more easily scored, other more complex measures must include specific criteria for scoring (Henning, 1987). Some test developers devise "cutoff" scores or basal/ceiling levels to determine the competence expected of a given child at a given age. Others rely on ratings agreed upon by several evaluators to define competence. In the development of scoring procedures, the most efficient way to determine how children should score on tests is to establish norms by administering the test to a population of children similar to those to whom the test will be administered. After norming, test developers can gain greater knowledge about the effectiveness of their tests by seeking "concurrent validity." That is, they may administer several different tests to the same population of students. If students score at comparable levels on each of those tests, it is possible that all of the tests are measuring the same elements. In addition, the same test can be administered to students at two different times, appropriately spaced. If their performance is the same on the two tests, one can assume that the test has measured skills accurately. In other words, the test shows "reliability" or accuracy of measurement.

Although careful thought has been put into the development of language proficiency measures, "comprehensive, flexible assessments don't currently exist" (LaCelle-Peterson & Rivera, 1994, p. 66) for ELLs. It has been difficult to establish norming procedures (Ulibarri, Spencer, & Rivas, 1981) since there are so many populations in need of language proficiency assessments, many of whom use a dialect in their primary language. At present, "available instruments, in general, do not possess psychometric reliability and validity, yet educators continue to use available instruments because no better measuring devices currently exist" (Rivera & Simich, 1981, p. 39).

In addition, as Merino and Spencer (1983) point out, it has been extremely difficult to establish concurrent validity among these tests.

> There are substantial reasons to doubt the comparability of these oral language proficiency instruments across languages. The use of these instruments to diagnose a child's relative level of proficiency in English and Spanish is subject to serious question. School personnel should not assume that a child's performance in one language version can necessarily be compared to results in the other. Placement into special programs, based on relative levels of English and Spanish proficiency as defined by these tests, should not be undertaken. (pp. 27–28)

We emphasize this caveat that language proficiency tests are still lacking in validity and reliability and that their norms have been established primarily with English-speaking populations. Still, to be informative about what is available, we list in the Appendix at the end of this chapter some of the standardized tests currently used to measure language proficiency among young ELLs. We include the tests that are described in the most recent resources on measurement and evaluation of ELL children.

ALTERNATIVES TO STANDARDIZED MEASURES

There is increasing agreement among practitioners and policy makers that alternatives to standardized measures must be developed and used if traditional patterns of testing are to change (Darling-Hammond, 1994; Fournier, Lansdowne, Pastenes, Steen, & Hudelson, 1992). As noted earlier, at present there are few large-scale attempts to change the nature of testing for bilingual or ELL children, although the need for change has been recognized (LaCelle-Peterson & Rivera, 1994). LaCelle-Peterson and Rivera (1994) point out that norms for a test's reliability and validity are typically based on an English-speaking population. Thus tests become primarily measures of knowledge of English, not of literacy, mathematics, or other content.

The current focus is on developing alternative *performance-based assessment measures*. These often are still dependent on knowledge of English, but they are potentially more flexible than standardized tests. Performance-based measures, which include teacher-created alternatives, are ways of tapping *what children actually can do in classrooms and centers*. They depart from the usual multiple-choice format of standardized tests and focus more on the processes of development and learning and not discrete products. Moreover, the theoretical framework for performance-based assessments often includes multiple skills, abilities, and intelligences (Gardner, 1983), in contrast to traditional testing theory, which assumes that an individual possesses a measurable general level of intelligence. The view of intelligence as multifaceted calls for assessment that is also multifaceted.

Performance-Based Assessment Measures

Multifaceted performance-based assessments can range from an audio-taped language sample to a child's singing of "Happy Birthday" (Wexler-Sherman, Gardner, & Feldman, 1988). They can be oral, written, "performative," as in a dance, or visual/artistic. Because they may be documented in a variety of ways, they are by nature less language-dependent than traditional tests. Early childhood teachers often find it natural to observe children as they engage in varied activities, although careful assessment (compiling written records based on observations) is time-consuming. As interest in this kind of assessment grows, some administrators in schools, centers, and school districts provide guidelines for what and when teachers should assess, so that individual teachers do not need to invent a system for themselves. Moreover, administrators believe that in order to be useful and credible, alternatives to standardized tests need to be applied consistently to all children of all teachers.

Thus some schools and school districts provide a framework for teachers to follow that combines teachers' observations and required samples (Copeland, 1994). Required samples of children's painting, block-building, or oral language may be collected three times during the year (fall, winter, and spring). In addition, there may be teacher-selected and/or child-selected pieces that demonstrate ability or skill not included in the required samples or that reflect a unique aspect of a child's development. These assessment frameworks generally include multiple domains of development, including social, cognitive, emotional, aesthetic, and physical, as well as specific objectives for children's learning. Frameworks like this have the advantage of developing according to the needs of a district or school, at a pace that suits staff and teachers. Further, local efforts can be flexible in responding to teacher feedback.

Performance-based assessment *systems* are also available commercially and have many of the characteristics of informal teacher-based ways of assessing children. *The Work Sampling System* (Meisels, Dichtelmiller, Dorfman, Jablon, & Marsden, 1993), for example, consists of three main components: developmental checklists, portfolios, and summary reports. There is a checklist for each age/grade from preschool-age 3 to third grade, and each contains observable behaviors in the domains of personal and social development, language and literacy, the arts, social studies, mathematical thinking, scientific thinking, and physical development. Portfolios consist of samples of children's products in these seven domains. Three times a year the teachers are asked to rate samples from each domain as "developing as expected" versus "needs development." Further, five other samples that may integrate abilities across domains are chosen by the teacher or child for each child.

Thus a performance-based assessment system *is* an alternative to standardized tests, tapping what children can do at different times of the year. Because the system's creators have established the domains of interest and the behaviors to be included in the checklists, *The Work Sampling System* is a kind of compromise between standardized tests, which are narrow in focus and administered at a single point in time, and teacher-created ways of assessing, which we discuss next.

Teacher-Created Ways of Assessing

Teachers in early childhood settings have traditionally used informal ways of assessing how children develop and learn. Observation, or taking notice by watching and listening, has been fundamental to teachers' understandings of the children in their classrooms (Almy & Genishi, 1979). In fact, their basic ways—observing, developing checklists, recording children's talk and progress in literacy, taking photographs—are well represented in the performance-based assessment system just described. In this section we present three early childhood teachers' ways of assessing bilingual and ELL children in public school settings, from prekindergarten to grade 1.

Doreen Murphy's Prekindergarten. Doreen Murphy is a teacher in the school district cited earlier (Copeland, 1994) in which all prekindergarten and kindergarten teachers are involved in documenting children's progress. Her class consists of English speakers, with the exception of Josefina, who began the school year speaking Spanish and no English. During the fall, Mrs. Murphy heard very little English from Josefina. By the winter (mid-January), however, Josefina was using a combination of English and Spanish as she engaged in activities with other children. Listen to her as she "reads" a book by describing its pictures to a friend.

Josefina: Sylvia, here. (*Sylvia moves chair so they can sit together.*) Sylvia, stop. I told you, no squishing.

Josefina (reading): *Su mama* [her mother] sleeping. Yesterday. No, I no told
you to come here. *No tengo* [I don't have]. I got to go, Ma.

This is an excerpt from a longer conversation that Mrs. Murphy wrote down
during her monthly focus on children's spoken language. She wrote it on a form
that is part of the *Primary Language Record* (Centre for Primary Language
Education, 1988) called "Observations and Samples," which can be used over
a period of time to show how language is used in a variety of settings. Mrs.
Murphy has a form for every child in her class.

Adding to the same form, in June Mrs. Murphy recorded the following
excerpt during center time. Josefina is on the rug, "reading" as the teacher
would:

Josefina: Goldilocks. Sylvia, I read the pictures. Sylvia, come here (*laughs as
another child falls*). He falls.
Mrs. M (to two boys throwing something): Apologize, please.
Josefina: Say you're sorry. Sylvia, come here.
Gerard: I got Goldilocks too.
Josefina: Right, it's Goldilocks, Mrs. Murphy.
Mrs. M: Yes.
Josefina: See, I told you it's Goldilocks (*"reading"*). The mother and the
daddy are going to go down, down, down. Here is the pages. It's too hot.
She fall down on the floor. You sit on the mommy. What's that bed?
Sylvia: Bed.
Josefina: You sit on the mommy bed. The mommy go home. "You eated my
food. You eated my food. You ate all my food."

By the end of the school year, Josefina speaks only English with her peers, using
some immature forms that English-speaking prekindergartners might also use
("eated") but then correcting herself immediately. Mrs. Murphy's monthly focus
on talk enables this systematic record of Josefina's progress in a "regular" classroom where she is surrounded by English speakers.

Marla Powell's Prekindergarten. In a different kind of classroom, a bilingual prekindergarten in which many of the children come from Spanish-
speaking families, teacher-created assessments are enriched by the teacher's
knowledge of the children's language *and* culture. Pre-K teacher Marla Powell
tells her own assessment story.

A learning environment which involves a language other than English
may also involve a cultural perspective that is outside of the main-

stream. Thus the teacher in a bilingual classroom will need to be "fluent" in two cultures, as well as in two languages. This fluency, or cultural literacy, is a prerequisite for quality teaching, which includes quality assessment.

Before a teacher can begin to assess and evaluate young students, she must be able to understand and interpret the children's expressions. This understanding is limited if she considers only the grammar of the language and is not familiar with the children's culture. One example might be the use of the term *maestra*, literally "teacher." In many Dominican families, this term is seen as one of respect and honor. To many teachers raised in the U.S., *maestra* might be interpreted as a generic and not very respectful term, leading them to say, "My name is Ms. So-and-so." If a child continued to use *maestra*, how might she or he be viewed by a teacher out-of-touch with the students' background?

I've also learned about the importance of being aware of current trends within the children's lives. Examples range from Barney to the Power Rangers, popular action figures. While screening a child last week [a school district requirement], I noticed that although he couldn't name the colors, he could say "Jason" and point to the red crayon and "Tommy" and point to the green crayon [Jason is the red Power Ranger, Tommy, the green one]. If I did not know anything about the Power Rangers, I would have dismissed these comments as meaningless. . . .

One of the most important endeavors of the early childhood teacher who wants to improve her assessment skills is to get organized at or before the beginning of the school year. I have learned that this is imperative to conducting fair and timely assessments. I make a schedule which lists, month-by-month, the types of assessment I will conduct.

Ms. Powell includes in her assessments children's dictations. As she writes what children say, she sometimes distinguishes between what they say in English and in Spanish, using a red marker for English and a blue one for Spanish. This may help children distinguish between the two languages. She also has children "draw a person" three times a year, providing directions in both Spanish and English. Most of Ms. Powell's assessments, however, are done on an ongoing basis. She focuses on every aspect of the curriculum, from early literacy experiences to free play to spoken language in an informal interview with each child, and embeds her interpretations of children's progress in her knowledge of their culture. In her own words:

One very critical aspect of assessment in a bilingual classroom is that it *must* be ongoing. Children may make a gradual move toward greater usage of a second language or may make a more rapid change. Some children may continue to choose their dominant language in a large-group setting, while using their second language in less formal, and possibly less pressured, settings. In order to assess a child's current level, a teacher must be continually observing and recording a child's linguistic attempts, in varied settings.

Cira Focarino's First Grade. Cira Focarino, a first-grade teacher in a "regular" classroom in which almost all the children are Chinese, expresses similar beliefs. She is an acute listener as well as one who maintains an ongoing written dialogue with her children as they keep journals throughout the year. Journal keeping is the core of her language arts curriculum because it enables children to use a variety of abilities—speaking, drawing, writing, socializing for pleasure, asking for or giving help—as they become writers and readers. That process is gradual and may be a real challenge for the six children in her class who are ELLs, or ESLs as they are called in Ms. Focarino's school. In her words, ESL learners rely on nonverbal abilities.

> In the beginning of the year, the journal may be a picture which is more developed than the "story." I'll use their story picture to aid in completing the word story. But the picture is a valuable story as is, until they [the children] are willing or able to tell about the picture in words. (Genishi, Dubetz, & Focarino, in press)

Like Ms. Powell and Mrs. Murphy, Ms. Focarino watches for nonverbal cues from the children as she makes decisions about when ESL learners are ready to accept correction of errors (editing) in their journals.

> To differentiate between the students who are just coping and those who are ready to tackle the editing . . . it is mostly a nonverbal thing that I get from the kids, like it's their body tensing if I have their journal right there and they're sitting in the chair, how comfortable they are. Also . . . if they're writing the same sentences over and over again, and don't change their subjects and don't change the length of their journals, that shows me that they're not confident to go further. . . . If I see growth, then I know they're ready for like just a tiny bit of editing. . . . I just get that whole sense of who can take not a piece of criticism, but a correction. . . . Some kids will only write correctly spelled words. . . . Some of the kids are just not ready. . . . It's just on a one-to-one. Everybody's different. (Genishi, Dubetz, & Focarino, in press)

Making progress in literacy learning involves risk since children share their successes and errors with the rest of the class during "journal share." Like other teachers whose assessments guide their curricula, Ms. Focarino watches for the times when learners are ready to take risks, to show what they know publicly.

CONCLUSION

This overview of assessment illustrates the complexity of the challenge to create equitable means of assessing bilingual and ELL children. The "science" of measurement is not nearly flexible enough to take into account the multiple situations in which young children learn and live. By sampling current standardized instruments and classroom practice, we have attempted to show the strengths and weaknesses of the varied approaches.

Because of the ever-changing nature of children's learning and their increasingly diverse linguistic and cultural backgrounds, our position is that the development of performance-based assessment, particularly teacher-created ways, must be supported. We are aware that a major obstacle to teachers' creation of their own ways of assessing is a lack of time. As Barbara Frogel, a pre-K teacher who engages in alternative assessment, said so pointedly, "Standardized tests take into consideration the value of time." Our recommended next step for administrators and school personnel is not to rely only on time-saving standardized measures, but to focus instead on this critical element of time. What changes can be made in the school day so that teachers have the time to reflect on how their own assessments can guide their curricula? Like other significant aspects of school reform, the reallocation of time presents a challenge that must be met if alternatives to standardized tests are to fulfill the promise they offer, especially to the growing number of ELLs in early childhood classrooms.

NOTE

1. ELL is a term used by LaCelle-Peterson and Rivera (1994). We choose to use it as well because it emphasizes the *learner* of English and not his or her limitations, highlighted in the more well-known term *limited English proficient* (LEP).

APPENDIX
Selected Standardized Tests Used for Placement in Bilingual Programs

Title: Basic Inventory of Natural Language (BINL), 1977
Author: Charles H. Herbert

Publisher: CHECpoint Systems, Inc.

Age Range: Grades K–6, 7–12

General Description: The BINL employs a "language sampling" approach. Children are asked to talk about pictures in groups of six or fewer. Each child's conversation is tape-recorded until 10 sentences have been recorded for an individual. That sample is then scored according to specific criteria described in the scoring manual regarding fluency, average sentence length, and average level of complexity.

Title: Language Assessment Battery (LAB), 1984

Author: Prepared by Board of Education of the City of New York

Publisher: Riverside Publishing Co.

Age Range: Grades K–2, 3–6, 7–12

General Description: The LAB makes use of black and white pictures to evaluate the "effectiveness" of a child in English and Spanish. Students are given tasks to perform in listening, speaking, reading, and writing. They are individually assessed first in English and, if they score below the twentieth percentile, then in Spanish. Their effectiveness is determined by rank percentile—the higher the rank, the more "effective" the language skills.

Title: Bilingual Syntax Measure (BSM), 1976, 1980

Authors: Marina K. Burt, Heidi C. Dulay, and Eduardo Hernandez

Publisher: Psychological Corporation

Age Range: Grades K–2

General Description: The BSM makes use of eight cartoons to engage students in conversation with the test administrator, who asks questions such as, "Who is that?" and "What would happen if. . .?" Students' responses and conversation are rated according to five levels of proficiency with reference to "level of grammaticality in overall language" and "level of syntactic structure" attained. Examples of correct and incorrect responses are given for scoring at each level.

Title: Language Assessment Scales (LAS), 1981–82, PRE-LAS, 1985

Author: Edward A. De Avila and Sharon E. Duncan

Publisher: CTB/McGraw-Hill

Age Range: Grades Pre-K, K–5, 6–12

General Description: Using standards based on the language proficiency of monolingual speakers, the LAS are organized in six sections, which include tasks in following directions, identifying objects, matching pictures to descriptions presented by the examiner, repeating sentences, completing brief story sequences, and retelling stories told by the examiner.

Title: Language Proficiency Measure (LPM), 1985

Publisher: Tucson Unified School District

Age Range: Grades K–2

General Description: The LPM was developed to measure listening comprehension and speaking ability in Spanish and English. The listening comprehension tasks involve seven instructions to the child which he or she acts out. The child is asked to tell a story based on a wordless picture story, and a conversation between examiner and child is also recorded and assessed according to specific criteria.

Title: Expressive One-Word Picture Vocabulary Test (EOWPVT–R), 1990
Author: Morrison F. Gardner
Publisher: Academic Therapy Publications
Age Range: Ages 2–11

General Description: The EOWPVT–R assesses a child's level of functioning with reference to his or her expressive vocabulary for instructional purposes. The child is asked to name objects and to note common elements among pictures to demonstrate abstract thinking. The test is sequenced to move from very simple to increasingly more complex. Scores are determined along a continuum ranging from a child's basal level to his or her ceiling level. There are English and Spanish versions of the instrument.

Title: Early Screening Inventory (ESI), 1983
Author: Samuel J. Meisels and Martha Stone Wiske
Publisher: Teachers College Press
Age Range: Ages 4–6

General Description: The ESI is designed to be used as one component in a total screening process to identify children who may be in need of special education. It measures visual-motor skills, language comprehension, verbal expression, the ability to reason and count, and the ability to remember auditory sequences. There is also a draw-a-person task and a letter-writing portion (not scored; used to assess fine-motor control and to compare with the visual-motor copying task in the first section). The child is scored according to developmental cutoff scores and evaluated according to whether he or she should be rescreened, placed in special education, or placed in a regular classroom. The instrument includes a parent questionnaire. The ESI is available in English and Spanish versions.

REFERENCES

Almy, M., & Genishi, C. (1979). *Ways of studying children.* New York: Teachers College Press.

Barrows-Chesterfield, K. (1985). Test review. In J. Mitchell, Jr. (Ed.), *The ninth mental measurements yearbook* (Vol. 2, pp. 807–808). Lincoln: Buros Institute, Lincoln Nebraska Press.

Centre for Primary Language Education/Inner London Education Authority. (1988). *Primary Language Record.* Portsmouth, NH: Heinemann.

Charlesworth, R., Fleege, P. O., & Weitman, C. J. (1994). Research on the effects of group standardized testing on instruction, pupils, and teachers: New directions for policy. *Early Education and Development, 5,* 195–212.

Copeland, S. (1994). *The use of early childhood developmental portfolios for kindergarten screening and changing teaching practice.* Unpublished dissertation proposal, Teachers College, New York.

Darling-Hammond, L. (1994). Performance-based assessment and educational equity. *Harvard Educational Review, 64,* 5–30.

Fournier, J., Lansdowne, B., Pastenes, Z., Steen, P., & Hudelson, S. (1992). Learning with, about, and from children: Life in a bilingual classroom. In C. Genishi (Ed.), *Ways of assessing children and curriculum: Stories of early childhood practice* (pp. 126–162). New York: Teachers College Press.

Gardner, H. (1983). *Frames of mind: The theory of multiple intelligences.* New York: Basic Books.

Genishi, C. (Ed.). (1992). *Ways of assessing children and curriculum: Stories of early childhood practice.* New York: Teachers College Press.

Genishi, C., Dubetz, N., & Focarino, C. (in press). Reconceptualizing theory through practice: Insights from a first-grade teacher and second-language theorists. In S. Reifel (Ed.), *Advances in early education and day care* (Vol. 7). Greenwich, CT: JAI Press.

Grace, C., & Shores, E. F. (1992). *The portfolio and its use: Developmentally appropriate assessment of young children.* Little Rock, AR: Southern Association on Children Under Six.

Graham, R. C. (1978). Test review. In O. K. Buros (Ed.), *The eighth mental measurements yearbook* (Vol. 1, pp. 233–234). Highland Park, NJ: Gryphon Press.

Haber, L. (1985). Test review. In J. Mitchell, Jr. (Ed.), *The ninth mental measurements yearbook* (Vol. 2, pp. 808–811). Lincoln: Buros Institute, Lincoln Nebraska Press.

Henning, G. (1987). *A guide to language testing: Development, evaluation, research.* Cambridge, MA: Newbury House.

LaCelle-Peterson, M. W., & Rivera, C. (1994). Is it real for all kids? A framework for equitable assessment policies for English language learners. *Harvard Educational Review, 64,* 55–75.

Ligon, G. (1985). Test review. In J. Mitchell, Jr. (Ed.), *The ninth mental measurements yearbook* (Vol. 2, pp. 328–329). Lincoln: Buros Institute, Lincoln Nebraska Press.

Meisels, S. J., Dichtelmiller, M., Dorfman, A., Jablon, J. R., & Marsden, D. B. (1993). *The Work Sampling System.* Ann Arbor, MI: Rebus Planning Associates.

Merino, S., & Spencer, M. (1983). The comparability of English and Spanish versions of oral language proficiency instruments. *NABE Journal, 7*(2), 1–31.

National Association for the Education of Young Children & National Association of Early Childhood Specialists in State Departments of Education. (1991). Guidelines for appropriate curriculum content and assessment in programs serving children ages 3 through 8. *Young Children, 46*(3), 21–38.

Powers, S., Johnson, D., Slaughter, H. B., Crowder, C., & Jones, P. B. (1985). Reliability and validity of the language proficiency measure. *Educational and Psychological Measurement, 45,* 959–963.

Rivera, C., & Simich, C. (1981). Issues in the assessment of language proficiency of language minority students. *NABE Journal, 6*(1), 19–39.

Ulibarri, D., Spencer, J., & Rivas, G. (1981). Language proficiency and academic achievement: A study of language proficiency tests in their relationship to school ratings as predictors of academic achievement. *Journal of the National Association for Bilingual Educators, 5,* 47–80.

Wexler-Sherman, C., Gardner, H., & Feldman, D. H. (1988). A pluralistic view of early assessment: The Project Spectrum approach. *Theory Into Practice, 27*(1), 77–83.

CHAPTER 5

The Mexican–American War: The Next Generation

Howard L. Smith and Paul E. Heckman

Many of the boundaries found in society are based on myths, misconceptions, and fears about differences in language and culture. Schools, as products of the communities they serve, often perpetuate these divisions by segregating students of one language and culture from those of another language and culture. Long before children fully understand the written system of language, they formulate beliefs about the status of specific languages and cultures. These early formed and most often erroneous perceptions can continue throughout their lives.

Using longitudinal, qualitative data, we explore a playground incident that reflects the pernicious effect that linguistic and cultural segregation had on hundreds of children in a bilingual elementary school. The incident prompted the elementary school to change its grouping practices at every grade level.

THE PLAYGROUND INCIDENT

There was plenty of warning of what was to come. Indeed, the conflict was the result of years of misunderstanding and separation. But no one took notice.

It began with an innocent exchange. Soon came the insults: "Stinkin' wetbacks!," *Gringos estúpidos!* Then a push was returned with a shove. One may even have spat at another. Still shouting insults in their respective languages, the "Mexicans" quickly ran to one end of the field, while the "Americans" assembled on the other.

Someone threw a rock. The other side retaliated. Back and forth they went. Sharp-eyed warriors would occasionally hit their targets. For those who witnessed the incident, the passion of the participants would have been more fitting of military soldiers defending their countries with the latest weapons of the time. In truth, this conflict between two groups of fourth graders with a pile of rocks and stones lasted only about 30 minutes on the playground of an American elementary school.

While shocking, this conflict appears to reflect a deeper and more complex set of tensions that existed within the school long before the 1990–91 academic year. For reasons of anonymity, the school will be referred to as Proyecto Uno School and throughout the chapter names of all students and school personnel have been changed.

Following are conditions that existed at Proyecto Uno School and circumstances that led to the rock-throwing incident:

On Monday, November 19, 1990, the two fourth-grade classes had substitute teachers because their regular teachers were attending a workshop, hoping to learn strategies to accommodate English- and Spanish-dominant students during occasional mixed-language activities. However, no workshop would have prepared them for what they found when they returned. In the following discussion, which is a composite of several interviews conducted after the incident occurred, four students (Kay, Joe, Ira, and Pi) describe the incident to a university interviewer.

Kay: It was our class against his, right?

Joe: . . . there was a bilingual class and . . . an English class.

Ira: We, we were playing like chasing each other like cops and robbers.

Kay: . . . they would call us names and . . .

Pi: . . . the English kids would call us like wetbacks, dirty Mexicans, and stuff. . . .

Joe: And we got real mad.

Ira: And then they were hiding behind bushes with rocks and throwing at us. . . . They got in a big group like that and started throwing rocks at us. So we threw the rocks back.

Pi: Even the girls were throwing rocks at, at us.

Kay: They were throwing rocks . . . at everybody and all the teachers had to come out . . . and told everybody to get into the classroom. . . .

Ira: And we got in trouble . . . someone did get hurt.

Kay: [A student] threw a rock . . . and it hit me right here. . . .

Eva: It happened during lunch break. . . .

Although this incident lasted only a half hour, it has served as a topic of discussion for several years. Students and professionals of this school community have pondered the event continually. It would appear that this conflict transcended the intermediate (fourth, fifth, and sixth) grades and the playground. When information from that time is considered along with recent data, the conflict appears to reflect a pervasive belief system that originated in the early grades and manifested itself in actions of teachers and students (Nias, South-worth, & Campbell, 1992) in the classrooms, corridors, and on the playground.

We explore here some of those beliefs and the ways in which they were reified in the school community, as well as those characteristics of the school's culture (Sarason, 1982; Smyley, 1991) that at one time may have engendered what one teacher referred to as a "very ugly and bloody" battle.

At the time of the rock fight, Proyecto Uno School had just begun a collab-orative restructuring program with the College of Education at the University of Arizona (Heckman, 1990), creating the Educational and Community Change (ECC) Project. Today, teachers and students report that there is a new school climate and that the rock fight could not occur now. What has changed during the intervening years? Has the school's collaboration with the ECC Project played any role in this transformation? To discern the changes that may have occurred within the school culture and the possible contributions the project has made to that culture, we explore four questions: (1) Do the students and faculty today have beliefs similar to those that existed at the time of the conflict? (2) If beliefs have changed, what new beliefs have developed? (3) What has contributed to the creation of these new shared beliefs? (4) Have new tensions arisen in the school culture as old ones have been resolved? Answers to these questions may suggest that beliefs and tensions are ever present and must be regularly examined and altered over time if school cultures are to reinvent themselves.

PROYECTO UNO SCHOOL

Proyecto Uno School is located just 60 miles north of Mexico. A number of students (as well as their parents) were born in Mexico, and most have rela-tives who still live there. Not surprisingly, the teachers estimate that 95% of the students speak Spanish in varying degrees. In addition to a common origin, the families of the 387 members of the student body have a similar socioeconomic status: According to school records, nearly 95% qualify for federally funded meals at the school. Their parents are predominately blue-collar and working poor. Such indicators are characteristic of groups that historically have been ill-served by public schools (Thornburg, Hoffman, & Remeika, 1991).

At the time the incident occurred, Proyecto Uno students received class-room instruction in either Spanish or English. These two class groups were known as the monolingual (English) track and the bilingual (Spanish) track. Students in the first group were considered sufficiently fluent to receive their instruction exclusively in English. Those in the bilingual track were Spanish dominant and were taught almost exclusively in Spanish. On the first day of enrollment, the school office staff asked parents about their child's language background and then assigned students to a particular track according to the parents' responses to three questions.

1. What was the first language the student learned to speak?
2. What is the language spoken most often by the student?
3. What is the language most often spoken in the student's home regardless of what the student speaks?

DATA SOURCES

We rely on three interrelated sources to answer our questions: (1) interviews, (2) field notes, and (3) journal entries.

Interviews

During the first 2 years of the ECC Project, structured interviews with students and faculty were conducted on a variety of topics. These interviews were audiotaped, transcribed, edited for accuracy, and then coded. An initial set of codes was created a priori to reflect the descriptive (rather than inferential) nature of the data. For example, FE signified "feelings"; LE "learning (how children learn)"; LI "learning issues"; PB "problem(s)/barrier(s)"; SB "student behavior"; SF "staff," and ST "student(s)." As new topics and issues arose, the research staff modified the list of codes, categories, and their definitions.

Coding of the interviews was a three-step process that began with the edited transcript, a first coding by one researcher, a second coding by a different researcher, and a consensus meeting where differences were identified and reconciled. For further analysis, the coded transcript was then entered into a computerized ethnographic program.

Two years after the incident, a formal interview protocol (see Appendix) referencing the rock fight was developed and administered to students and teachers who were involved. These interviews were transcribed and edited for accuracy. Because all responses were based on highly contextualized questions, they were coded in a manner that was not similar to the initial interviews of the study.

For this investigation, 21 teacher interviews and 67 student interviews (completed over a 30-month period) were examined. Using the ethnographic procedures, we were able to locate passages that reflected staff and student views on the issues raised.

Field Notes

Throughout the first 3 years of the ECC Project, conversations occurred between members of the school and the project team in the teachers' lounge, in the library, in classrooms, and in the main office. Project staff maintained field notes to recall what was said in these conversations. The field notes also contain observations made by the project team during classroom participation. As suggested by Spradley (1980), when project staff and teachers collaborate in school activities, they acquire "knowledge people use to interpret, experience and generate behavior" (p. 6).

Journals and Student Writing

Journals kept by some teachers, as well as students' views in their writings about the incident, are the final source of information. Portions of these writings also will be examined in what follows.

FIVE "COMMON SENSE" EXPLANATIONS

After reviewing the available data, we perceived five reasons offered by the school to explain the conflict. In some ways they may be considered "common sense" explanations, because, while plausible, they were not accompanied by any solid evidence when they were reported by the school member. The first two were mentioned only once throughout the data. The remaining explanations have been encountered repeatedly in the data sources since the time of the incident.

Theory 1: The "Haves" Versus the "Have-Nots"

When interviewed, May, a fourth-grade teacher, suggested that the ridicule of poverty might have been a possible cause of the battle between the students.

Interviewer: What was happening, deep down, between the kids?
May: I think that some of the kids were feeling attacked. They were, they were being made fun of [interrupted]
Interviewer: Because of . . . ?
May: . . . for what they were, the language they spoke, or something from home, you know?
Interviewer: Ummm.
May: "Oh, you live in that ugly house that's falling down." Stuff like that. Real personal things.

Interviews with other participants, however, offer no support for this theory. No other respondent shared this view. Moreover, the relative economic homogeneity of the population suggests that it would have been difficult for students to view one group as significantly more economically advantaged than another.

Theory 2: Street Gangs

A second possibility was suggested by a student who observed the incident. He said that the battle may have been gang related. No one else, involved or uninvolved in the fight, mentioned gang activity as the source of the conflict. Also, neither the city police department nor the school resource officers could relate this incident to gang activity in the area.

Theory 3: Muddled Group Identity

Following the rock fight, some teachers commented that the mixing of the students was the cause. The 2 fourth-grade classes involved in the conflict had been participating in limited exchanges for special activities and subjects. Going against a school tradition that had been in place for a decade, the 2 fourth-grade teachers decided not to work exclusively with one language group. Their students were obligated to work with both teachers and both languages. May recalls some of the reactions of her colleagues when they began to mix the students.

May: [Many] people . . . saw that as a totally negative thing. . . . I think some of them thought we were out of our minds. [However,] I think some people were willing to give us a chance and think about how brave we were for trying to do this.
Interviewer: You mean brave for mixing the children?
May: Yeah. I think some of them were leery of what we were doing. And I think some of them were willing to give us a chance to see what [would happen].

Through their daily encounters with two teachers and two languages, students not only were developing cognitively but were also reassessing their beliefs on language-based grouping. Joy, a fourth-grade teacher, recalls having overheard students arguing: "She's my teacher." "No, she's my teacher." Their mixing, even on a limited basis, forced the students and their teachers to re-examine long-held beliefs regarding language-based grouping within the school.

Theory 4: "Nationalism"

A fourth theory emerged. When interviewed, staff members felt the cause of the problem was language-based "nationality": Students in the bilingual track were often taunted as foreigners or aliens by those in the monolingual track (who identified more with American culture than Mexican culture). It is note-worthy that many who were mocked were not recent arrivals, but had resided in the United States for as long as 6 years. Equally noteworthy is the fact that some students in the English-dominant group had been born in Mexico or had recently arrived in the area themselves. However, students in this latter group had one advantage: They were considered English speakers (hence American) because of the language track to which they were assigned.

Moving beyond the issue of "which is your classroom?" the implication here is "which culture is yours?" Students were heard making ethnic slurs and insults as they struggled with the idea of nationality.

A sixth-grade teacher describes how the school initiated the language-based division in the early grades and the resultant hostility between the student groups.

> [The] classes were divided into monolingual strand and bilingual strand. . . . They were brought up in their strand since kinder[gar-ten] . . . [and the] recent arrivals . . . [from Mexico were assigned to the] bilingual strand [track]. . . . There was this division going on of "those *Chicanos*" and "*los mojados*.". . . [See Table 5.1 for a descrip-tion of terms.] There were lots of fights.

Other teachers also reported that they knew of children making ethnic slurs. Here Joy discusses the animosity.

Joy: The monolingual kids would put down the Spanish speakers all the time.
Interviewer: You'd witness this?
Joy: Oh yeahhhhh. Oh yeahhh.
Interviewer: What are some things they would say?
Joy: Oh, they would just . . . they'd call them "wetbacks," or they would tell them about the immigration coming or, you know, "How come you don't learn English yet?" and just a lot of different things. You know, talk about them in English and knowing that they don't understand.

Another staff member also had heard students exchange insults: "You see, the kids that Joy had [in her class] called the other ones *guachos* because they were from Mexico. They felt that they were American because they were born here." Children interviewed reported that during the years before the fight occurred "they would call us names like 'wetback' and stuff or say 'we hate Americans.'"

The following interview with two students who had been on opposite sides of the conflict illustrates interpersonal and intrapersonal tension regarding nationality:

Joe: We were mad, like, a lot, like, we started to throw rocks a lot, a lot of rocks like that.

Interviewer: What were you mad about?

Joe: . . . they would say like the Mexicans they say were like rats . . .
(*moments later*)

Kay: And they would call us, um, gringos. They would call us, um, "Oh those gringos don't know nothing."
(*seconds later*)

Interviewer: You got mad because you were being called Mexican? What do you . . .

Kay: I mean, no, they were calling us gringos and we weren't gringos.

Interviewer: Oh.

Joe: And they were calling us Mexicans.

Kay: I don't know. I don't even think they were calling . . .

Interviewer: And you aren't Mexican?

Joe: I'm an, I'm an American. But . . .

Kay: You're a Mexican American. I mean you're Spanish American.

Joe: I'm Chicano. Whatever that is.

Theory 5: Language and Grouping

As stated before, the school had been providing instruction in two tracks, English and Spanish. According to the school staff, this had been the practice since 1975. From kindergarten through sixth, each grade level had both an English-speaking teacher and a Spanish-speaking counterpart. Although all teachers interviewed were able to articulate a positive reason for the grouping, during the years following the incident they also were able to see the flaws in such segregation. Various teachers made comments to the effect that this language-based division was so strong that "our kids never played together." Dee, a sixth-grade teacher at that time, recounted the atmosphere of the school.

Oh, it was difficult. Even on the playground. Bilingual kids would be playing over on this side and the monolingual kids would be [over here] "and never the twain shall meet." [It was the] same way in the cafeteria. It was terrible. I mean segregated. . . . Civil segregation.

Several months later, during a meeting of educators and researchers, teachers commented on the school's practice of separating human resources. Chapter I (reading resource) teachers were assigned to work within one language track. Special education teachers were also language-bound. Students labeled bilingual were in contact exclusively with Hispanic faculty. The school afforded them little opportunity to interact with Anglo staff or students who spoke English. According to Joy, with one exception, the bilingual track was taught exclusively by Hispanic teachers. Another teacher noted the effect:

> I used to get kids from . . . [another teacher's class] for reading. Some of the kids . . . were a little bit hesitant. They were bright kids, but yet they were hesitant, because they were . . . out of their element—they were out of that security of their own little classroom where . . . [Spanish] was spoken all the time.

Material resources also were segregated. Teachers reported that there were no Spanish materials in the English-language classes. All Spanish materials were reserved and sent to the bilingual classes. The library resources were overwhelmingly in English. Signs on the teachers' doors would have the title "Monolingual" or "Bilingual." The former district director of bilingual education programs informed us that Proyecto Uno School had been known as "Little Mexico."

LANGUAGE AND CULTURE DEFINED

Within Proyecto Uno School, qualitative attributes were assigned to individuals depending on the language that they spoke. Several words and phrases that suggest beliefs about the languages and cultures found within this school appear throughout the interviews (as illustrated through excerpts in this chapter), in the dialogue discussions, during class observations, and in impromptu conversations with students and adults (see Table 5.1). The first four terms in the table commonly refer to nationality or cultural membership (Anzaldúa, 1987). However, when these words were used in the Proyecto Uno School community, they communicated the student's perceived language abilities or the academic track to which the student belonged.

The two words in Table 5.1, "bilingual" and "monolingual," are also of interest. At Proyecto Uno School, these terms are unconditionally synonymous with "Spanish speaking" and "English speaking," respectively. Any student perceived as Spanish dominant is classified as bilingual, irrespective of her or his knowledge of any other language. In the same manner, a child taught in the English-speaking track is referred to as monolingual, notwithstanding that a student could have knowledge of two (or more) languages.

Table 5.1. Terms used in Proyecto Uno School. For the etymology of the term *Chicano*, see Anzaldúa, 1987.

TERM	STANDARD DEFINITION	SCHOOL DEFINITION	PEJORATIVE
Chicano	U.S. citizen or resident Mexican descent	U.S. and Mexican culture English speaking	Society: No School: No
Mexican-American	Being of Mexican and U.S. descent	U.S. and Mexican culture English speaking	Society: No School: No
Spanish-American	Being of Spanish and U.S. descent	U.S. and Mexican culture English speaking	Society: No School: No
Mexican	Being of Mexican origin	Mexican culture Spanish dominant	Society: No School: Yes
Bilingual	Having two languages	Mexican culture Spanish dominant Spanish monolingual	Society: No School: Yes
Monolingual	Having one language	U.S. culture English dominant English monolingual	Society: No School: No
Wetback	A laborer who illegally enters the U.S.	Mexican/Foreigner Spanish dominant	Society: Yes School: Yes
Mojado	Spanish translation of "wetback"	Mexican/Foreigner Spanish dominant	Society: Yes School: Yes
Guacho	Mexicans not from northern areas of Mexico	Mexican/Foreigner Spanish dominant	Society: Yes School: Yes
Gringo	hostile, contemptuous term for American	American/Non-Mexican English dominant	Society: Yes School: Yes

Table 5.1 also lists terms that are considered derogatory in any normal context. As a group, they refer in some way to culture, origin, or nationality. Both "wetback" and *mojado* originally referred to the Mexican nationals who entered Texas via the Rio Grande. A *guacho* is a person who comes from the central or southern regions of Mexico (unlike most of the school community, which is primarily from the north). The core of the word *gringo* is Anglo-Saxon culture. It is not the offensiveness of these four words that is intriguing, but rather the language-based criteria for their selection. More specifically, irrespective of birthplace, ancestry, or nationality, *it would appear that labels were applied to students according to their language use at the school.*

When Table 5.1 is re-examined, it seems that at Proyecto Uno School the need to establish language membership (group membership) was so strong that concepts of nationality, origin, culture, and linguistic abilities were distilled into two categories: English speaking and Spanish speaking. A cursory review of the words listed indicates that a grouping system had developed regarding cultural characteristics and language abilities. Once a student's language group was determined, he or she was treated in accordance with the status of that language. Conklin and Lourie (1983) remind us that "language functions not only to communicate social information but also to define and maintain social roles" (p. 114). In many schools, Proyecto Uno included, students who are not considered English dominant are often the object of derision. This suggests not only beliefs about which language had greater importance in the school but also the interrelationship of language, culture, and society.

> Society decrees that certain people be more highly thought of than others—because they are economically, culturally, or politically more powerful. To the extent that social identity is tied to language, actual linguistic forms become "good" or "bad" language according to the social standing of the individuals and groups who use them. (Conklin & Lourie, 1983, pp. 114–115)

The rewards earned for speaking the language or dialect of prestige have been well documented (e.g., Crawford, 1992; Heath, 1983). Edwards (1982) argues that the issue of "whose language counts" for purposes of schooling, is reflected and reinforced by the balance of power and prestige between social groups. As such, language-based academic tracks are "socially constructed barriers to learning where the linguistic insensitivity and intolerance of teachers made them so" (p. 514).

Negative attitudes toward recent immigrants and their languages is not a new issue in the United States. The following is an excerpt from a letter written by Benjamin Franklin, dated May 9, 1753:

> Those [Germans] who come hither are generally the most ignorant Stupid Sort of their own Nation, and as Ignorance is often attended with Credulity

when Knavery would mislead it, and with Suspicion when Honesty would set it right; and as few of the English understand the German Language, and so cannot address them either from the Press or Pulpit, 'til almost impossible to remove any prejudices they once entertain.... Now they come in droves.... Few of their children in the Country learn English. (Crawford, 1992, p. 19)

Throughout the data, students and teachers commented on the school's beliefs regarding language at the time. Joy said, "I believe that the monolingual students thought that they were better than Spanish-speaking students because they had learned English." Dee concurred, "[The English-dominant] students perceived themselves to be in a higher category—smarter than, or better than—[the Spanish-dominant students].... There was a lot of resentment."

There were teachers who also realized that their personal belief system was biased. Joy said:

I think I felt that way too, not outwardly. I didn't show it. But, I do believe that I thought that way because I didn't know that they knew as much as I did—because we never talked about it.... [After] I had more chances to talk with students from May's class, I remember thinking to myself, "Wow, these kids really are smart." You know? And all this time I didn't know this, because I didn't understand the language.

She was not alone in her feelings. In a private conversation, another teacher confessed that before the school mixed its entire student body, she thought that "people who didn't speak English weren't as smart" as she.

These comments seem to suggest that the separation of these children greatly contributed to the fight. We will argue, however, that membership in a given class group did not by itself provoke the conflict. Rather, teachers and students shared a set of beliefs about the two languages and the cultures associated with those languages. These beliefs underlie both the separation and the conflict. When considered as a Gestalt-like system, beliefs about language, grouping, and nationality (or cultural identity) appeared to be the root of this Mexican–American War.

In review, for members of this school community the issue of national origin was supplanted by cultural identification. Cultural identification was defined by language use within the school. For the students, language use within the school was preordained by the language track to which each student was assigned when he or she enrolled in the school. Once enrolled, children were seldom transferred to another language track.

In this section we have discussed how language was used to indicate group membership. We also examined how language was accompanied by beliefs, attitudes, and values held by users and also by persons who did not speak the language. Moreover, we saw how the beliefs regarding language are "often confounded with attitudes toward the users of that language" (Grosjean, 1982, p. 117).

CHANGES BEGIN TO OCCUR

Between 1990 and 1993, the students and faculty at Proyecto Uno School contemplated, developed, and enacted changes in school practices. While negative connotations about other cultures and languages have existed in the United States for years, the members of this school community began to understand that these views required attention, and the teachers made efforts to change them. The faculty agreed in the spring of 1991 to group students in new ways.

Language Grouping

Nearly 3 years after the rock fight, the school no longer separates English-dominant and Spanish-dominant students and teachers from each other. Each class is a bilingual class, and students and teachers are expected to work in both languages. As Joy explains:

> Students are learning—predominately Spanish-speaking students are learning more English and speaking more English; predominately English-speaking students are learning and speaking more Spanish. So, it's really an ideal bilingual situation. I'm learning more Spanish and speaking more Spanish. And May doesn't even teach ESL in her classroom with just her students. All the ESL they're getting [is] from the mixing of the students. And I see a lot of it happening and happening quicker than I've seen before.

Mixed-Aged Grouping

Another notable change at the school is the practice of multiage grouping. The school refers to the early childhood group (preschool through first), primary group (second and third), and intermediate (fourth through sixth). In this way, students and teachers experience the benefits of working across levels and ages; grouping is much more heterogeneous. Joy offers her rationale for mixing students in this way:

> Our original motive for mixing them were, was that last year there were, there were many problems with conflicts between the 2 fourth-

grade classes because of the separation—we thought it was because of the separation from the bilingual to the monolingual. So, at the very beginning of the year, we thought—in order to try to put an end to that—we would mix—we would start mixing the classes. . . . Socially I believe the students are really benefiting—out of learning to get along with each other and seeing the value of being bilingual. Prior to this, attitudes of students, of my fourth-grade students in my class, have, has been of, um, almost an attitude of being superior to anybody who doesn't speak English.

Her colleague May shares a similar belief.

I like to have . . . all different levels mixed up because they learn from each other. The slower kids can get help from the kids who aren't having any problems. And the kids who aren't having any problems learn to have patience with some of those who may have problems. So I think it works a lot on the social abilities also—having them all mixed up and learning to work with different people.

NEW COLLABORATIONS

Students and teachers frequently mention new collaborations that have taken place as well as a decrease in fighting in the school yard. The following response by a student illustrates the correlation between the new class groupings and the decrease in playground battles.

I think it's funner because we're together now. We don't fight anymore. We do math together, we go play together, we eat lunch together . . . I'm happy that we're friends again—that we play together and do things together—like when we went to Camp C—we went together. We slept in cabins and some English kids in the cabin and some Spanish kids and we slept together in the cabin and then we would go hiking together.

With the advent of the ECC Project, teachers began to learn from each other. In the passage that follows, May describes to the interviewer how another staff member, Lee, decided to use tables, in lieu of rows of desks, in the classroom.

At first Lee didn't want to have anything to do with this. Lee just couldn't stand the change, and, and Lee wasn't going to try anything. . . . And it was that one week before school started where we were setting up our rooms and getting desks or tables or whatever it was we wanted. . . . Lee was strictly a desks-and-rows person. . . . Lee saw somebody's room and they talked a little bit and she got excited about it. She said, "Hey, I want to try that. It might work well, you know." So Lee did. And Lee was real happy with . . . [replacing the desks with tables].

Teacher-colleagues and their students have done rotation activities that allow each teacher to share an area of strength with all students, such as a particular subject area. Resource teachers are no longer "pull-out specialists." They go into the classes and work with teacher-colleagues and students to explore literacy, mathematics, science, and many other topics.

Also, students are now given the opportunity to set agendas and to teach others. The intermediate students share reading time with the younger students to foster greater literacy experiences. Parents have been invited from the community to create and support research projects. Several parents have come in to plant vegetables and flowers on school grounds. Others teach children how to prepare traditional foods. Community members have come to discuss the nuts and bolts of their professions (e.g., "What is mathematics?" "What do engineers do?" "What is chemistry?" "What is music?"). These experiences appear to be assisting in redefining a new view of teaching and the knowledge and skills that schools might promote for children and adults.

NEW BELIEFS EMERGED

Beliefs about the importance of collaboration and heterogeneity appear to be replacing views that mandate separation and homogeneity. Teachers and children are exchanging ideas, negotiating tasks, and creating practices and school structures together. They now encourage individuals with diverse interests and experiences to come together. For instance, younger children work with older children. Teachers of younger children interact with teachers of older students. Students who appear to have greater literacy skills engage in activities with those who may not have as many skills.

Also, the use of English and Spanish no longer separates children and adults. Instead, children and teachers are using greater amounts of both English and Spanish in classroom work. Recent immigrant children are not separated from children whose families have resided in the community for years. The strength of the language and culture that each child brings to any activity is encouraged. The diverse strengths of the students and teachers are utilized to encourage new learning for each other.

EVIDENCE SUGGESTS IMPORTANCE OF DIALOGUE

At the time of this writing, the many experiences and events recorded in the data are still being examined and analyzed by the school and ECC Project staff. For that reason, conclusions regarding the conditions for reinvention will not be proposed at this time.

However, there is strong evidence in the data to suggest that at least weekly dialogue sessions, initiated by the project, encouraged teachers to (1) challenge old beliefs and teaching practices and replace them with new ones (Connor & Heckman, 1993; Heckman, Confer, & Hakim, 1994), and (2) introduce and explore these new beliefs and values in the classroom.

Working within the framework of the dialogue concept, after every session participants return to their classrooms to put into practice their new theories and beliefs. During the succeeding dialogue sessions, teachers describe results of new thinking and practices, as well as changes that are occurring in pre-existing beliefs.

Beliefs and actions are interrelated and cyclical. Attention to one promotes changes in the other. As existing practices are examined, new beliefs are explored and suggest new actions. New beliefs encourage newer beliefs; new actions encourage newer actions.

The conditions that have been discussed here, as well as general beliefs about culture and language, were explored in dialogue sessions. Alternative explanations and methodology were addressed for language acquisition, and the implications of these alternatives for practice were examined. Through dialogue, all participants were encouraged to create alternative beliefs about language and culture.

In the dialogue sessions at Proyecto Uno School, the rock-throwing incident became a vehicle for teachers to explore general beliefs about culture and language as well as the school's language-based tracking tradition. The 2 fourth-grade teachers began to discuss their own beliefs about why the fight occurred and what might be done to prevent a similar circumstance from arising.

The teachers felt that any misgivings they had about mixing students were outweighed by the need for the students to work together. They immediately united both groups on a full-time basis, creating a single bilingual fourth-grade class with two teachers. These ideas and practices were also discussed in dialogue sessions.

The experiences with these "try-out" activities helped encouraged later efforts of other colleagues to examine the separation practices across all grades. In addition, the problems that these two teachers faced as they tried out different practices to accommodate the mixing also focused dialogue discussions as well as small-group conversations among others.

COLLABORATIVE TENSIONS

Apparently, some teacher and student beliefs and actions have changed in classrooms and in the school. However, new conditions within an organization will create a new set of dynamics. A criterion for determining the power of any new structure is the degree to which it effectively addresses new problems as they arise.

In their interviews after the rock fight, students and teachers noted new issues that were arising in the school. For example, as discussions about language and literacy development have taken center stage in various staff dialogue sessions and private meetings, questions about the nature of language-appropriate instruction have arisen.

Language dominance is no longer a consideration in Proyecto Uno's structure of classrooms. In essence, every teacher has a bilingual class, and those teachers who are not bilingual team-teach with a teacher who is bilingual. However, some, such as Joy, who have made commitments to bilingual education question their support of bilingualism when they do not speak a second language: "Sometimes I felt like, am I . . . hypocritical to value bilingualism when I'm not bilingual. Is that hypocritical?"

During several dialogue sessions, teachers also voiced their concern over the possibility of losing their jobs at the school because they did not speak Spanish fluently. Wong-Fillmore (1992) examines antibilingual education movements and notes how a school can be balkanized over the issue of hiring and seniority. "One way this is achieved is to make it appear that each bilingual teacher hired means one 'regular' teacher put out of work" (p. 375). The following excerpt from an interview with Joy lends credence to Wong-Fillmore's assertion and highlights a new tension in the school based on a new language issue:

> The policy right now is if . . . you're bilingual, you got your job, no problem. Doesn't matter how many years you have. Doesn't matter anything. That if you have a bilingual endorsement over something, you don't have anything to worry about. And I don't think that's fair. Personally. I don't think it's fair. [For example] Jan [a monolingual colleague] has been teaching for 22 years—one of the best teachers I've ever met and it's not fair [for job security to hinge on bilingualism].

Team-teaching also has posed challenges. Although most teachers are predisposed to collaborating in some way with colleagues, learning new ways to interact on a professional level raises additional questions: (1) While some staffers have been at the school for many years, each year brings some changes in personnel. Is it fair to expect teachers to enter into collaboration when they really don't know each other? (2) One goal is to create rich experiences across languages. What should happen when two teachers wish to collaborate but neither is bilingual? (3) Teachers are constantly encouraged to work with colleagues. How do teachers collaborate when they have conflicting views (e.g., whole language vs. phonics, ESL vs. biliteracy development)?

A third new tension arises in this context—"How do you do it?" Spanish-dominant and English-dominant students share the same classroom. Every teacher at Proyecto Uno School in essence has a bilingual class. Students from special education are now mainstreamed for the greater portion of the day. Primary students are sometimes taught with intermediate students. Basals or standard textbooks and teachers' manuals cannot address what to do under these new conditions at this school.

The ECC Project seeks to encourage "indigenous invention" (Heckman & Peterman, 1994) based on the view that human beings are endowed with unlimited imagination to create. The challenge is to establish the conditions for unleashing such creativity, which will generate new learning opportunities (the unknown) using past and present experiences (the known). Experiences in the project thus far have been hopeful. Nevertheless, the question remains—Can it be done?

CONCLUSION

In this study, we examined a rock fight that occurred between two groups of elementary students. The student body was of a common ethnic origin as well as socioeconomic status. In addition, 95% of them spoke Spanish to some degree. As the students and teachers deliberated on the conditions that preceded the battle, they attributed the fight to a more profound conflict that existed within their particular school community.

While many studies exist that confirm the negative educational consequences of differentiation and conflict based on gender (e.g., Noddings, 1991), race (e.g., Brown, Carter, & Harris, 1978; McCarthy, 1988), social class (e.g., Short, 1991; Sigmond, 1988), and poverty (e.g., Menacker, 1989), the tension and subsequent social stratification at Proyecto Uno School revolved around beliefs about culture and language that were beneath the language-based tracking tradition of this school. As we have seen, it was not the grouping as such, but rather the belief system of the teachers and students of this school, that attached positive and negative values to membership in a particular language track. The example offered here, our analysis, and what evolved have direct implications for early childhood education. The ill effects of language stratification in the early life of a child can be lasting, and the longer children experience the subtle and direct effects, the more pernicious the practice.

Members of this community invariably stated that there were negative attributes associated with the Spanish track, and positive with the English track. When the old grouping practice was discontinued at the school, the professionals and children reported that fighting occurred less frequently. Through collaboration in the ECC Project—in dialogue and other teacher-driven activities—new beliefs and actions developed. These altered beliefs and actions, in turn, were the basis for new professional and classroom practices.

The ECC Project seeks to determine the conditions for reinventing education in the two collaborating schools during its 1990 to 1998 tenure. At the time of this writing, the project had completed 4 years at Proyecto Uno School. In the remaining years, university and school staff will continue to explore the reinvention of schooling so that several languages and cultures are celebrated, and diversity and heterogeneity are seen as advantageous and necessary to the development of the children, the adults, and the community.

As we question and redefine school practices of pedagogy and theory, we are confident that through collaboration we will be able to alter the patterns of success for children and free the genius within us all.

Perhaps Chico, a participant in the "Mexican–American War," tells the story best in his reflection.

> Just because we were born in [the United States] does not mean we are not Mexican. To tell you the truth, I cannot remember how it [the rock fight] happened or why it happened. I think that it was stupid because we were all Mexicans.
>
> I think that it is okay that other people see [the story about the Mexican–American War] only if other people do not get ideas—like prejudice.
>
> I am just glad that we are friends. I have learned that it doesn't matter—what color of your skin. We are all the same in a lot of ways!!

APPENDIX: INTERVIEW PROTOCOL

March 1, 1993

Thanks for making some time for me. I'm trying to recreate the scuffle that happened between the intermediate students a couple of years ago. Sometimes people call it the fight between the Mexicans and the Americans. I had heard so much about it, that I thought it would be good to capture your understanding of the event.

I'm going to stop the interview in about 45 minutes. If you'd like to go on we can negotiate.

So again, it's that day back in November. Tell me what you remember.

Which kids were involved? Were any not involved?
How long did the fight last?
How did it stop?
At what point did you become involved?
What caused the fight? Was it something all-of-a-sudden?
[If historic reasons are given]
Do you think those same things exist [at the school] today?
Why?/Why not?
Has anything changed?
What has been done to eliminate these [causes]?
Do you find that new tensions have developed in place of the old tensions?
[If suggested]
Are they based on the same conflict of language and culture?
Who else in the school would be good to talk to about this?
Do you think she or he would say about the same thing [you said], regarding
the causes of that fight and the changes?

REFERENCES

Anzaldúa, G. (1987). *Borderlands La Frontera: The new mestiza.* San Francisco: Spinster/Aunt Lute.

Brown, F., Carter, D., & Harris, J. (1978). Minority students, ability grouping, and career development. *Journal of Black Studies, 8*(4), 477–488.

Conklin, N., & Lourie, M. (1983). *A host of tongues: Language communities in contact.* New York: Free Press.

Connor, C., & Heckman, P. E. (1993). *Teachers' voices in school reinvention: Initial themes from the Educational and Community Change Project.* Unpublished manuscript, University of Arizona, College of Education, Tucson.

Crawford, J. (1992). *Language loyalties: A source book on the official English controversy.* Chicago: University of Chicago Press.

Edwards, A. (1982). Perspective: Language difference and educational failure. *Language Arts, 59*(5), 513–519.

Grosjean, F. (1982). *Life with two languages: An introduction to bilingualism.* Cambridge, MA: Harvard University Press.

Heath, S. B. (1983). *Ways with words: Language, life, and work in communities and classrooms.* Cambridge: Cambridge University Press.

Heckman, P. E. (1990). *Altering patterns for success for at-risk children.* Unpublished manuscript, University of Arizona, College of Education, Tucson.

Heckman, P. E., Confer, C., & Hakim, D. (1994). Planting seeds: Understanding through investigation. *Educational Leadership, 51*(5), 36–39.

Heckman, P. E., & Peterman, F. (1994). *Indigenous invention: New promise for school reform.* Unpublished manuscript, University of Arizona, College of Education, Tucson.

McCarthy, C. (1988). Rethinking liberal and radical perspectives on racial inequality in schooling: Making the case for nonsynchrony. *Harvard Educational Review,* *58*(3), 265–279.

Menacker, J. (1989). Poverty as a suspect class in public education equal protection suits. *West's Education Law Reporter, 54*(4), 1085–1098.

Nias, J., Southworth, G., & Campbell, P. (1992). *Whole school curriculum development in the primary school.* London: Falmer Press.

Noddings, N. (1991). The gender issue. *Educational Leadership, 49*(4), 65–70.

Sarason, S. B. (1982). *The culture of the school and the future societies* (rev. ed.). Boston: Allyn & Bacon.

Short, G. (1991). Perceptions of inequality: Primary school children's discourse on social class. *Educational Studies, 17*(1), 89–106.

Sigmond, S. (1988). Remarks on social inequality and measured cognitive abilities in schools. *Western Journal of Black Studies, 12*(4), 210–214.

Smyley, M. A. (1991). Organizational cultures of schools: Concept, content, and change. In S. Conley & B. Cooper (Eds.), *The school as a work environment: Implications for reform* (pp. 20–41). Boston: Allyn & Bacon.

Spradley, L. P. (1980). *Participant observation.* New York: Holt, Rinehart and Winston.

Thornburg, K. R., Hoffman, S., & Remeika, C. (1991). Youth at risk: Society at risk. *Elementary School Journal, 91*(3), 199–208.

Wong-Fillmore, L. (1992). Against our best interest: The attempt to sabotage bilingual education. In J. Cummins (Ed.), *Language loyalties: A source book on the official English controversy* (pp. 367–376). Chicago: University of Chicago Press.

CHAPTER 6

Socialization and the Development of Cooperative, Competitive, and Individualistic Behaviors Among Mexican American Children

George P. Knight, Martha E. Bernal, and Gustavo Carlo

Considerable research has focused on the impact of cultural background on the development of the social behavior styles of Mexican American children. This research has examined a wide variety of social behaviors. Among the most investigated ethnically relative dimensions, however, is the development of cooperative, competitive, and individualistic social behaviors. In a chapter resulting from the "First Symposium on the Mexican American Child," McClintock, Bayard, and McClintock (1983) provided a thorough review of the research addressing the socialization of cooperative, competitive, and individualistic social behaviors among Mexican American children. While the present chapter will update that review by citing some subsequent research, the primary purpose of this chapter is to present a theoretical model focusing on sociocultural experiences and the development of cognitive abilities from a cognitive social learning perspective. The description of this model focuses on the development of cooperative, competitive, and individualistic social behaviors, but the model probably applies equally well to any number of value-based behaviors.

DEFINITION AND MEASUREMENT OF COOPERATIVE, COMPETITIVE, AND INDIVIDUALISTIC SOCIAL BEHAVIORS

The considerable research literature on the cooperative, competitive, and individualistic social behaviors of Mexican American children has been based on a number of different conceptual and operational definitions. In part, the variability in operational definitions is the result of different conceptual definitions of these constructs. For example, some researchers have viewed cooperation, competition, and individualism as a structural process variable having to do with interaction style. In this view, cooperation is the process of working together in a coordinated fashion on a particular task, whereas competition is the process of working against one another on a particular task, and individualism is the process of working alone. In contrast, other researchers have viewed cooperative, competitive, and individualistic behaviors as an outcome variable having to do with preferred reward distributions. These latter researchers have investigated behaviors as an index of a desired distribution of available resources between oneself and another. In this chapter, we will discuss the research using the latter of these two conceptual definitions because the more recent research has tended to assess preferred reward distributions.

Several theoretical frameworks (e.g., Kagan, 1977; McClintock & Van Avermaet, 1982) have specified the most likely preferred reward distributions in situations where children have either direct or indirect control over the rewards they will receive and those that a peer will receive. Although these theoretical frameworks sometimes have used quite different labels to refer to specific reward-distribution preferences, they have suggested conceptually very similar, if not identical, distribution preferences. The measures in this research paradigm generally put children into a situation where their decision behavior affects the rewards they will receive as well as those of a peer. In this type of interdependent situation, the child's decision-making process usually includes consideration of his or her rewards, but not necessarily a peer's rewards. Theoretically, the most likely reward distribution preferences are three that loosely can be considered as cooperative, two that loosely can be considered competitive, and one that is considered individualistic.

Cooperative Reward-Distribution Preferences
1. *Equality*—minimizes the difference between the child's and the peer's rewards
2. *Group enhancement*—maximizes the dyad's rewards regardless of the specific distribution between the child and the peer
3. *Altruism*—maximizes the peer's rewards regardless of the effect on the child's own rewards

Competitive Reward-Distribution Preferences
1. *Superiority*—maximizes the child's own rewards relative to the peer's rewards
2. *Rivalry*—minimizes the peer's rewards regardless of the effect on the child's own rewards

Individualistic Reward-Distribution Preference
  1. *Individualism*—maximizes the child's own rewards regardless of the effect on the peer's rewards

There is a substantial body of evidence that lends support to the validity of the measures used to assess these reward-distribution preferences (see Knight & Chao, 1991; Knight, Cota, & Bernal, 1993).

Recently, some researchers (Chao, Knight, & Dubro, 1986; Knight, Berning, Wilson, & Chao, 1987; Knight, Dubro, & Chao, 1985) have suggested that there are considerable differences in the empirical likelihood of each of these six preferences. This research has provided no clear evidence of altruism or rivalry preferences and only a low frequency of group-enhancement preferences among Anglo American children under 12 years of age. Thus, it appears as though the most frequently preferred distributions among Anglo American children are equality, superiority, and individualism. Further, the patterns of decision making and verbal explanations of decision making obtained in past research (e.g., Knight & Kagan, 1977a, 1977b) suggest that equality, superiority, and individualistic reward distributions may be the most common among Mexican American children as well.

EQUAL SHARING OF REWARDS AS PART OF A MEXICAN AMERICAN VALUE SYSTEM

A central assumption of the socialization model presented in this chapter is that the preference for the equal sharing of rewards is based on a value system linked to the Mexican American ethnicity and is transmitted through socialization experiences. Although equality, superiority, and individualistic reward distributions may be the most common among Anglo American and Mexican American children, a substantial body of research has yielded the consistent finding that cooperative (equality and group-enhancement) reward distributions occur more often among Mexican American than Anglo American children (e.g., Knight & Kagan, 1977a; Madsen, 1971; McClintock, 1974). Such findings support the assumption that Mexican American children prefer equal sharing of rewards, and therefore that such preference reflects a Mexican American ethnic value.

In addition, investigations of theoretically relevant subsets of the Mexican American and Mexican populations also support this assumption. For example, Knight and Kagan (1977b) compared the reward distribution behaviors of second-generation Mexican American children (one or both parents born in Mexico), third-generation Mexican American children (one or more grandparents born in Mexico, but both parents born in the United States), and Anglo

American children. This study revealed significant linear trends indicating that, at least for second- and third-generation Mexican American children, there is an apparent loss of cooperative values in favor of competitive values through successive generations. Kagan and Madsen (1971) found that Mexican American children preferred equal divisions of rewards less often than Mexican children did but preferred equal divisions of rewards more often than Anglo American children did. In addition, the preference for equal sharing of rewards has been related to self-evaluations in a manner consistent with the assumption that these preferences reflect an ethnic value. For example, Kagan and Knight (1979) found that among second-generation Mexican American children, high self-esteem was associated with a preference for equal reward distributions. In contrast, among third-generation Mexican American and Anglo American children, high self-esteem was associated with a preference for unequal and competitive reward distributions (Kagan & Knight, 1979). These patterns are precisely what one would expect if the equal sharing of rewards were a Mexican American ethnic value transmitted through socialization experiences that are changing in response to the ecological demands of the urban Anglo American environment.

While these reward-distribution preferences and the group differences in preferences have been clearly demonstrated in an experimental paradigm, research has not isolated the specific naturalistic behavioral referents or values for such experimentally elicited behaviors. However, a likely candidate is demonstrated in the frequent reminders to Mexican American children to behave in a manner consistent with the term *bien educado,* which refers to good breeding or upbringing. The value of *bien educado* includes politeness and respectful behavior toward others. Behaviors such as allowing others to precede in entering doorways, bringing a chair for guests to sit on, and sharing with another child some reward, such as ice cream, are part of this value. A child who has been *bien educado* would know how to behave in many social contexts because many behaviors are regulated by this generalized value. If one accepts that a number of behaviors such as the aforementioned are subsumed under the rubric of the generalized value, then the preference for equal reward distributions might best be likened to sharing with others and understood as a value-based behavior that results from the Mexican American child's socialization experience.

A SOCIALIZATION MODEL

If the relatively greater preference for equal sharing of rewards among Mexican American children is based on an ethnic value system, then the mechanisms for the transmission of this preference probably entail socialization. A number of authors have suggested that socialization experiences are likely causes of the observed reward-distribution preferences of Mexican American children (e.g., Kagan, 1977; McClintock, Bayard, & McClintock, 1983). However, while there has been some discussion and some empirical research on potential socialization antecedents, the precise mechanisms through which these reward-distribution preferences are socialized are not clear. As McClintock and coauthors (1983) indicate, "there exists neither a commonly agreed upon definition of culture, nor a general theory of how culture may mediate differences in members' behaviors." In this chapter we will present a theoretical model that suggests the mediational relationships involved in the transmission of values linked to ethnicity that lead to a preference for the equal sharing of rewards.

This socialization model (see Figure 6.1) includes four basic clusters of variables: (1) family background, family structure, and the broader social ecology; (2) socialization by familial and nonfamilial agents; (3) ethnic identity; and (4) cognitive development. The nature of the Mexican American family background, family structure, and the broader social ecology lead to specific socialization content from both familial and nonfamilial socialization agents. The content information from these familial and nonfamilial socialization agents influences the child's ethnic identity, which includes, among other factors, the knowledge of and degree of acceptance of ethnic values. The child's ethnic identity, which we will characterize as a domain of the child's self-concept, in turn influences the child's social behaviors. Thus, this model suggests several mediational relations. The socialization variables mediate the relation between family variables and ethnic identity. Ethnic identity mediates the relation between the socialization variables and social behavior. Furthermore, the development of cognitive skills, and the specific socialization practices used by socialization agents, moderates the acquisition of ethnic identity and the expression of ethnic values in behavior.

Although this model focuses on the transmission of the ethnic value for equal reward distributions, it may be applicable to a wide variety of value-based social behavior patterns that are linked to ethnicity. Further, it is important to note that this model of the socialization of Mexican American children is highly probabilistic. That is, some Mexican American children may engage in equal sharing of rewards in highly familiar situations because they are required to by their family, rather than because they have an ethnically based value. In this case, however, we would not expect these children to necessarily share rewards equally in novel situations with peers, as has been the case in most of the research comparing Mexican American and Anglo American children. Similarly, some Mexican American children may equally share rewards and may have acquired a value for sharing through the socialization process, but this value may not be associated with their ethnicity. In this case the mediator is some other

Figure 6.1. A theoretical socialization model of the cooperative, competitive, and individualistic social behaviors of Mexican American children.

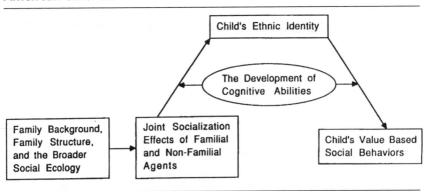

feature of the child's self-concept rather than ethnic identity. In addition, this model is probabilistic in that the ethnically based value system may be overridden in situations where the social pressure to compete is intense. Finally, one should note that the model also may include recursive influences. That is, it is very possible that hypothesized causal agents in this model, such as socialization, will both influence and be influenced by the child's ethnic identity and behavior. Indeed, individual differences in children's behavior may be a reflection of ethnic identity and may elicit specific socialization experiences.

Family Background, Family Structure, and the Broader Social Ecology

Several authors (Kagan, 1977; Keefe & Padilla, 1987; Martinez, 1977; McClintock et al., 1983) have discussed the variables associated with the family background, the family structure, and the broader social ecology that influence the socialization experiences of the Mexican American child. In considering the processes through which these types of variables may lead to specific socialization experiences, it is important to note that these variables probably do not function independently.

The family background variables that probably are related to parental and familial socialization goals are the families' generation in the United States and the parents' ethnic identity. The generation of the family in the United States and the nature of the parents' acculturative adjustment determine the range of possible exposure of the family to a traditional Mexican cultural value system, which, in turn, may have an impact on socialization goals. Similarly, the degree to which the Mexican American parents identify with their ethnic heritage may be related to the ethnic identity they would like their children to acquire, as well as to the specific information the parents attempt to communicate to their children about their ethnic background.

The family structure variables related to the parents' socialization goals are the strength of familial interdependence, the pattern of status relationships within the family, and the family size (see McClintock et al., 1983, for more details). Strength of familial interdependence consists of feelings of family solidarity as well as attachment and commitment to the family. There is some empirical evidence regarding the presence of close family ties among Mexican American families (Domino & Acosta, 1987; Jones, 1948; Kearns, 1970; Keefe, 1979; Keefe, Padilla, & Carlos, 1979; Rusmore & Kirmeyer, 1976; Steward & Steward, 1973, 1974). For example, Rusmore and Kirmeyer (1976) demonstrated that in the Mexican American family, compared with the Anglo American family, there are closer relations and greater loyalty among members, more frequent visitation of relatives, parental encouragement of family-centered orientations in their children, fewer opportunities for children to bring friends home, less freedom for children to play away from home, greater disapproval of children contradicting authority, and fewer decision-making opportunities for children. Similarly, Johnson, Teigen, and Davila (1983) found parents of Mexican background to be relatively demanding and restrictive of their children, compared with Anglo American parents. While caution is advocated regarding the generalizability of results pointing to stronger interdependence among Mexican American families, McClintock and coauthors (1983) have speculated about the implications of these characteristics for the Mexican American child's exposure to nonfamilial peers, and in turn for their reward-distribution preferences. Thus, the relatively limited exposure of Mexican American children to nonfamilial peers may make their Anglo American peers less relevant referents for social comparison and modeling, and thereby reduce the value of competitive (superiority) reward distributions to these Mexican American children.

The pattern of family relationships consists of the relative strength of bonds and the specific interaction styles among individuals within the family. Lewin (1975, described in McClintock et al., 1983) demonstrated that the first-generation Mexican American family is characterized by relatively strong mother–child bonds and relatively weak husband–wife bonds. Hoppe, Kagan, and Zahn (1977) found Mexican American children more often avoid conflict with their mothers than do Anglo American children. Martinez and his colleagues (1977; Martinez, Martinez, Olmedo, & Goldman, 1976) found that the Mexican American mother, in contrast to the Anglo American mother, is considered the more important role model through adolescence; whereas the Mexican American father is considered relatively strong, slow, passive, and calm. These types of family relationships not only may provide specific types of socialization experiences but may lead parents to strive for specific socialization outcomes and thereby to socialize their children in specific ways.

Family size consists of the number of individuals considered part of the family unit. Mexican American families generally contain a large number of children (Grebler, Moore, & Guzman, 1970; Keefe, 1979). This relatively large family size may influence parental socialization goals because it is more likely for children to assume some responsibilities (e.g., caring for other family members), it requires firm conflict regulation and conflict resolution strategies, and it influences the resource allocation rules within the family. There is some evidence of ethnic differences in conflict regulation and resolution in mother–child interactions (Hoppe, Kagan, & Zahn, 1977) and in material reward allocation (Kagan & Knight, 1984).

The broader social ecology also has been suggested as an important determinant of the socialization of Mexican American children (Kagan, 1984; Keefe & Padilla, 1987; Martinez, 1977). This broader social ecology includes environmental characteristics such as the urbanization level of the community in which the child lives, the socioeconomic status of the family and the community, and the nature of the minority status of the Mexican Americans in the community and the prevailing views of the broader society regarding Mexican Americans. In many ways a relatively rural and/or a relatively low socioeconomic environment may lead to socialization experiences that foster interdependency, respect for others, and more sharing of resources. In contrast, a more urban environment may lead to socialization experiences that foster independence, competitiveness, and more reliance on social supports that are external to the family. Minority status may lead to considerable variability in socialization experiences simply because the minority child generally has direct contacts with the minority group as well as the dominant Anglo American group. The Mexican American child also may encounter unique socialization experiences because she or he is a minority. There has been some empirical demonstration of a relation between the social behaviors of children and urbanization level (e.g., Kagan, Knight, Martinez, & Espinoza-Santana, 1981) and socioeconomic status (Knight & Kagan, 1977a).

In summary, the socialization model suggests that characteristics of the family background, the family structure, and the broader social ecology are important determinants of the socialization content provided by numerous socialization agents, and to a lesser degree the socialization practices to which Mexican American children are exposed. Unfortunately, much of this is speculative because there is little direct evidence of this causal link. Furthermore, in at least one investigation (Knight & Kagan, 1982) the number of children in the family was unrelated to either the reward-distribution behavior of Mexican American children or the Mexican American–Anglo American behavior differences that would be expected from this model. Moreover, it is probably necessary to examine the joint influences of these types of family and social ecology variables on socialization experiences in order to adequately understand this process.

Familial and Nonfamilial Socialization Experiences

One of the most significant functions of socialization is the transmission of values. By socialization, we refer to the process through which prescriptions and prohibitions are transmitted to members of the social group, as well as the impact of events or processes that are ongoing as the child becomes socialized and that have an influence on that socialization. Thus the family purposefully creates opportunities for the child to learn values, while agents such as the media may communicate value-based information that also has an impact on socialization but without purposeful intent. Cooperative, competitive, and individualistic reward-distribution patterns are products of socialization, assuming that these behavior patterns are value-based. Furthermore, the multiple familial and nonfamilial socialization agents may or may not be consistent in the socialization content or practices presented to the child.

The traditional socialization view generally presented in the literature has focused on the family (including siblings and the extended family) as important socialization agents. More recent conceptualizations (e.g., Hetherington & Parke, 1988) have considered socialization agents outside the family as well as the reciprocal roles of the socialization agents and the child. We conceptualize socialization in the broadest possible sense, including not only familial but nonfamilial socialization agents, with particular emphasis on the joint or interactive influence of these agents. Familial socialization agents include parents, siblings, and the extended family. Nonfamilial socialization agents include teachers, peers, other persons with whom the child regularly interacts, and the media (especially television).

To the extent that the family is ethnically identified, the child will be enculturated or ethnically socialized. Because a child from an ethnic minority will most likely interact with the dominant Anglo American group, it is important to consider the nature of these interactions in the child's socialization. For most Mexican American children these interactions probably become more significant when the child enters school and gradually adapts or acculturates to the dominant society. As Berry (1980) has indicated, the nature of the contacts will be determined by the characteristics of the dominant group and by the nature of the interactions between the minority and dominant groups. The child's experiences in contact with the dominant group may range from very positive to very negative depending on two major factors: (1) child characteristics—including the child's ethnic family orientation, ethnic appearance, socioeconomic status, and the ethnic neighborhood and school composition; and (2) dominant group characteristics—including the attitudes, behaviors, and related characteristics of the members of the dominant group.

In examining the socialization process it is imperative to consider both the specific socialization practices and the content material that is being socialized. The socialization practices through which the Mexican American child may acquire ethnic values, can be grouped into four general types (Bandura, 1977).

1. *Direct instruction*—verbal exhortations reflecting the appropriateness of various behavioral alternatives
2. *Modeling*—observational learning through identification with, and imitation of, significant others
3. *Feedback*—rewards and punishments indicating the appropriateness of various behavioral alternatives
4. *Other-generated experience*—selective exposure to environments that guide behavior and that are determined by the socialization agent

Whether or not these socialization practices lead to the acquisition of ethnic values depends on the content communicated through these practices. For example, the Mexican American child is more likely to acquire ethnic values if the socialization agents instruct the child in the appropriateness of ethnic values, express ethnic values while fostering identification with the model and the imitation of the behaviors representing these values, reward behaviors consistent with ethnic values and punish behaviors inconsistent with ethnic values, and create sociocultural experiences that demonstrate and encourage ethnic values and behaviors. While the content communicated through these practices is probably most important in determining the Mexican American child's acceptance of ethnic values, the specific practices utilized by the socialization agents also are likely to influence the child's acceptance of ethnic values. For example, among young children some of the practices (e.g., feedback) may be more impactful than others (e.g., direct instruction or modeling) because of the child's limited abilities when attempting to abstract and encode socialization rules. The consistent use of all of these general types of socialization practices may more rapidly lead to the acceptance of ethnic values, at least among some children, because the multiple sources of information may help in abstracting and encoding rules regarding the appropriateness of various behaviors. Moreover, other behaviors such as acceptance of the child and a generously positive/nurturant parent–child relationship may enhance the child's receptiveness to the ethnic values communicated by the socialization agent.

The pattern and nature of consistencies and inconsistencies in the ethnic teaching derived from the familial and nonfamilial sources are of special relevance to the understanding of the Mexican American child's ethnic identity and ethnic values. Various patterns of familial/nonfamilial influences are possible.

For instance, one pattern involves a child who comes from a home where the family has recently immigrated from Mexico or has maintained strong ties with its Mexican background and has strong interdependency among the relatively large and extended family. This ethnic socialization is paired with nonfamilial influences that are consistent. That is, the child experiences a Mexican American community and school with a substantial or majority representation of Mexican Americans and with Mexican Americans in positions of authority (e.g., politicians, teachers, school administrators) who strongly encourage Mexican American traditions and values. This child is taught about his or her ethnic background and encouraged to adopt an ethnic value system by the familial and nonfamilial socialization agents. Such a child will most likely develop a positive ethnic identity, including an ethnic value system, and engage in behaviors such as the equal sharing of rewards.

A different, though conceptually consistent pattern, involves a child who comes from a family that immigrated several generations earlier and that has not maintained ties with its Mexican background. The family's interdependencies, size, and interaction patterns are not characteristically Mexican American, and the family teaches little or nothing about the Mexican American culture. The child experiences a community and school that have few Mexican American role models, and they are not in powerful positions and do not encourage Mexican American traditions and values. Such a pattern of familial and nonfamilial socialization influences may lead to a weak or negative ethnic identity in the child. Although the child may know that she or he is Mexican American, the child would probably have little knowledge about ethnic behaviors and values and may be less likely to prefer equally shared rewards.

Perhaps a more characteristic pattern, however, involves a child who experiences different and conflicting information from familial and nonfamilial socialization sources. If the child comes from a family that is ethnically identified as Mexican American, but experiences a community and a school that are composed primarily of the dominant Anglo American group, there may be considerable pressure on the child to conform to two different and inconsistent sets of behavioral expectations. This child develops a clear understanding that he or she is Mexican American and has considerable knowledge of Mexican American traditions, role behaviors, and values because the family teaches the child these things. The child experiences pressure from the family to behave in a manner consistent with its ethnic values, but also experiences pressure from nonfamilial agents to conform to the behavioral expectations of the dominant group.

The relative nature and degree of the familial and nonfamilial conflicting pressures will have an important bearing on the child's value system and value-based behaviors. The child may resolve these conflicting pressures in at least four ways. First, the child may behave in accordance with the Mexican American values and therefore function well within the family but become relatively isolated from the dominant group. Second, the child may behave in accordance with the expectations of the dominant group and experience conflict within the family. Third, the child may learn to function in socially appropriate ways in both Mexican American and Anglo American settings. However, some settings with varying Mexican American and Anglo American composition may not provide consistent or clear cues for socially appropriate behaviors, and may create conflict with the family or the dominant group. Fourth, the child may not behave in accordance with the expectations of the family or the dominant group. This may be the case when the child joins with others to form a group that promotes its own expectations and values (e.g., when the child joins a gang).

In summary, there are a variety of socialization practices through which a number of socialization agents may communicate a number of value systems (Olejnik & McKinney, 1973) to the child (cf. Bandura, 1977). Indeed, research has demonstrated reward contingency and modeling effects on Mexican American children (e.g., Kagan & Madsen, 1971; Rosenthal & Zimmerman, 1972). To the extent that these agents communicate a consistent message regarding the appropriate value system, the resulting values and behaviors of the child are predictable. That is, if the socialization agents consistently pressure the child to engage in equal sharing of rewards and to avoid relatively advantaged reward distributions, it is very likely that the child will value equality and behave accordingly. As the message regarding the appropriate value system begins to vary among socialization agents, the resulting values and behaviors of the child become less predictable. That is, if some socialization agents pressure the child to equally share rewards while others pressure the child to divide rewards competitively or individualistically, the child may adopt one of these values and reject the others or may adopt context-specific values and behaviors.

Ethnic Identity

Ethnic identity is a set of ideas about one's own ethnic group membership and is an important dimension of self-concept. Ethnic identity is a part of a Mexican American individual's self-concept in much the same way in which gender identity is a part of self-concept (e.g., Huston, 1983). As such, ethnic identity plays a role in producing individual differences in behavior. Rotheram and Phinney (1987) defined ethnic identity as "one's sense of belonging to an ethnic group and the part of one's thinking, perceptions, feelings, and behavior that is due to ethnic group membership." Recent theoretical frameworks (see Bernal & Knight, 1993) have identified five components of ethnic identity.

1. *Ethnic self-identification*—the categorization of oneself as a member of one's ethnic group
2. *Ethnic constancy*—the knowledge that one's ethnic characteristics are unchanging and permanent across time, settings, and transformations

3. *Ethnic knowledge*—the knowledge that certain behaviors, traits, and values are relevant to one's ethnic group
4. *Ethnic role behaviors*—varying behaviors that manifest ethnic cultural values, styles, customs, traditions, and language
5. *Ethnic preferences*—feelings and preferences about one's ethnic group membership

While ethnic knowledge and ethnic preferences are most central to the preference for equal sharing of rewards, if indeed this preference is tied to an ethnic value, it is also likely that the five components are somewhat integrated. For example, it is unlikely that a child could have ethnic knowledge or ethnic constancy without having some ethnic self-identification. On the other hand, the child could have some ethnic self-identification without understanding ethnic constancy or having ethnic knowledge. Furthermore, the specific nature of the child's ethnic preferences and whether or not the child engages in ethnic role behaviors are probably not totally dependent on the other ethnic identity components. It is also likely that the Mexican American child's knowledge and acceptance of ethnic values are dependent on the specific information communicated about ethnicity, primarily by family members. Additionally, evaluation of one's ethnicity is heavily influenced by the responses of others, particularly members of the dominant culture.

The Role of Cognitive Development

The development of cognitive abilities plays an important role in the timing of the socializing of Mexican American children. Cognitive development moderates the abstraction and encoding of socialization rules presented by socialization agents, the nature and complexity of the child's ethnic identity, and the enactment of internalized values in relatively novel situations. While the specific socialization content communicated to the child influences the nature of the child's ethnic identity, cognitive development influences the rate of acquisition and the complexity of the child's ethnic identity.

As Bandura (1977) has suggested, learning is to a large extent an information processing activity and any limitation in the information processing system may limit the rate of learning. Thus, the learning that occurs during socialization is dependent on, among other cognitive skills, the abilities to abstract and encode rules of conduct. Given the evidence of developmental changes in the information processing system (e.g., Flavell, 1985; Kail & Hagen, 1977) and given that values are more cognitively complex than ethnic behaviors (such as, speaking Spanish or eating frijoles), ethnically based values and the associated behaviors probably develop somewhat later than simpler ethnic behaviors. There may be considerable individual differences in the rate at which Mexican

American children acquire a value for cooperative reward distribution, in part because different socialization practices have an impact on the child's processing. That is, children whose parents consistently use combinations of socialization practices designed to enhance the children's understanding will most likely acquire ethnically based values at an earlier age than children whose parents are inconsistent. For example, children whose parents reward equal sharing of rewards and at the same time verbally describe the appropriateness of sharing equally will understand and adopt a sharing value at an earlier age than children whose parents only use feedback. In the former case, the verbal information may help the child correctly abstract the appropriate rule rather than requiring the child to make inferences about the reasons for rewards and punishments. The utility of feedback has been demonstrated by Rosenthal and Zimmerman (1972) in their study of the effect of feedback and modeling on the performance of Mexican American children on a conservation task. Performance on conservation tasks is conceptually linked to the understanding of conservation of ethnicity or ethnic constancy and in turn to the acquisition of ethnic values.

As noted, ethnic identity among Mexican American children may be an important dimension of self-concept. Harter's (1983) self-system theory suggests that the nature of ethnic identity may be, in part, a function of cognitive development. An application of the developmental principles suggested by Harter's theory to the concept of ethnic identity suggests that once very young Mexican American children have some concept of ethnicity, they are likely to have a fairly empty label for their ethnic self-identification (e.g., I'm Mexican American because my mother said so); not understand ethnic constancy; have very simple global and behavioral knowledge of ethnic roles (e.g., I speak Spanish); engage in highly specific and day-to-day ethnic behaviors (e.g., I eat frijoles); and have little preference for ethnic behaviors (i.e., simply do as the family does). In contrast, older children who have sufficient cognitive abilities for their self-concept to include trait-level characteristics, are likely to have relatively meaningful labels for their ethnic self-identification (e.g., I'm Mexican American because my parents came from Mexico); understand ethnic constancy; have trait-level knowledge of ethnic roles (e.g., Mexican Americans like me are cooperative and respectful); engage in more, as well as more value-based, ethnic role behaviors (e.g., I go to church to visit the Virgin of Guadalupe from Mexico); and have considerable preferences regarding their ethnicity (e.g., I'm proud to be Mexican. I like to sing Mexican songs).

Even after Mexican American children have acquired a value for the equal sharing of rewards, they still may not be capable of enacting that value in some situations. Enacting a value for equal sharing requires the specific information processing abilities characteristic of the mathematical nature of this task (Chao, Knight, & Dubro, 1986; Knight, Dubro, & Chao, 1985). Thus, while Mexican

American children may value a cooperative reward distribution, the specific options available to them or the nature of the situation may make it difficult or impossible for them to accurately identify and enact an equal sharing of rewards. In this case the child may indeed value and want to share rewards equally, but will not do so because she or he does not know how to.

CONCLUSION

In this chapter we have presented a model of the socialization of the ethnically based value for cooperative reward distributions. This model suggests that the family background, family structure, and broader social ecology are causally linked to the content that is socialized by familial and nonfamilial agents. The socialization content is, in turn, causally linked to the nature of the child's ethnic identity, including the acceptance of values that guide behavior. The model also suggests that the child's cognitive development and the socialization practices through which the socialization content is transmitted are causally linked to the timing of the development of the child's ethnic identity and the respective behaviors. That is, the child's cognitive abilities at any given point during development may limit his or her abilities to abstract and encode socialization rules, to develop a complex ethnic identity that includes trait-level descriptors and values, and to enact in novel situations those behaviors characteristic of ethnic values.

In addition to presenting this model, we have reviewed the research bearing on the processes described in this model. It is apparent that while there has been considerable research on Mexican American–Anglo American differences and recent research on the Mexican American family, there has been little research bearing directly on many of the most important features of this model. Further, there is little or no research directly assessing any of the mediational relationships specified in this model. The one exception is the study by Knight, Cota, and Bernal (1993) in which the viability of the socialization aspects of this model was assessed using structural equation modeling. This recent investigation indicates that the greater the mother's ethnic knowledge and ethnic preferences, the more she teaches about the ethnic culture; and the more her child identifies with ethnic self-labels, the more her child knows about the culture and the greater the child's ethnic preferences. Further, those children whose ethnic identification was stronger engaged in more cooperative resource allocations. Clearly, more comprehensive and extensive research is necessary if we are going to fully understand the acquisition of the value for cooperative reward distributions among Mexican American children.

Furthermore, understanding the acquisition of cooperative social values among Mexican American children has a number of potentially important implications for early childhood education. For example, Kagan (1984) has suggested that the traditional educational policy in the United States has resulted in a structural bias against Mexican American values and achievement. That is, if the traditional classroom fosters and relies on competitive values in supporting the educational mission, then Mexican American children may underachieve because their own culturally prescribed value system may be incompatible with that promoted in the classroom. Recognizing this incompatibility may allow the educational system to modify the instructional system to accommodate individual and ethnic differences in values. One such instructional modification may be the use of cooperative learning environments as a context in which the achievement of children with either cooperative or competitive values may be stimulated (e.g., Kagan, 1984; Knight & Bohlmeyer, 1990; Sharan, 1990).

REFERENCES

Bandura, A. (1977). *Social learning theory.* Englewood Cliffs, NJ: Prentice-Hall.

Bernal, M. E., & Knight, G. P. (Eds.). (1993). *Ethnic identity: Formation and transmission among Hispanic and other minorities.* Albany: State University of New York.

Berry, J. W. (1980). Acculturation as varieties of adaptation. In A. M. Padilla (Ed.), *Acculturation: Theory, models, and some new findings* (pp. 9–25). Boulder, CO: Westview Press.

Chao, C. C., Knight, G. P., & Dubro, A. F. (1986). Information processing and age differences in social decision-making. *Developmental Psychology, 22,* 500–508.

Domino, G., & Acosta, A. (1987). The relation of acculturation and values in Mexican Americans. *Hispanic Journal of Behavioral Sciences, 9,* 131–150.

Flavell, J. H. (1985). *Cognitive development.* Englewood Cliffs, NJ: Prentice-Hall.

Grebler, L., Moore, J. W., & Guzman, R. C. (1970). *The Mexican American people.* New York: Free Press.

Harter, S. (1983). Developmental perspectives on the self-system. In E. M. Hetherington (Ed.), *Handbook of child psychology: Socialization, personality, and social development* (Vol. 4, 275–385). New York: John Wiley.

Hetherington, E. M., & Parke, R. D. (Eds.). (1988). *Contemporary reading in child psychology* (3rd ed.). New York: McGraw-Hill.

Hoppe, R. W., Kagan, S., & Zahn, G. I. (1977). Conflict resolution among field independent and field dependent Anglo American and Mexican American children and their mothers. *Developmental Psychology, 13,* 591–598.

Huston, A. C. (1983). Sex-typing. In P. H. Mussen (Ed.), *Handbook of child psychology* (Vol. 4, pp. 387–467). New York: John Wiley.

Johnson, D. L., Teigen, K., & Davila, R. (1983). Anxiety and social restriction: A study of children in Mexico, Norway, and the United States. *Journal of Cross-Cultural Psychology, 14,* 439–454.

Jones, R. C. (1948). Ethnic family patterns: The Mexican family in the United States. *American Journal of Sociology, 53,* 450–452.

Kagan, S. (1977). Social motives and behaviors of Mexican American and Anglo American children. In J. L. Martinez, Jr. (Ed.), *Chicano psychology* (pp. 45–86). New York: Academic Press.

Kagan, S. (1984). Interpreting Chicano cooperativeness: Methodological and theoretical considerations. In J. L. Martinez, Jr. & R. H. Mendoza (Eds.), *Chicano psychology* (2nd ed., pp. 289–333). Orlando, FL: Academic Press.

Kagan, S., & Knight, G. P. (1979). Cooperation–competition and self-esteem: A case of cultural relativism. *Journal of Cross-Cultural Psychology, 10,* 457–467.

Kagan, S., & Knight, G. P. (1984). Maternal reinforcement style and cooperation–competition among Anglo American and Mexican American children. *Journal of Genetic Psychology, 145,* 37–46.

Kagan, S., Knight, G. P., Martinez, S., & Espinoza-Santana, P. (1981). Conflict resolution style among Mexican children: Examining urbanization and ecology effects. *Journal of Cross-Cultural Psychology, 12,* 222–232.

Kagan, S., & Madsen, M. (1971). Cooperation and competition of Mexican, Mexican American, and Anglo American children of two ages under four instructional sets. *Developmental Psychology, 5,* 32–39.

Kail, R., & Hagen, J. W. (1977). *Perspectives on the development of memory and cognition.* Hillsdale, NJ: Erlbaum.

Kearns, B. J. (1970). Childrearing practices among selected culturally deprived minorities. *Journal of Genetic Psychology, 116,* 149–155.

Keefe, S. E. (1979, Summer). Urbanization, acculturation, and extended family ties: Mexican Americans in cities. *American Ethnologist,* pp. 349–362.

Keefe, S. E., & Padilla, A. M. (1987). *Chicano ethnicity.* Albuquerque: New Mexico Press.

Keefe, S. E., Padilla, A. M., & Carlos, M. L. (1979). The Mexican American extended family as an emotional support system. *Human Organization, 38,* 144–152.

Knight, G. P., Berning, A. L., Wilson, S. L., & Chao, C. C. (1987). The effects of information-processing demands and social-situational factors on the social decision making of children. *Journal of Experimental Child Psychology, 43,* 244–259.

Knight, G. P., & Bohlmeyer, E. M. (1990). Cooperative learning and achievement: Methods for assessing causal mechanisms. In S. Sharan (Ed.), *Cooperative learning: Theory and research* (pp. 1–22). New York: Praeger.

Knight, G. P., & Chao, C. C. (1991). Cooperative, competitive, and individualistic social values among 8–12 year old siblings, friends, and acquaintances. *Personality and Social Psychology Bulletin, 17,* 201–211.

Knight, G. P., Cota, M. K., & Bernal, M. E. (1993). The socialization of cooperative, competitive, and individualistic preferences among Mexican American children: The mediating role of ethnic identity. *Hispanic Journal of Behavioral Sciences, 15,* 291–309.

Knight, G. P., Dubro, A. F., & Chao, C. C. (1985). Information processing and the development of cooperative, competitive, and individualistic social values. *Developmental Psychology, 21,* 37–45.

Knight, G. P., & Kagan, S. (1977a). Development of prosocial and competitive behaviors in Anglo American and Mexican American children. *Child Development, 48,* 1385–1394.

Knight, G. P., & Kagan, S. (1977b). Acculturation of prosocial and competitive behaviors among second- and third-generation Mexican American children. *Journal of Cross-Cultural Psychology, 8,* 273–284.

Knight, G. P., & Kagan, S. (1982). Siblings, birth order and cooperative–competitive social behavior: A comparison of Anglo-American and Mexican-American children. *Journal of Cross-Cultural Psychology, 13,* 239–249.

Lewin, E. (1975). *Mothers and children: Latin American immigrants in San Francisco.* Unpublished doctoral dissertation, Stanford University.

Madsen, M. C. (1971). Developmental and cross-cultural differences in the cooperative and competitive behavior in young children. *Journal of Cross-Cultural Psychology, 2,* 365–371.

Martinez, J. L., Jr. (1977). Cross-cultural comparison of Chicanos and Anglos on the semantic differential: Some implications for psychology. In J. L. Martinez, Jr. (Ed.), *Chicano psychology* (pp. 29–43). New York: Academic Press.

Martinez, J. L., Jr., Martinez, S. R., Olmedo, E. L., & Goldman, R. D. (1976). The semantic differential technique: A comparison of Chicano and Anglo high school students. *Journal of Cross-Cultural Psychology, 7,* 325–334.

McClintock, C. G. (1974). Development of social motives in Anglo-American and Mexican-American children. *Journal of Personality and Social Psychology, 29,* 348–354.

McClintock, C. G., & Van Avermaet, E. (1982). Social values and rules of fairness: A theoretical perspective. In J. Grzelak & V. Derlega (Eds.), *Living with other people: Theory and research on cooperation and helping* (pp. 43–71). New York: Academic Press.

McClintock, E., Bayard, M. P., & McClintock, C. G. (1983). The socialization of social motivation in Mexican American families. In E. García (Ed.), *The Mexican American child: Language, cognition and social development* (pp. 143–161). Tempe, AZ: Center for Bilingual Education.

Olejnik, A. B., & McKinney, J. P. (1973). Parental value orientation and generosity in children. *Developmental Psychology, 8,* 311.

Rosenthal, T. L., & Zimmerman, B. J. (1972). Modeling by exemplification and instruction in training conservation. *Developmental Psychology, 6,* 392–401.

Rotheram, M. J., & Phinney, J. S. (1987). Introduction: Definitions and perspectives in the study of children's ethnic socialization. In J. S. Phinney & M. J. Rotheram (Eds.), *Children's ethnic socialization: Pluralism and development* (pp. 10–28). Beverly Hills: Sage.

Rusmore, J., & Kirmeyer, S. (1976). *Family attitudes among Mexican American and Anglo American parents in San Jose, California.* Paper presented at the 56th annual meeting of the Western Psychological Association, Los Angeles.

Sharan, S. (Ed.). (1990). *Cooperative learning: Theory and research.* New York: Praeger.

Steward, M., & Steward, D. (1973). The observation of Anglo- Mexican- and Chinese-American mothers teaching their young sons. *Child Development, 4,* 329–337.

Steward, M., & Steward, D. (1974). Effect of social distance on teaching strategies of Anglo-American and Mexican American mothers. *Developmental Psychology, 10,* 797–907.

CHAPTER 7

Diverse Families

Francisco A. Villarruel, David R. Imig, and Marjorie J. Kostelnik

In contemporary society, the term *diversity* has been used to describe the racial and ethnic variation among children and the families in which they live. Focusing on the family as a developmental context, this chapter examines the issues relevant to the provision of services in early childhood education programs that can build upon the strengths of the family context. Included is a discussion of a new framework that educators and researchers might consider in an effort to understand the impact of families in the formative years of childhood, especially the cultural and ecological contexts that affect development. In considering the influence of families on the development of young children, the vast majority of research has focused on the negative outcomes associated with racial-ethnic status of children in the United States and has not addressed the broad range of potential developmental topics, except to seek support for ethnic perspectives on specific stage theories of development. Such an approach has left unanswered a variety of research questions about the development of children from diverse racial and ethnic groups, and, more important, implications for early childhood practice.

A central tenet of this chapter is the provision of a framework for early childhood educators to develop an understanding of family relations, interactions, strengths, and barriers. One of the many theories that have contributed to this perspective is social capital. J. S. Coleman (1988) defined *social capital* as consisting of the mutuality of obligations and expectations that bind people together, the capacity among people to share information, and the acceptance of norms regulating behavior. This thesis explains variations in how well different racial and ethnic groups have "succeeded" in this country as resulting from the extent to which groups value success, are persistent in work, and are willing to defer gratifications—characteristics associated with "middle-class" culture (Glazer, 1975).

103

THE CHANGING OF AMERICA

Children enrich the present, promise an unbroken continuation of life and family, and are a value to society because they embody the future. Yet for many children today, future prospects are becoming increasingly mixed. While governments as well as families accept responsibility for ensuring the well-being of children, investment in education and the provision of safe and wholesome environments in which they can live has become increasingly more difficult. Social changes, for example, have become more commonplace among families. The growing divorce rate, economic hardship, and increases in never-married mothers have placed more children in single-parent homes during the formative years. As recently depicted in the National Kids Count Data book, female-headed families are much more likely to experience economic hardship (Center for the Study of Social Policy, 1992). Moreover, the entrance of more mothers (both married and single parent) of young children into the labor force has placed more children in the care of nonfamily members.

In addition to social-structural transformations such as those, new demographic patterns have emerged that have heightened our awareness of the need to focus renewed attention on how to build upon diversity in early childhood programs. The impact of demographic changes is best reflected in childcare settings and early childhood classrooms, where students represent many ethnic, cultural, and linguistic backgrounds. An evolving educational priority has focused attention on the conditions that appear to affect students and, in particular, children of color (Lerner, 1991; Trueba, 1989).

Changing Demographics

The United States is undergoing a demographic transition: It is becoming a multicultural society. During the 1990s it will shift from a predominately white society rooted in Western culture to a world society characterized by three large racial and ethnic minorities. All three minorities will grow in both size and population, while the still significant white majority will continue its relative decline in numbers (Riche, 1991).

One contributing variable to the changing population is the current pattern of immigration. During the 1980s, the United States received 6 million legal immigrants, up from 4.2 million during the 1970s and 3.2 million during the 1960s. Fewer of these immigrants are of European origin than in the past. The recent immigrants also tend to have more children than the non-Latino white population, as do Latinos and African Americans.

In addition to immigration patterns, childbearing patterns also play a role in the diversity of our society. Recent census data reveal that fertility rates are still higher for minority groups than for non-Latino whites. In 1988, Latino

Table 7.1. Demographic trends and the transformation of America's children (population under 18 years old).

	1980		1990	
	Number	Percentage	Number	Percentage
Total children	63,754,960	28.1%	63,604,432	25.6%
European-American	50,085,021	78.6%	47,628,229	74.9%
Minority children	16,719,434	26.2%	19,797,121	31.1%
African American	9,395,912	56.2%	9,584,415	48.4%
Latino*	5,627,956	33.7%	7,757,500	39.2%
Asian American	1,044,601	6.0%	2,083,387	10.5%
Native American	555,735	3.3%	696,967	3.5%
Other Minorities	2,673,691	16.0%	3,611,434	18.2%

People of Latino origin may be of any race, and, thus, may be double counted in other racial minority categories.

women had the highest rate, with 96 children per 1,000 women aged 15 to 44; African American women had a rate of 87 per 1,000, compared with 63 per 1,000 for European Americans. As a result, two-thirds of minority families had children in 1990, compared with fewer than half of the non-Latino white families. Thus, as depicted in Table 7.1, the number of minority children in the United States has increased substantially, while the number of nonminority children has decreased (Center for the Study of Social Policy, 1992).

The changing demographics also are influencing the diversity within minority communities. The 1990 census gives an accurate picture of the growing diversity in our nation. In that year, for example, 12% of Americans identified themselves as African American, 9% as Latino, 3% as Asian or Pacific Islander, 1% as American Indian, and 4% as "other." As each group grows, diversity within groups will grow too.

These same data indicate that between 1980 and 1990, the Hispanic population increased, from 6.4% of the U.S. population to 9%. This was a 53% increase. In contrast, the white population increased by 6%, African Americans by 13.5%, American Indians by 37.9%, "others" by 45.1%, and Asian or Pacific Islander by 107.8%. As a whole, the increase in the Latino population represented an increase of approximately one-third (34%) of the growth of the U.S. population during the 1980s (Chapa & Valencia, 1993; Hernandez, 1993).

While the Hispanic growth of the 1970s and 1980s was expected, it was not uniform among Latino groups. Among all Hispanics, the Mexican population decreased slightly from 62% of all U.S. Latinos in 1970 to 61% in 1990. By the same token, however, the actual number of Mexicans in the U.S. increased. In contrast, the Puerto Rican and Cuban groups have remained at about 12% and 5%, respectively, while also growing in terms of their absolute population. Latinos from other countries (e.g., El Salvador, the Dominican Republic, Colombia, Guatemala, Nicaragua, Ecuador, Honduras, Peru, Panama), while smaller in overall population, increased by slightly more than 2 million between 1970 and 1990 (Chapa & Valencia, 1993; Hernandez, 1993).

The Significance of Diversity

Contrary to what many people seem to think, there is no such thing as "the typical" American or American-minority family. Families are as diverse as race and ethnicity. In recent years, the primary model for individual, familial, and community development has seen the introduction of a variety of transformations and differences. The "traditional" nuclear family, which consists of two "natural" parents and their children, for example, is no longer the norm of family life. However, this image of the family is still believed to be normal and desirable culturally, socially, and psychologically (Anderson & White, 1986; Hernandez, 1993; Lerner, Castellino, Terry, McKinney, & Villarruel, in press). Remarried, never-married, single-parent, and cross-cultural families are quickly becoming the dominant family structure.

Nonetheless, the family system remains the central institution for early child development. Ethnicity, in turn, generally has been regarded as the primary institution for the development of values, attitudes, life-styles, customs, rituals, and personality types of individuals who identify with a particular ethnic group (Mindel, Habenstein, & Wright, 1988). The maintenance of ethnic identification and solidarity ultimately rests on the ability of the family to socialize its members into the ethnic culture and thus to channel and develop future behavioral and interpersonal norms as well as family life-styles. What is becoming increasingly more apparent is that as the diversity of cultures increases, so too does the diversity within families, especially with respect to roles, norms, and patterns of communication. We will return to this point later in the chapter.

The Impact of Diversity on the Young Child

Appreciating the significance and validity of the child's and family's language, culture, and communication strategies is a challenge. With so many children from a variety of language and cultural groups within early childhood settings, the need to move from appreciation to actions that go beyond acknowledging that diversity has become increasingly more important, especially in larger urban areas.

During early childhood the family is the major institution for the socialization. The transition to formal schooling, however, marks a critical period in the child's life, signaling an end to insulated security and innocence for all children, and perhaps more so for culturally/linguistically diverse children. Only after non-English-speaking children or those whose way of life is very different from the mainstream American life-style have entered school or have had certain encounters with children from the mainstream do they become aware of their "deviance" and hence their minority status (Gibson & Ogbu, 1991). From then on, they may experience years of stress, confusion, conflict, and defeat—both in and outside of school.

It is important to underscore that behaviors are governed by cultural norms, values, beliefs, and practices. Therefore, behavioral characteristics of one culture group can be markedly different from those of another. Consequently children from culturally diverse groups tend to have noticeable behaviors that, similar to physical and linguistic differences, quickly differentiate them from children of the dominant culture (Thomas, Chess, Sillen, & Mendez, 1974). Since there is no absolute standard for judging social and personal conduct, and as long as the statistical model is applied to psychosocial measurement, minority young children who bring to school their home and cultural upbringing are at risk of being considered deviant (Cummins, 1989).

Heterogeneity in Early Childhood Education

Early childhood professionals are working with increasingly varied populations of children. As described earlier, such trends are expected to continue over the coming years. Knowing this, educators and researchers have identified a wide array of variables that account for the heterogeneous nature of early childhood classrooms. Some of these include differences among children in terms of ability (Barbour, 1990; Glickman, 1991), age and achievement of developmental milestones (Katz, Evangelou, & Hartman, 1990; McKee, 1991), gender (Soderman & Phillips, 1986; Stanford, 1992), socioeconomic status (Allington, 1983; Dawson, 1987), religious orientation (Haynes, 1992), cultural beliefs and racial-ethnic identity (Jenson & Warstadt, 1990), family composition (Washington, 1988; Zill, 1989), learning styles (Anderson, 1988; Gardner, 1983;

Kovalik, 1986), and the parenting styles children experience at home (Baumrind, 1983; Maccoby & Martin, 1983; Sroufe & Cooper, 1989). The major thrust of current educational practices is how to accommodate these differences in ways that maintain the dignity of each child while also enhancing learning and achievement. Early childhood educators are thus expected to look at children within the context of their family, culture, and community and to create age-appropriate as well as individually appropriate living and learning environments. These accommodations manifest themselves in many different ways, but are most evident in changing classroom routines, curricula, and approaches to parent involvement (Kostelnik, Soderman, & Whiren, 1993). It is our premise that differences in family system structures also should be included as contributing to early childhood heterogeneity.

THE ECOLOGICAL CONTEXT OF EARLY CHILDHOOD

Children are born and carry out their lives within an ecological context. This context includes both the biological makeup bestowed on them by their parents and the environment in which they develop. That environment encompasses the nuclear and extended family, and extra-familial settings such as neighborhood, childcare center or elementary school, culture, and society. These contexts often overlap and are embedded within one another, influencing children in complex, interconnecting ways.

Analyzing the Ecological Contexts

The contexts of young children may be best represented as a series of concentric rings, with each ring influencing and being influenced by others (Bronfenbrenner, 1986, 1989). A graphic representation of this conceptualization is offered in Figure 7.1

The Biological Context. At the contextual core is the child endowed with a particular biological heritage. Genetic givens include gender, temperament, and a timetable for the emergence of intellectual, emotional, and physical capabilities. In addition, young children have an innate predisposition to act on the environment, to learn, and to seek social stimulation as well as form bonds with other people (Sroufe & Cooper, 1989). Yet, because each child comes into this world as a unique being, all these factors combine to create a singular context for his or her future development.

The Immediate Context. Development is further influenced by the immediate environment—all the people, objects, settings, and resources with which the child has direct contact. At first, this context is dominated by the

Figure 7.1. A social-ecological framework or development. (Adapted from Bronfenbrenner, 1986, 1989; Perkins, Ferrari, Covey, and Keith, 1994.)

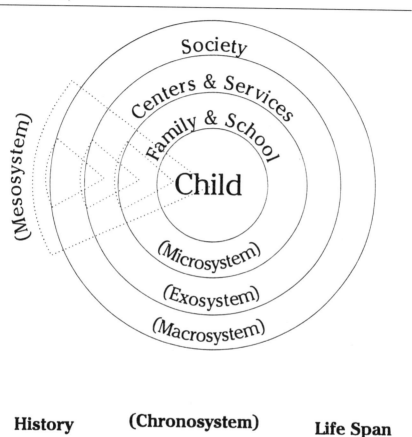

family. Eventually, additional settings (e.g., family childcare home, childcare center, school, playground, or neighborhood) become increasingly influential.

The Socioeconomic Context. All the immediate settings in which children find themselves are further embedded in a broader socioeconomic context. The impact of social and economic factors on children's development is frequently ancillary but profound. For instance, the materials provided in a classroom and the curricula children encounter at school are shaped by educators, parents, and school boards using resources within a particular community. Indirectly, all of these general economic factors and community-based beliefs have an impact on each child.

The Societal-Cultural Context. Individuals, families, schools, and communities exist within a society and a culture and are greatly influenced by these, the broadest of all environments. The societal-cultural context is defined by the belief patterns shaped by groups of people and is depicted as the outermost ring in Figure 7.1. These beliefs shape the structure of various societal institutions (e.g., legal, economic, religious, and political systems) and other social structures such as social class. In addition, within and across societies there exist culture groups that share more narrowly defined beliefs, norms, and values, and that differ from one another in their basic approaches to living. Essential cultural variations exist regarding the way human beings relate to one another, the significance of time, personality types most valued, how humans relate to nature, and fundamental notions of whether human beings are innately good or bad (Berns, 1989). Also, there is increasing evidence that cultural differences influence all elements of childrearing, such as the following (York, 1991):

Age-related expectations of children
Interest in and concern over children acquiring certain skills by a particular age
Sleep patterns and bedtime routines
Children's role and responsibility in the family
Toilet training
Diet and mealtime behavior
Discipline and child guidance techniques
How adults talk to children
How adults show affection to children
Importance of gender identity and particular sex roles
Dress and hair care
Illness and approaches to cures and remedies
Use of supplementary childcare
Acceptance of, meaning of, and response to crying
Child's attachment to adults, separation from adults

As a result of how different families approach these issues, some children grow up learning that cooperation is more highly valued than competition, and others the reverse (see also Chapter 6, this volume). One family might interpret a child's assertive behavior as a positive sign of independence, while another would be dismayed at the child's lack of deference. In some families, children are encouraged to revere nature; in some they are taught to control it. Which belief system prevails for children is a function of the familial and cultural-historical contexts in which they find themselves.

Contextual Relationships and Impacts

None of the contexts described above exists in isolation. None exerts its influence apart from the rest. They are interdependent, both influencing and being influenced by others. For instance, children are not passive recipients of environmental impacts. They actively contribute to their own development and to the creation of the contexts in which they live and learn. Knowing this, for example, we observe that a resistant child frequently elicits rule-related confrontations with adults and that such behavior, in turn, prompts the child to become increasingly resistant. Similarly, the family environment may be strengthened or weakened by changes that occur in the socioeconomic context surrounding it. However, because its influence is bi-directional, families also affect socioeconomic forces, demanding alterations in services and community organizations to support their changing needs. This interdependence among contexts makes it clear that intervention with the child will have an impact on the other contexts within which he or she functions, such as the family. Also, what goes on in the family will influence the child's behavior in the early childhood program.

The Essential Nature of Children's Families

As pointed out earlier, during the early childhood period it is the immediate context of the family that has the greatest influence on the child. The family is responsible for meeting the child's physical needs as well as for socializing the child. Family members provide children with their first social relationships, models for behaviors and roles, a framework of values and beliefs, and intellectual stimulation (Bobbitt & Paolucci, 1986). All such functions take place through direct and indirect teaching; in constructive and sometimes destructive ways; more or less successfully. Furthermore, all additional environmental influences are channeled to some extent through the family. For instance, it is via the family that children gain access to economic resources and that they learn the customs of their cultural group. The first attitudes toward education, work, and society that children encounter are in the family. Parents arrange for out-of-home care and make the initial entree into a school for their children. They also promote or inhibit opportunities for peer and community contact. If parents are stressed by the hardships of poverty, the uncertainty of losing a job, or the prospects of marital dissolution, their ability to meet the needs of their young children is jeopardized. If such parents receive help or support from relatives, friends, or social institutions, the home environment they create for their children may be enhanced. In short, the significance that biological variables, other immediate environments, and socioeconomic and societal-cultural factors have for children is always mediated by decisions and interactions within families (Sroufe & Cooper, 1989). Thus, to better understand what is happening to young children in America, it is useful to put forth a current perspective of families.

FAMILY SYSTEM STRUCTURES

Familial, cultural, and environmental meanings play an important role in the processes used by families to cope with and adapt to the demands of educational institutions (Boss, 1988; Imig, 1993; Kantor & Lehr, 1975). In examining families within our increasingly pluralistic society, there are multiple cultural dimensions to address (Allison & Takei, 1993; Baca Zinn & Eitzen, 1992; Gibson & Ogbu, 1991; Lerner, 1991; McLoyd, 1991). Families, for example, have been characterized with respect to their racial, ethnic, and socioeconomic group membership; the sociocultural history of the group; immigration status; time in residence; geographical location (i.e., urban, suburban, rural); and region of the country. While we do not underestimate the importance of these issues, we turn to a broader issue that has an impact on teaching and on social interactions among diverse children, families, teachers, and educational settings.

A great deal of knowledge of family systems involves tacit assumptions, that is, taken-for-granted knowledge that often is not made explicit (Bowers, 1984). As a result, we experience many of our judgments as part of the natural order of things, rather than as reflections of values that may be specific to our own (or someone else's) culture. Thus, professionals' impressions of families' functioning styles may be expected to be influenced by their own, often unexamined, cultural and experiential assumptions. Unless we can step outside of our own framework, it can be difficult to see strength in behaviors that reflect different assumptions; it can be difficult to understand that a feature that appears at first glance to be a deficit may actually be a resource.

With regard to family structures and roles, for example, Wright, Salleby, Watts, and Lecca (1983) argued that pervasive stereotypes, such as matriarchy among African Americans and machismo among Latinos, fail to acknowledge the strengths of these patterns—the requirements for both responsibility and authority inherent in these roles. Correa (1989, 1991) underscores this point in relation to the challenge of establishing collaborative relationships with families from diverse backgrounds, by suggesting that the belief system held by the family may actually be a strength for working with children and their families. Inherent within this perspective, however, is the notion that the patterns of communication and interaction can be discerned and, more important, used as the basis upon which strategies for interaction and teaching can be built.

Principles describing human communication hold that behavior is governed by patterns incorporating constancy and variety feedback. That is, either people tend to do more-of-the-same (structured), or they tend to do something different (flexible). Because communication is an interpersonal phenomenon, behavior may reflect collaborative or noncollaborative acts. People can behave in a conjoint manner (connectedness), or they can act in the absence of others (separateness) (Constantine, 1986; Galvin & Brommel, 1991). When dimensionally ordered in an orthogonal relationship, these behavioral options result in the articulation of four basic family system structures (see Figure 7.2).

1. Structured-connected (closed)
2. Flexible-separate (random)
3. Flexible-connected (open)
4. Structured-separate (synchronous)

Each of these four family structures, when considered in its "pure" form, represents a unique paradigmatic way of perceiving, interpreting, and understanding life phenomena. Each type has a unique perspective of what makes life meaningful, how time should be viewed and used, what constitutes love and caring, how information and ideas are handled, how decisions are made, and how children should be raised and taught.

Structured-Connected Families (Closed)

The structured-connected or closed family type employs strategies that conform to "normative" cultural prescriptions and expectations. Conformity to societal expectations and maintenance of the status quo provide a sense of stability and security unlike that experienced by any of the other three typal structures. Because cultural prescriptions and expectations differ, we sometimes confuse behavioral diversity with structural diversity. Constantine (1986) provides a case in point. Bereavement following the death of a family member may differ given the cultural context. In structured-connected European American families, the expression of grief may reflect an attempt to remain calm and collected, while struggling to maintain public control. In structured-connected Lebanese families, the bereaved are expected to wail loudly and publicly. Behaviorally these two families are opposites; structurally they are similar. They are also similar from an interactional perspective. Observation of both types of families would reveal a qualitative similarity in the interaction patterns among family members. In each family, whether patriarchal or matriarchal in orientation, opposition to prescribed expectations would be discouraged. In the

Figure 7.2. A model of basic family system structures.

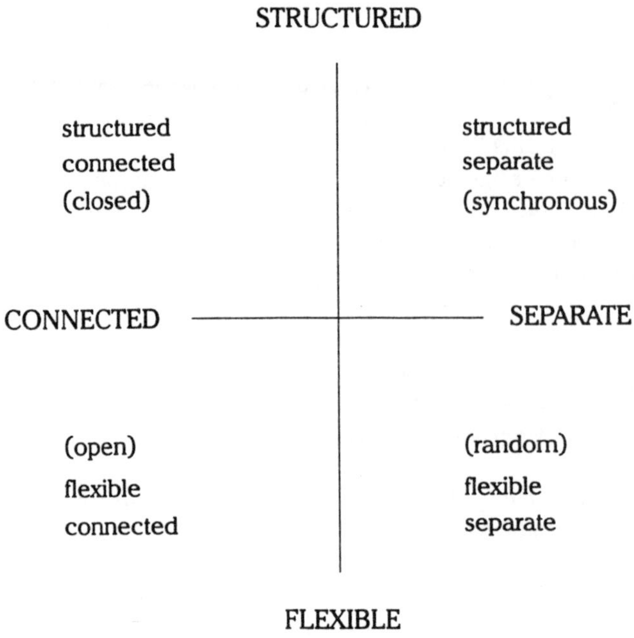

STRUCTURED

structured	structured
connected	separate
(closed)	(synchronous)

CONNECTED ———————————— SEPARATE

(open)	(random)
flexible	flexible
connected	separate

FLEXIBLE

structured-connected European American family, public expression of grief would be subtly controlled by a priori comments from the family authority figure(s), suggesting that it would be important to manifest signs of strength by behaving in a stoic and controlled manner. At any sign of a public display of "emotional weakness," the authority figure might give the "offending" individual nonverbal cues intended to remind the person to maintain his or her composure. Conversely, for the structured-connected Lebanese family, the authority figure(s) would encourage, reinforce, and "expect" public expressions of grief. Interestingly, if both of these families were in attendance at the same funeral, one can only guess how they might assess each other's behavior; however, it is likely they would consider themselves as behaviorally different from one another, not knowing that from a structural perspective they were very much alike.

Analogous behavioral differences are likely to manifest themselves in early childhood classrooms. For instance, the cultural standard for one group (e.g., European Americans, Germans) may be that infancy equals the first 12 months of life, and for another (e.g., Japanese) that infancy ends at approximately 5 years of age (York, 1991). Children raised in the former circumstances may be breast fed for a few months then weaned to a cup before the end of the first year. Discipline begins early with adults saying no and slapping the child's hand. As the child moves into the preschool years, demands for more grown-up behavior increase. By the time such children enter elementary school, they are expected to know how to behave so that teachers can get on with a cognitive agenda. Youngsters brought up under the second set of conditions may be breast fed for 2 to 4 years and allowed to have a bottle until they enter kindergarten. Discipline begins at the end of this period, with the school expected to play a major role in the socialization process.

Although the outward manifestations of child behavior that result from these two cultural orientations may look very different, the methods for socializing the child according to the appropriate standard will look much the same in both families if each personifies a structured-connected system. For instance, adult family members will provide verbal and nonverbal cues to children about what behaviors are expected. Modeling, direct instruction, consequences, and rewards may be used to uphold the cultural norm. Also, there will be relative cohesion among family members across generations.

Flexible-Separate Families (Random)

Because societal expectations are intended to maintain the social order, minimize individual "antisocial" behaviors, and shape personal identity through group participation and belonging, the flexible-separate or random family type represents the antithesis of the structured-connected family type. In the flexible-separate type each family member is "expected" to do what is meaningful to him or her as an individual person. In the classroom, for example, a student coming from a flexible-separate family type might have considerable difficulty in conforming to a structured-connected oriented teacher and participating in collaborative activities. A child in a flexible-separate family is socialized to develop intuitive and instinctive capacities, to rely on individual and subjective strengths, and to expand, if not significantly stretch, conventional boundaries in search of the undiscovered. Time is viewed as discretionary and flexible rather than consistent and predictable. No ideas are too extreme, and conflict is expected and need not be resolved—differences are a sign of individuality and uniqueness.

Flexible-Connected Families (Open)

Seemingly, the most common type of family in mainstream U.S. society is the flexible-connected or open family. This family type represents the "ideal" portrayed in a great deal of contemporary media and literature. This family engages in a collective give-and-take among family members. It attempts to manage a balance between the need for collective order and structure, and individual freedom and choice. Time is viewed as flexible and adaptable; expressions of interpersonal coupling are authentic, genuine, and responsive. Information and ideas are important elements of decision making and have significant meaning for coping with change.

A child from this type of family "fits in" with the conventional educational context. Education is about ideas and information. The typical classroom "paradoxically" requires a tolerance of conformity, while requiring an individual capacity to recognize and utilize the resources and opportunities always available. The flexible-connected child knows when to be assertive, but also knows when to respond appropriately to authority. The child from an enabled flexible-connected family has been taught the skills of negotiating and balancing the "opposites" of life. Many teachers respond positively to children from this type of family.

Structured-Separate Families (Synchronous)

Perhaps one of the most difficult of all family structures for the educational system to understand is the structured-separate or synchronous family system. Contemporary educational institutions favor children coming to school with a blend of structured-connected (closed) and flexible-connected (open) attributes. Teachers tend to be positively disposed to children who "recognize" the importance and relevance of positivistic, empirical, and objective educational methodologies and have an insatiable desire for the conventional presentation of information and ideas—children who are willing to engage in discussion, "bat around" ideas and dialogue. This is not the child from a synchronous family.

The synchronous family appears to be connected to the rhythms and spiritual truths of the natural environment—a perhaps cosmos. Knowledge of life is derived not through conventional verbal communication, as in the case of the closed and open families, but through life experiences and insights. Separately experienced events, often implicitly planned for children by the experienced family members, merge in a coincidental manner to create an explicitly uncommunicated yet implicitly "understood" sense of bonding, coupling, and "just knowing" among family members. Often the notion of family coincides with the community. The community or tribe or clan can be the family.

The notion of explicitly uncommunicated yet implicitly understood sense of knowing can be understood in the example of the Japanese concept of *Amae*. It is important to note before presenting this example, however, that cross-cultural differences in childrearing patterns are, in theory, intended to encourage the development of qualities and attitudes needed for expected adult roles, which differ from society to society (Hoffman, 1988; Super & Harkness, 1981).

The concept of *Amae*, as described by Bell (1994), represents a synchronous parenting technique that defines and establishes the parent–child interactions that extend throughout the period of infancy. Specifically, during the first 5 to 6 years of life, every need of the child is met as soon as it is expressed. Utilizing a Western definition of parenting style, parents would be described as "spoiling" or overindulging their children. As the infant develops, needs are perceived or met prior to overt expression. In other words, the relationship that is established is based on the perspective of positive dependency. While this relationship might be viewed as a symbiotic relationship in Western society, in Japan it is critical to the development of the young child, and as a consequence of its significance, remains intact until the next phase of development, which begins at approximately age 6. It is not until this point that independence between child and parent is noted.

Thus, as illustrated in this example, the theme of positive dependency represents the concept of *knowing* (i.e., the synchronous version of empathy) and caring (Bell, 1994). When one has made emotional contact with another, then one is moved to know the other. As illustrated by *Amae*, an outcome of positive dependency is restraint: When one cares for another and understands the other's needs, one exercises restraint so as not to be a burden. Thus, the family can adjust to children with developmentally and environmentally changing needs and interests as a consequence of this positive dependency.

Beyond Communications: Structural Diversity in Families

The challenge of providing developmentally appropriate early childhood services to an increasingly culturally diverse society is not trivial. Embedded within the challenge of service delivery to a pluralistic community or classroom is the task of identification of and sensitivity to family priorities, resources, and concerns in a nonjudgmental mode that at once respects families' varying functioning styles and also offers services consonant with the beliefs of professionals and the systems they represent.

In addition to not making an effort to develop an understanding of distinctive communication styles, practitioners often overlook differential concepts of family structure and identity. Typically, professionals from mainstream American backgrounds tend to recognize the parents of a child as the main authority in the family. In so doing, however, professionals overlook cultural assumptions concerning what constitutes a family, how lines of family responsibility are drawn, and, more important, how families interact and communicate. This assumption can be a major source of conflict and misunderstanding between professionals, parents, and children.

In Native American families, for example, freedom traditionally allowed to children on reservations is based on a sense of community responsibility, rather than individual family responsibility, for children (Everett, Proctor, & Cartmell, 1983; Lewis, 1982). Professionals working with such families may readily apply their own assumptions about family structure and responsibility and, in so doing, may fail to recognize the strengths that may accrue from a broader assumption of community responsibility for children. Another culturally bonded aspect of family structure is the definition of biological family. The existence of informal co-parenting and informal adoption by godparents, extended family, or friends has been documented among working-class Mexican, Puerto Rican, African American, and Native American families (García, 1992; Garcia-Preto, 1982; Lewis, 1982; McAdoo, 1992; Moore-Hinds & Boyd-Franklin, 1982). Such events are not interpreted as evidence of neglect or lack of interest on the part of parents but are understood by their communities as acceptable actions for the good of the family as a whole.

As Laosa (1984, 1988) argues, the history of the United States is really a history of distinct ethnic and racial groups with contrasting patterns of cultural traditions, historical circumstances, and access to societal resources. Therefore, we must accept the notion that the evolution of family forms is the outcome of a process of adaptation to cultural, social, and economic circumstances.

IMPLICATIONS AND CONCLUSION

In this chapter, we have attempted to provide a panoramic, although detailed, view of two systemic parameters—culture and family structure—that may differentiate family systems in the United States and, as such, have an impact on a child's ability to learn. This initial overview provides only a starting point along a continuum of dimensions that early childhood educators should consider when working with culturally, ethnically, linguistically, and economically diverse children and their families.

In order to understand differences and strengths among family systems and communication, early childhood educators and students need to learn to recognize developmental equivalences in patterns of behavior. That is, all children have learned many of the same things—language, category systems, interpersonal communication styles—before they come to school. Although these accomplishments may look quite different, their developmental adequacy should not be questioned. There are a number of "equally" good ways to shape children. When children do not respond to the social and cognitive expectations of school, the teacher should look first for a developmentally equivalent task that the child does know. If in doubt, professionals should assume that culturally different children are normal and should look again, recognizing that their vision may be clouded by their own cultural myopia. It is by assuming developmental equivalence that adults can begin the search for the fit between their

understanding, a child's understanding of a situation, and the skills or competencies necessary for a task to be performed.

If what is meaningful is also relevant, then how can educators better recognize and accommodate institutional environments to the needs and "ways of
knowing" of children socialized in structurally diverse families? By structurally
diverse we are not referring to the variety of physical structures of families,
such as single-parent families, traditional families, dual working families, step-
families, or other alternative family forms, but to the paradigmatically, interac-
tionally, and perceptually diverse families. Children from each of the paradigmatically diverse families perceive, interpret, understand, and know the
"objective" world in a different (diverse) fashion. It is the responsibility of educators, beginning with their initial interactions with the child and in observing
the child's interactions with parents and peers, to recognize and respect this
paradigmatic and perceptual diversity. Further, it can be argued that it is in all
likelihood the responsibility of educators (and parents) to facilitate a multipara-
digmatic perceptual capacity and appreciation in children. Thus, it is essential
not to value some ways of achieving developmental milestones over others,
since young children are particularly sensitive to how adults value them. Hilliard and Vaughn-Scott (1982) and Hale-Benson (1986), for example, point out
that because the behavior of African American children is so different from that
of their European American peers, they often are judged to be deficient in their
development rather than just different. The result is that healthy and normal
children who are are at risk for being diagnosed as learning disabled or emo-
tionally impaired.

Where discrepancies exist between the cultural patterns of home, community, and school, teachers must plan to bridge these gaps. The essential task is
to create new and shared meanings between the teacher and children—new
contexts that give meaning to the knowledge and skills being taught. The challenge is to find personally interesting and culturally relevant ways of creating
new contexts for children—contexts in which school skills are meaningful and
rewarding. Moreover, school learning is most likely to occur when family values
reinforce school expectations. This does not mean that parents must teach the
same things at home that teachers do in school. It does mean that parents and
community must project school achievement as a desirable and attainable ideal
if the children are to build it into their own sense of self (Kostelnik, Soderman, & Whiren, 1993).

Finally, the same "contexts" do not have the same meanings to children
from different groups, and the assessment of learning outcomes therefore presents a formidable problem as children may misunderstand the meaning of a
teacher's request for information, knowledge, and skills (Kagan, 1991). The
meaning of words, gestures, and actions, for example, may be quite different,
without either the adult or the child recognizing the discrepancy. Similarly, cur-

riculum materials may take on meanings different from what the teacher intended, and they may be interpreted differently by the various children in the class depending on their background. Evaluation of children's knowledge and understanding is difficult, and until teachers have built a common "classroom culture and language" with children, they will be unable to assess accurately what children know or can do. Formal assessment should be delayed until teachers and children have built a set of socially constructed shared meanings.

Thoughtful teachers can use developmental principles to create meaning for the new context of multicultural learning communities—to attach new learning to that which has already been achieved, and to safeguard children's self-image and self-confidence while they expand their knowledge and skills. In order to achieve this difficult, but workable, system, we recommend that professionals be made aware, in both preservice and continuing educational experiences, of the growing body of ethnographically derived information on cultural minority groups in the United States and on the processes that may influence acculturation.

Moreover, early childhood professionals should be trained in the use of open-ended approaches to understanding and working with child and family strengths. Such approaches may include the development of informal interview scales, such as a family resource and inventory scale focusing on family structure, that could be included in enrollment or school orientation materials. Such information would further educators' awareness of variations among families and provide a background against which a classroom climate could be created that is sensitive to this dimension of children's lives. The creation of parent involvement strategies that allow children, their families, and teachers to exchange ideas and develop mutual understandings is also desirable. This latter approach provides early childhood professionals an opportunity to develop an appreciation and understanding of the families' normative, albeit different, strategies of social interaction and teaching.

Acknowledgments. The preparation of this chapter was supported in part by a grant from the W. K. Kellogg Foundation. The authors would like to thank Dr. Alice Whiren for her comments and suggestions on an earlier draft of this manuscript, and Ms. Dee Sylvester and Ms. Deborah Johnson for their clerical assistance.

REFERENCES

Allington, R. L. (1983). The reading instruction provided readers of different abilities. *Elementary School Journal, 83,* 548–558.

Allison, K. W., & Takei, Y. (1993). Diversity: The cultural contexts of adolescents and their families. In R. M. Lerner (Ed.), *Early adolescence: Perspectives on research, policy, and intervention* (pp. 51–69). Hillsdale, NJ: Erlbaum.

Anderson, J. A. (1988). Cognitive styles and multicultural populations. *Journal of Teacher Education, 29,* 2–9.

Anderson, T. Z., & White, G. D. (1986). An empirical investigation of interaction and relationship patterns in functional and dysfunctional nuclear families and step-families. *Family Process, 25,* 407–422.

Baca Zinn, M., & Eitzen, D. S. (1992). *Diversity in families* (2nd ed.). New York: HarperCollins.

Barbour, N. H (1990). Flexible grouping: It works! *Childhood Education, 67,* 66–67.

Baumrind, D. (1983). Rejoinder to Lewis's reinterpretation of parental firm control effects: Are authoritative families really harmonious? *Psychological Bulletin, 94,* 132–142.

Bell, D. C. (1994, November). *The origins of nurturance norms in the family.* Paper presented at the 24th annual NCFR Preconference Theory Construction and Research Methods Workshop, Minneapolis.

Berns, R. M. (1989). *Child, family, community.* New York: Holt, Rinehart and Winston.

Bobbitt, N., & Paolucci, B. (1986). Strengths of the home and family as learning environments. In R. J. Griffore & R. P. Boger (Eds.), *Child rearing in the home and school* (pp. 47–60). New York: Plenum.

Boss, P. (1988). *Family stress management.* Newbury Park, CA: Sage.

Bowers, C. A. (1984). *The promise of theory: Education and the policies of cultural change.* New York: Longman.

Bronfenbrenner, U. (1986). Ecology of family as a context for human development: Research perspectives. *Developmental Psychology, 22,* 723–742.

Bronfenbrenner, U. (1989). Ecological systems theory. In R. Vasta (Ed.), *Annals of child development* (Vol. 6, pp. 187–249). Greenwich, CT: JAI Press.

Center for the Study of Social Policy. (1992). *Kids count data book.* Washington, DC: Author.

Chapa, J., & Valencia, R. R. (1993). Latino population growth, demographic characteristics, and education segregation: An examination of recent trends. *Hispanic Journal of Behavioral Sciences, 15,* 165–187.

Coleman, J. S. (1988). Social capital in the creation of human capital. *American Journal of Sociology, 94* (Suppl.), 95–120.

Constantine, L. L. (1986). *Family paradigms.* New York: Guilford Press.

Correa, V. I. (1989). Involving culturally diverse families in the educational process. In S. H. Fradd & M. J. Weismantel (Eds.), *Meeting the needs of culturally and linguistically different students: A handbook for educators* (pp. 13–144). Boston: College Hill.

Correa, V. I. (1991). Family based applications. In C. V. Morsink, C. C. Thomas, & V. I. Correa (Eds.), *Interactive teaming. Consultation and collaboration in special programs* (pp. 247–276). New York: Merrill.

Cummins, J. (1989). A theoretical framework for bilingual special education. *Exceptional Children, 50,* 111–119.

Dawson, M. M. (1987). Beyond ability grouping: A review of the effectiveness of ability grouping and its alternatives. *School Psychology Review, 16,* 348–369.

Everett, F., Proctor, N., & Cartmell, B. (1983). Providing psychological services to the

American Indian children and families. *Professional Psychology: Research and Practice, 14,* 588–603.

Galvin, K. M., & Brommel, B. J. (1991). *Family communication: Cohesion and change.* New York: HarperCollins.

García, E. E. (1992). "Hispanic" children: Theoretic, empirical, and related policy issues. *Educational Psychology Review, 4,* 69–93.

Garcia-Preto, N. (1982). Puerto Rican families. In M. McGoldrick, J. K. Pearce, & J. Giordano (Eds.), *Ethnicity and family therapy* (pp. 164–186). New York: Guilford Press.

Gardner, H. (1983). *Frames of mind: Theory of multiple intelligences.* New York: Basic Books.

Gibson, M. A., & Ogbu, J. U. (1991). *Minority status and schooling: A comparative study of immigrant and involuntary minorities.* New York: Garland Press.

Glazer, N. (1975). *Affirmative discrimination.* New York: Basic Books.

Glickman, C. (1991). Pretending not to know what we know. *Educational Leadership, 48,* 4–8.

Hale-Benson, J. E. (1986). *Black children: Their roots, culture and learning styles.* Baltimore: John Hopkins University Press.

Haynes, C. C. (1992). Living with our deepest differences: Religious diversity in the classroom. In D. A. Byrnes & G. Kiger (Eds.), *Common bonds: Anti-bias teaching in a diverse society* (pp. 23–38). Wheaton, MD: Association for Childhood Education International.

Hernandez, D. J. (1993). *America's children: Resources from family, government, and the economy.* New York: Russell Sage Foundation.

Hilliard, A., & Vaughn-Scott, M. (1982). The quest for the minority child. In S. Moore & C. Cooper (Eds.), *The young child: Reviews of research* (Vol. 3., pp. 63–83). Washington, DC: National Association for the Education of Young Children.

Hoffman, L. W. (1988). Cross-cultural differences in childrearing goals. In R. A. Levine, P. M. Miller, & M. M. West (Eds.), *Parental behavior in diverse societies* (pp. 99–122). San Francisco: Jossey-Bass.

Imig, D. R. (1993). Family stress: Paradigms and perceptions. *Family Science Review, 6,* 45–55.

Jenson, G. O., & Warstadt, T. (1990). *Ranking critical issues facing American families.* Washington, DC: National Association for the Education of Young Children.

Kagan, S. L. (1991). *The care and education of America's young children: Obstacles and opportunities.* Chicago: University of Chicago Press.

Kantor, D., & Lehr, W. (1975). *Inside the family: Toward a theory of family process.* New York: Harper Colophon.

Katz, L. G., Evangelou, D., & Hartman, J. A. (1990). *The case for mixed-age grouping in early education.* Washington, DC: National Association for the Education of Young Children.

Kostelnik, M. J., Soderman, A. K., & Whiren, A. P. (1993). *Developmentally appropriate programs in early childhood education.* New York: Macmillan.

Kovalik, S. (1986). *Teachers make the difference.* Oak Creek, AZ: Susan Kovalick and Associates.

Laosa, L. M. (1984). Social policies toward children of diverse ethnic, racial, and language groups in the United States. In H. W. Stevenson & A. E. Siegel (Eds.), *Child development research and social policy* (Vol. 1, pp. 1–109). Chicago: University of Chicago Press.

Laosa, L. M. (1988). Ethnicity and single parenting in the United States. In E. M. Hetherington & J. D. Arasteh (Eds.), *Impact of divorce, single parenting, and stepparenting* (pp. 23–49). Hillsdale, NJ: Erlbaum.

Lerner, R. M. (1991). Changing organism–context relations as the basic process of development: A developmental contextual perspective. *Developmental Psychology, 27,* 27–32.

Lerner, R. M., Castellino, D., Terry, P. A., McKinney, M. H., & Villarruel, F. A. (in press). The ecology and parenting: A developmental contextual perspective. In M. H. Bornstein (Ed.), *Handbook of parenting: Vol 2: Ecology and Biology of Parenting: Part 1: Ecology of Parenting.* Hillsdale: Erlbaum.

Lewis, R. G. (1982). *Strengths of the American Indian family.* Tulsa, OK: National Indian Child Abuse and Neglect Resource Center.

Maccoby, E. E., & Martin, J. K. A. (1983). Socialization in the context of the family: Parent–child interaction. In P. H. Mussen (Ed.), *Handbook of child psychology: Vol. 4. Socialization, personality, and social behavior.* New York: Wiley.

McAdoo, H. P. (1992). A portrait of African American families in the United States. In S. E. Rix (Ed.), *The American women, 1990–91: A status report* (pp. 71–93). New York: Norton.

McKee, J. S. (1991). The developing kindergartner: Understanding children's nature and nurturing their development. In J. S. McKee (Ed.), *The developing kindergarten: Programs, children and teachers* (pp. 65–119). East Lansing: Michigan Association for the Education of Young Children.

McLoyd, V. C. (1991). What is the study of African American children the study of? In R. Jones (Ed.), *Black psychology* (3rd ed., pp. 419–440). Berkeley: Cobb & Henry.

Mindel, C. H., Habenstein, R. W., & Wright, R. (1988). *Ethnic families in America. Patterns and variations* (3rd. ed). New York: Elsevier Press.

Moore-Hinds, P., & Boyd-Franklin, N. (1982). Black families. In M. McGoldrick, J. K. Pearce, & J. Giordano (Eds.), *Ethnicity and family therapy* (pp. 84–107). New York: Guilford Press.

Perkins, D. F., Ferrari, T. M., Covey, M. A., & Keith, J. G. (1994). Getting dinosaurs to dance: Community collaborations as applications of ecological theory. *Home Economics Forum, 7,* 39–47.

Riche, M. F. (1991). We're all minorities now. *American Demographics, 14,* 26–34.

Soderman, A., & Phillips, M. (1986). Education of young males: Where are we failing them? *Educational Leadership, 44*(3), 70–72.

Sroufe, L. A., & Cooper, R. G. (1989). *Child development: Its value and course* (2nd ed.). New York: Knopf.

Stanford, B. H. (1992). Gender equity in the classroom. In D. A. Byrnes & G. Kiger (Eds.), *Common bonds: Anti-bias teaching in a diverse society* (pp. 87–104). Wheaton, MD: Association for Childhood Education International.

Super, C. M., & Harkness, S. (1981). Figure, ground, and gestalt: The cultural context of the active individual. In R. M. Lerner & N. A. Busch-Rossnagel (Eds.), *Individuals as producers of their own development: A life-span perspective* (pp. 69–86). New York: Academic Press.

Thomas, A., Chess, S., Sillen, J., & Mendez, O. (1974). Cross-cultural study of behavior in children with special vulnerabilities to stress. In D. F. Ricks, A. Thomas, & M. Roff (Eds.), *Life history research in psychopathology* (pp. 53–63). Minneapolis: University of Minnesota Press.

Trueba, H. T. (1989). *Raising silent voices: Educating the linguistic minorities for the 21st century.* New York: Newbury House.

Washington, V. (1988, January). Demographics: Part I. *Trends in Early Childhood Education,* pp. 4–7.

Wright, R., Salleby, D., Watts, T. D., & Lecca, P. J. (1983). *Transcultural perspectives in the human services.* Springfield, IL: Thomas.

York, S. (1991). *Roots and wings.* St. Paul, MN: Toys 'n Things Press.

Zill, N. (1989). *Child trends: Summary report of the Select Committee on Children, Youth and Families.* Washington, DC: U.S. House of Representatives.

CHAPTER 8

Family Support: Diversity, Disability, and Delivery

Karen Shu-Minutoli

In recent years, the cultural diversity movement and the family support movement have been receiving a great deal of attention, consideration, and support. Interestingly, the practicing field and the literature rarely address how these two concepts interface with each other. Therefore, the purpose of this chapter is to discuss the interaction between family support service delivery and culturally diverse families with severely developmentally disabled young children.

The characteristics that culturally diverse families share will be extensively presented. Then, the development and rationale for the family support movement will be described, as well as the range of available services. Based on all of the information presented, the actual delivery of services to culturally diverse families will be surmised. Finally, practical suggestions for working with ethnic families will be presented.

CHARACTERISTICS OF CULTURALLY DIVERSE FAMILIES

In order to develop intervention programs that are effective and meaningful, it is essential that early childhood professionals familiarize themselves with the rich range of ethnic diversity among families. There is a significant amount of literature on how various ethnic groups differ from the majority culture, as well as how much they vary from each other. The heterogeneity within a single ethnic group can be just as pronounced as the differences between various culturally diverse populations. Rather than focusing on the differences within or between groups, this chapter will accentuate some of the central tendencies that culturally diverse families have in common.

Professionals must be cognizant not to develop stereotypes or overgeneralizations based on this limited presentation. While there are some similarities between ethnic groups, no one set of characteristics can truly describe all minority families. In every family, there are individual and family idiosyncrasies. Families react to situations in various ways that may or may not be culturally related. It is essential to differentiate the situation from the culture.

The reaction to a child with a severe disability is very personal, and cultural attitudes may be just one factor that influences the family's response. Socioeconomic status, national origin, regional differences, religious preference, degree of assimilation and acculturation, language proficiency, educational level, occupation, immigration history and status, length of time in the country, and family mobility and stability are a complex part of families' cultural matrix.

Language and Communication Style

Miscommunication is a common phenomenon among individuals from the same cultural background. When people from different language and cultural backgrounds interact, the likelihood of misunderstandings increases substantially. For example, most minority cultures rely on high-context communication, while the majority culture focuses on low-context intercourse. Low-context communication centers on exactly what is said during the interaction. The communication is straightforward, specific, and logical. High-context cultures focus on the subtle implicit messages of the interaction; for example, body language, gestures, facial expressions, what wasn't said, timing of silences, vibes, moods, gut feelings, gestures, environmental clues, symbolism, cryptic sentences, indirect storytelling, and shared experiences (Hanson, Lynch, & Wayman, 1990; Willis, 1992). In this context, verbal behavior doesn't really convey genuine meaning. Professionals unaware of these differences can leave an encounter feeling frustrated, puzzled, confused, and dissatisfied.

Nonverbal communication is a key component in any discourse with culturally different families. However, nonverbal behavior means different things to various cultures. The significance of eye contact, facial expressions, proximity, touching, body language, and gestures varies considerably. For many traditional cultures, making direct eye contact is considered disrespectful. Asian cultures may hide embarrassment by smiling or laughing. Latinos may prefer close conversational distances. Muslim cultures are deeply offended if the left hand is used to touch a person. Sitting in a seat higher than that of one's elders is considered rude by Samoans. In several cultures, beckoning a person with the index finger is obscene since it applies only to animals (Anderson, 1989; Hanson et al., 1990; Willis, 1992). It is essential to be aware of these nonverbal nuances when interacting with ethnically diverse families.

Traditional families may defer to authority figures by not expressing critical comments, arguments, or contradiction; not interrupting for clarification; refraining from asking questions; failing to make their needs known; avoiding eye contact, and restraining their emotions. This is considered showing proper respect (Anderson, 1989; Joe & Malach, 1992; Shu, 1989). Professionals often misinterpret this deferential attitude as lack of understanding or interest. While confrontation in these cultures is considered insulting, in black American culture, family members are more apt to openly state their opinion (Turner, 1987).

In many languages there are no equivalent terms to describe various types of disabling conditions (Chan, 1992; Joe & Malach, 1992). For instance, in Latin and Asian languages, there is no word for "mental retardation." People from those cultures often mistake the term as referring to mental illness, which suggests to these cultures that someone is crazy. Disabilities are culturally normed. Every culture has different parameters for normal and abnormal development. Some cultures accept a wide range of diversity in behavior and development, while other cultures are more narrowly defined (Florian, 1987; Gartner, Lipsky, & Turnbull, 1991; Harry, 1992). Thus, when initially presenting a diagnosis to culturally diverse families, it is imperative that the professional (or an interpreter) properly translate and help parents understand that the meaning and use of special terminology may differ from their culture.

Privacy, Trust, and Respect

Culturally diverse families need to preserve their privacy, trust the people they are dealing with, and feel respected by professionals. These are key concepts in developing cooperative relationships with minority families.

Family life is private, and intimate family matters should not be discussed with strangers. Families believe they are responsible for taking care of their own; outsiders cannot and should not be trusted (Chan, 1992; Gillis-Olion, Olion, & Holmes, 1986; Omdahl, 1987; Shu, 1989). By seeking outside help, the family believes they are displaying an inability to manage their own affairs and advertising their problems to outsiders. Among cultures where disabilities have considerable stigma attached to them, this perception is particularly intense. For example, unknown to friends and neighbors, children with disabilities are hidden in the home.

In a seemingly hostile environment, the preservation of privacy and the careful allocation of trust help families to survive. Social workers, teachers, nurses, and other professionals often are perceived as government officials that cannot be truly trusted. These families have real fears, such as that a disabled child will be taken out of their home or that they will be deported (Shu, 1989; Turner, 1987). Many of these families may have experienced racism, discrimination, and cultural insensitivity when dealing with public agencies (Florian, 1987; Joe & Malach, 1992).

Parents may view personal questions asked by professionals to be too intrusive. They may give minimal yes or no responses, no response, or the response that they think the interventionist wants to hear. Without trust, they will not openly express their concerns nor will they follow well-informed advice or suggestions (Chan, 1992; Omdahl, 1987; Turner, 1987).

Mutual respect is a stepping stone to the building of trusting relationships. As noted in the previous section, traditional families may show their respect for professionals by means of deferential behaviors. By the same token, culturally diverse families expect to be accorded respect by professionals. Being addressed in an informal manner, kidding around, casual dress, or poor manners are considered improper (Anderson, 1989; Gillis-Olion et al., 1986). For some cultures, this lack of professionalism indicates that the interventionist feels that they are not deserving of the same regard accorded to individuals in the majority culture.

Natural Supports

In times of stress or crisis, most families seek help from natural supports rather than from professionals. Natural supports are the informal helping network that people rely on for enduring emotional support. This network typically includes relatives, friends, neighbors, and coworkers (Hanson et al., 1990; Omdahl, 1987).

Although all families rely on natural supports, the network for culturally diverse families tends to be more exclusive and cohesive. Individuals in the mainstream culture are more apt to share their innermost feelings and thoughts with anyone who will listen, such as a stranger on the bus, an acquaintance, or a coworker. Due to the preservation of privacy and the need for trust, ethnic people are more likely to express themselves only within their network, which usually comprises individuals who share the same language and cultural background. This often includes ethnic community leaders or indigenous healers.

Randall-David (cited in Hanson, 1992) illustrated that when seeking help for psychosocial disorders, white Americans turned to counselors, psychiatrists, psychologists, social workers, and ministers. On the other hand, culturally different groups relied on agents such as *curanderos, espiritistas, santerios,* herbalists, diviners, medicine men, singers, root workers, voodoo priests, ministers, friends, and family members.

For most culturally diverse people, the extended family is the primary source of natural support (Anderson, 1989; Chan, 1992; Florian, 1987; Joe & Malach, 1992; Omdahl, 1987; Taylor, Chatters, Tucker, & Lewis, 1990). It may or may not be composed of blood relatives; the important factor is that the family considers them kin. They are people that can always be trusted and relied on when needed. There is a deep sense of obligation, caring, and commitment to one another. The members of the extended family take care of each other;

responsibilities are not passed onto strangers. Several generations may share the same living quarters, and parenting responsibilities may be shared with a number of close members. Elderly people are highly valued and respected in this network. Members may seek their assistance, advice, and involvement in all family decisions.

Religious organizations are often considered an extension of the biological family. Turner (1987) elaborated that

> Parents feeling helpless and fearing the future with a disabled child are in need of a great deal of support and encouragement. The past and present day evidence suggests that Black churches have been extensively involved in providing support to its members. That assistance can be in the form of material support, emotional support, and, or spiritual support, as well as, providing information and advice. . . . The Black culture historically has lived with a high degree of stress, anxiety and challenges. Survival meant adapting. Consequently, the birth of a disabled or high-risk child happens into a cultural system that has been molded to accommodate crisis. (p. 12)

For many ethnic groups, religion offers healing and spiritual release from the hardships they face. It provides a collective group of concerned and caring members to supply consistent emotional and social support and release in times of crisis and joy (Anderson, 1989; Gillis-Olion et al., 1986; Joe & Malach, 1992; Taylor et al., 1990; Turner, 1987; Willis, 1992).

Childrearing Practices

Ethnically diverse families tend to be more indulgent and permissive with their children during the early years. In particular, they are very reluctant to discipline exceptional children. This often takes the form of overprotecting them and treating them as perpetual children. This philosophy of encouraging dependency may incline parents to groom, dress, and generally do things for the child rather than encourage self-sufficiency. It is viewed as part of their parental duty and responsibility (Anderson, 1989; Chan, 1992; Shu, 1989). Conflicts may arise when professionals insist that parents foster independence at an early age.

The additional demands of a child with a severe disability can be greatly reduced when the child's care is shared by various family members. Culturally diverse families often rely on their extended families for baby-sitting. Unless they trust the caretaker, they will be reluctant to use an "outsider" (Anderson, 1989; Turner, 1987). Often, the parents may not be the primary caregivers. Thus, decisions made between the interventionist and the parents may be inappropriate and may be undermined or ignored by the primary caregiver unless that person is included in the decision-making process.

Beliefs About Disabilities

Some culturally diverse families have moralistic, spiritualistic, or superstitious beliefs regarding the cause of disabling conditions (Anderson, 1989; Chan, 1992; Gartner et al., 1991; Joe & Malach, 1992; Shu, 1989; Willis, 1992; Zuniga, 1992). They may believe that moral wrongdoing committed by the afflicted child or the child's parents or ancestors resulted in the child's condition; for example, an extramarital affair, gambling, an immoral ancestor, or breaking a tribal rule. Evil spirits are perceived to be another cause of disabling conditions; for instance, harmful wishes or curses by others, possession, witchcraft, and the evil eye. There are also superstitions regarding specific behaviors on the part of mothers during their pregnancy that are believed to cause handicapping conditions; for example, looking at ugly animals, bowling, knitting, using scissors, and eating or not eating specific foods.

For many cultures, spiritualists or healers may dispel evil spirits or provide spiritual protection by means of prayer, meditation, chants, amulets, lucky charms, offerings to appease the spirits, rituals, exorcisms, dances, and traditional ceremonies. Cures also could include herbs, plants, foods, animals, massage, coining (i.e., abrading the skin), or even old-fashioned recipes such as cod liver oil, sassafras tea, and various concoctions (Chan, 1992; Hanson et al., 1990; Joe & Malach, 1992; Willis, 1992; Zuniga, 1992).

Survival Priorities

There is substantial literature on the fatalistic orientation of culturally diverse families (Chan, 1992; Hanson et al., 1990; Joe & Malach, 1992). These families often are cited as having an external locus of control. They feel powerless to change the destiny of their severely disabled child. Due to this passive attitude, these families may not see the merits of intervention for a child. Zuniga (1992) cautioned that "if an individual is poor, of lower status, and socialized to be powerless, she or he will be less prone to take the lead or to be assertive in interpersonal interactions—especially with regard to decision making" (p. 161). Thus, a fatalistic viewpoint is often related to economic constraints rather than culture.

Unfortunately, culturally diverse families often face multiple problems, such as meager housing, living in an unsafe neighborhood, unemployment, inadequate nutrition, and poor health. They may experience racial tension and discrimination daily. In addition, they may be single parents, or both parents may work several jobs to make ends meet. Furthermore, recent immigrants may be experiencing cultural shock (Joe & Malach, 1992; Omdahl, 1987). Options for these families will be limited. Priorities may focus on their single-minded quest for survival rather than the implementation of professional recommendations. Time is a precious commodity for these families. Professionals' expectations for family participation must be realistic, sensible, and sensitive to the families' survival needs and priorities.

FAMILY SUPPORT SERVICES MOVEMENT

The Education of the Handicapped Act Amendments of 1986 (Public Law 94–457, Part H—Infants and Toddlers) influenced the development of the family support services movement. This law mandates that early intervention practitioners develop an Individualized Family Services Plan (IFSP) for families of children with developmental disabilities from birth to age 3. The IFSP is to be developed for and, particularly, *with* the family. The plan must identify the family's strengths, needs, and intervention goals. Intervention strategies should focus on the strengths, resources, and positive coping strategies of the family and ways in which professionals can support and strengthen family functioning. The law stresses the partnership between families and professionals. This is a significant departure from deficiency-oriented and reactive past practices.

Public Law 94–457 has helped to provide the impetus for the development of alternative strategies for assisting families. Traditional service delivery has been accused of undermining, disempowering, and supplanting families. Until the recent family support movement, families were confronted with two options: place their children in out-of-home settings or take care of their children at home with little or no assistance. Family support services provides a third option: receive assistance in caring for their children at home (Traustadottir, 1988).

Caring for a young child with a severe disability at home is extremely stressful on the entire family unit. Peterson (1987) delineated some of the specific sources of stress: additional expenses and financial burdens; actual or perceived stigma; heightened demands on time; difficulties with basic caretaking tasks such as feeding, bathing, and dressing; decreased time for sleep; social isolation from friends, relatives, and neighbors; reduced time for leisure or personal activities; difficulties in managing the child's behavior; interference with routine domestic responsibilities; pessimism, depression, and anxiety; constant fatigue; marital discord; and sibling reactions or difficulties. Therefore, families with members with severe disabilities may need economic, physical, psychological, and social relief in order to maintain a child at home.

The philosophical underpinnings of the family support movement come from the basic concepts of normalization and community integration. People with disabilities have the right to have a normal life-style, the right to be a part of the community, and the right to belong and live in a family setting. The focus of family support services is to keep families together by supporting them as a unit and empowering them to care for their own members. Given the appropriate support services, families can meet the extraordinary needs of their children with disabilities (Traustadottir, 1988).

This movement is also economically motivated. Family support can prevent expensive out-of-home placements and perhaps encourage families to take their children back home from other placements. Providing support to the family costs substantially less than residential out-of-home placements. In many cases, there is a push to return children to their families with little or inadequate family support systems in place. In addition, families willing to care for their children at home are not receiving the necessary support to prevent out-of-home placements (Shu-Minutoli, 1992).

Family support programs are still in their infancy. Their provision is not mandated by federal regulation. Many states are just beginning to develop services, and the mechanics are still unclear. According to Agosta and Bradley (cited in Singer & Irvin, 1989), 27 states have created at least some form of family support services. Traustadottir (1988) noted that there is tremendous diversity in the quality and quantity of family support services between states and even within a particular state. The lack of uniform regulations has resulted in considerable variation in eligibility requirements, number of families served, amount of money spent, and type of services provided.

The different types of family support services include, but are not limited to, systemic assistance; case management; financial assistance; home environmental adaptations; in-home assistance; respite care and childcare; education and training; support groups, counseling, and therapy; and other types of assistance (Shu-Minutoli, 1992). No state provides all or even most of these services.

DELIVERING FAMILY SUPPORT SERVICES TO CULTURALLY DIVERSE FAMILIES

Family support will be discussed in terms of how service delivery interfaces or interferes with the traditions and attitudes of culturally diverse families with young severely disabled family members. Table 8.1 reflects the cultural issues that may arise when providing family support services to ethnically diverse families (Shu-Minutoli, 1992). It is evident that the characteristics of language and communication style, and privacy, trust, and respect will interact with every type of family support service.

It is crucial that professionals effectively communicate with culturally diverse families and be sensitive and responsive to their communication style. Obviously, communication breakdowns will occur if the interventionist does not

Table 8.1. Cultural issues in the delivery of family support services.

TYPES OF FAMILY SUPPORT SERVICES	POSSIBLE CULTURAL ISSUES

SYSTEMIC ASSISTANCE
   Information
   Referral
   Advocacy
	Language and communication style
	Privacy, trust, and respect
	Beliefs about disabilities

CASE MANAGEMENT	Language and communication style Privacy, trust, and respect

FINANCIAL ASSISTANCE
   Line of credit   Vouchers
   Reimbursement   Allowances
   Cash subsidy
	Language and communication style
	Privacy, trust, and respect
	Natural supports
	Survival priorities

HOME ENVIRONMENTAL ADAPTATIONS
   Adaptive equipment
   Home modification
	Language and communication style
	Privacy, trust, and respect
	Child-rearing practices
	Beliefs about disabilities
	Survival priorities

IN-HOME ASSISTANCE
   Home health care   Chores
   Attendant care   Homemaker
	Language and communication style
	Privacy, trust, and respect
	Natural supports

RESPITE AND CHILD CARE
   Respite
   Child care
   Sitter service
	Language and communication style
	Privacy, trust, and respect
	Natural supports
	Child-rearing practices

EDUCATION AND TRAINING
   Parent training
   Sibling training
	Language and communication style
	Privacy, trust, and respect
	Child-rearing practices
	Beliefs about disabilities
	Survival priorities

SUPPORT GROUPS, COUNSELING, AND THERAPY
   Family support groups
   Parent support groups
   Sibling support groups
   Family counseling/therapy
	Language and communication style
	Privacy, trust, and respect
	Natural supports
	Beliefs about disabilities
	Survival priorities

OTHER ASSISTANCE
   Rent assistance   Utilities
   Vehicle modification Home repairs
   Transportation   Health insurance
   Special diet and clothing
	Language and communication style
	Privacy, trust, and respect
	Survival priorities

speak the family's language and/or is unfamiliar and insensitive to cultural norms and taboos, or if no interpreter (or an inappropriate one) is available.

Even if the professional is from the same ethnic background and/or speaks the same language, this does not guarantee effective interaction. The family and the interventionist must build a relationship based on mutual respect and trust. Compared with traditional child-focused services, family support services are intrusive on the entire family system. Culturally diverse families that highly value privacy may be reluctant to participate in some of these services unless they feel comfortable with the provider.

Thus, in delivering any type of family support services, it is fundamental that the interventionist effectively communicate with the families and that the families feel that they can trust the professional. These factors are the building blocks for cooperative relationships with families. Then the provider can truly assess the type of services the families really desire and need in order to support their disabled family member at home. Since these two themes are central to all types of family support services, they will not be further elaborated. However, they should be kept in mind as each type of family support service is discussed.

Finally, family support services are designed to enable and empower families to make informed choices. Families are asked to determine what types of support they need. Interventionists are encouraged to respect the family's decisions even if they disagree. Since culturally diverse families are accustomed to deferring to professionals, initially it may be difficult to convince them to actively participate in the decision-making process.

Systemic Assistance

The social services system is very complex, and most families have difficulty comprehending the process. For linguistically and culturally different families, language and cultural barriers significantly limit their access to, use of, and understanding of services (Shu, 1989). According to Yee (1988), "parents' unfamiliarity with the English language and with services for exceptional children often leaves them feeling overwhelmed when deciding how best to provide for their child. They may also feel immobilized by cultural constraints" (p. 50).

Cultural beliefs about disabilities can impair service utilization. Hanson (1992) stated, "The views held by families about causation and disability will influence their need or willingness to seek help or intervention" (p. 10). For instance, among Asian families, children with disabilities are viewed as bringing considerable shame, embarrassment, and disgrace to the entire family. Thus, seeking professional help would mean an admission of the problem to outsiders (Shu, 1989). Only when the problem becomes very disturbing will they seek help. Therefore, unless culturally responsive outreach programs are available, "the system" may fail to locate these concealed children. Moreover, even if these children are identified, the families may refuse to admit that a problem exists, decline assistance and services, and continue to view and treat their children as "normal."

Case Management

Effective case management is considered to be the key to successful delivery of family support services. The case manager is the bridge between the families and the system. The case manager should be knowledgeable about what types of family support services are available, how to tailor individualized services to meet each family's strengths and needs, and how to obtain these services. It is critical that ethnically diverse families effectively communicate with the case manager and trust and respect that person; otherwise they will not agree to receive assistance. The case manager can mean the difference between the family accepting and rejecting desperately needed services.

Financial Assistance

The interventionist must sensitively address the issue of financial assistance. It is important to be careful not to offend or humiliate families whose cultural heritage imposes strict pride and honor. This type of help may be expected and received from the extended family. Nevertheless, families may need additional financial assistance as they struggle to achieve the American dream. The financial aid should not intrude on family life and values. The bureaucratic red tape and paperwork can be very overwhelming, particularly for families that do not speak English and/or have limited education. The case manager needs to patiently help them throughout the application process.

Home Environmental Adaptations

When properly explained to families, home modifications, such as wheelchair ramps, widening doorways, safety railings in the bathroom, adjusting table heights, and changing heating or ventilation systems, will be valued and appreciated. It may be more difficult to explain the merits of adaptive equipment and positioning devices, such as an adapted spoon, special toileting chair, hand splints, and prone standers.

Most people are extremely reluctant to make individuals with disabilities do things for themselves, especially when they appear uncomfortable and unhappy. Many parents, whether ethnically diverse or not, will continue to feed their children even though the children could feed themselves if given the proper adaptive equipment and assistance. The rationale is that it is much easier and faster to do the task for the child, especially when the child is fussy. Furthermore, it is extremely difficult to make a child remain in specialized equipment if the child is crying.

This universal parent perspective is intensified for culturally diverse families. In traditional cultures, independence is not fostered for family members without disabilities, let alone for a child with special needs. Guilt feelings about the cause of the disability may render families helpless in promoting a child's independence and doing what is uncomfortable yet necessary for the child in the long run.

In-Home Assistance

If natural supports are available, ethnically diverse families may tend to rely on them for ongoing childcare and help with household duties. The primary issue is whether ethnically diverse families will allow strangers to regularly intrude in their home. Again, gaining their trust is essential in providing this type of service. For medically frail children, families may be much more responsive to professional assistance in the home. It is questionable whether families will allow outsiders to assist them with household responsibilities and chores.

Respite Care and Childcare

Respite care and childcare services provide the family with temporary relief from caring for the child with the disability and/or siblings. This assistance can last as long as a couple of weeks or as little as a few hours. Service provision may occur in an out-of-home setting or in the home. This enables parents to conduct business, deal with an emergency, or pursue a leisure activity.

Culturally diverse families may be extremely reluctant to utilize these services. They may feel that they are shirking their responsibility. It is unthinkable to leave their children with "outsiders," particularly for extended periods of time. This can be overcome by finding someone that the family can trust and feel confident will take care of the child in a sanctioned manner. Families with a solid natural support network may not need this type of assistance. Some family support programs will pay extended family members, friends, and neighbors to care for the child. Gartner and coauthors (1991) warned that this may change the natural development of friendships into a social service.

Education and Training

Ethnically diverse families may be less involved in training programs for several reasons. First, it is difficult to actively participate in school activities when there are substantial language and cultural barriers. Second, both immigrant parents usually work and put in extremely long hours. Thus, they have little time to spare for training. Third, parents expect and depend on professionals to train their child. They do not understand why they need to be involved (Shu, 1989). Even when families participate in training, there may be no follow-through. The intervention method may conflict with time-honored childrearing beliefs and attitudes. In addition, the person receiving training may not be the primary caregiver; for instance, the parent may receive the training but the aunt may be the primary caregiver.

Support Groups, Counseling, and Therapy

Culturally different families are less likely to use mainstream culture support groups, counseling, and therapy. This is due to language barriers; cultural differences; time constraints; cultural norms regarding the open expression of feelings, particularly to strangers; beliefs about disabilities that impede disclosure of the problem; and reliance on natural support groups. These type of services may be considered too intrusive by families that highly value their privacy. On the other hand, they may be willing to utilize support groups, counselors, and therapists that share the same linguistic and cultural background and values.

Other Assistance

Other types of assistance such as rent assistance, vehicle modification, transportation, special diet and clothing, utilities, home repairs, and health insurance can be very useful. For ethnically diverse families, it is easier to understand and utilize services that are practical and have tangible results. Accessing help in these areas may significantly improve their quality of life. For instance, the provision of transportation would be extremely helpful for families that do not have a car. Using public transportation to go to the doctor, hospital, and therapy sessions is extremely burdensome, unreliable, and exhausting.

SUGGESTIONS FOR WORKING WITH CULTURALLY DIVERSE FAMILIES

Early childhood interventionists need to respond to families proactively. The following are some practical guidelines for working effectively with culturally diverse families.

1. Be aware of your own cultural values, assumptions, and biases.
2. Find out more about ethnically diverse cultures in order to better understand, support, and appreciate their differences.
3. Do not make assumptions, generalizations, or stereotypes about specific ethnic groups; for example, all Native American families consult tribal healers.

4. Incorporate the cultural practices of the family into the intervention. Do not try to change the family life-style to fit the method. Adapt the technique to the family's learning style, life-style, and relevant beliefs and values.

5. Avoid being judgmental. Respect and accept the family's folk beliefs and cures. Do not openly challenge, scoff, or ridicule their traditional attitudes. Try to work through or around these convictions. Allow the family to practice indigenous cures if they are not harmful to the child or contraindicated with critical therapeutic methods. If the family's cures do interfere, sensitively explain it to the family.

6. Remember that each family has its own unique characteristics. Find out what makes them special. Always look for the family's strengths.

7. Effectively communicate with the family. Write and speak to the family in clear, jargon-free language. Be certain that your manner conveys respect and is not condescending. Be cognizant of cultural norms for verbal and nonverbal communication. Utilize qualified translators and interpreters.

8. Convey regard, warmth, and concern for the child and the family's welfare. In verbal and written communications, focus on the child's strengths. Your genuine sincerity will overcome many language and cultural barriers.

9. Show the family that you respect them. Use formal forms of address, properly pronounce their names, engage in proper protocol, dress and act professionally, be courteous, convey interest, listen to their ideas, acknowledge their concerns and feelings, respect their insight and experience, encourage their contributions, and respect and honor their decisions.

10. Allow enough time to develop a good rapport with the family. Slow down your communication style; relax and discuss pleasantries. Accept small tokens of hospitality such as a beverage or snack. Ethnically diverse families do not feel that every moment must be verbally charged. They highly value silence and forethought before speaking. Remember to give the family time to think and respond to what has been presented. Respect their need for privacy. When they trust you, they will share their personal problems and concerns.

11. Capitalize on each family's natural support network by involving extended family members and significant others. Give parents the option to include them in the intervention process. View these kinship and friendship bonds as invaluable resources and enlist their assistance in helping to support the family. Be aware of family organization and roles. Who really is the primary caretaker or caretakers? Who actually makes the ultimate decisions in the family?

12. Become knowledgeable about resources in the ethnic community. Enlist the help of community leaders or organizations (e.g., religious organizations, volunteer groups, cultural societies, social clubs, youth centers) to intercede or interface with the family. Recruit and train ethnically diverse

community members, peer parents, or college students to assist in the provision of family support services.

13. Culturally diverse families highly value interpersonal relationships and social events. Plan social functions such as potluck dinners or picnics, and celebrate various ethnic heritage events. Preparing ethnic food is particularly important because food is an integral part of the culture. Families are very proud to share their customs and traditions with the mainstream culture. This is an excellent way to develop a positive relationship with families.

In conclusion, it is imperative that professionals be aware of the possible cultural issues that may have an impact on the delivery of family support services to culturally diverse families with disabled children. Although the spirit of the services is to assist families, for many ethnically diverse families, it translates to more outsiders attempting to intrude on their privacy. Gross (cited in Gartner et al., 1991) warned, "What one culture considers help, the other culture considers an imposition—or just plain bizarre" (p. 49). Professionals need to be cognizant that when they enthusiastically forge a partnership with culturally diverse families, they may not always be greeted with open arms. Like other families with problems, culturally diverse families do need support and assistance. The important point is that early childhood interventionists need to be prepared to deliver these services in a nontraditional manner and in a fashion that is most comfortable for the families.

REFERENCES

Anderson, P. P. (1989). Issues in serving culturally diverse families of young children with disabilities. *Early Child Development and Care, 50,* 167–188.

Chan, S. (1992). Families with Asian roots. In E. W. Lynch & M. J. Hanson (Eds.), *Developing cross-cultural competence: A guide for working with young children and their families* (pp. 181–256). Baltimore, MD: Paul H. Brookes.

Florian, V. (1987). Cultural and ethnic aspects of family support services for parents of a child with a disability. In D. K. Lipsky (Ed.), *Family supports for families with a disabled member* (pp. 37–51). New York: International Exchange of Experts and Information in Rehabilitation, World Rehabilitation Fund, Inc.

Gartner, A., Lipsky, D. K., & Turnbull, A. P. (1991). *Supporting families with a child with a disability: An international outlook.* Baltimore, MD: Paul H. Brookes.

Gillis-Olion, M., Olion, L., & Holmes, R. L. (1986). Strategies for interacting with black parents of handicapped children. *Negro Educational Review, 37*(1), 8–16.

Hanson, M. J. (1992). Ethnic, cultural, and language diversity in intervention settings. In E. W. Lynch & M. J. Hanson (Eds.), *Developing cross-cultural competence: A guide for working with young children and their families* (pp. 3–18). Baltimore, MD: Paul H. Brookes.

Hanson, M. J., Lynch, E. W., & Wayman, K. I. (1990). Honoring the cultural diversity of families when gathering data. *Topics in Early Childhood Special Education,* *10*(1), 112–131.

Harry, B. (1992). Making sense of disability: Low-income, Puerto Rican parents' theories of the problem. *Exceptional Children, 59*(1), 27–40.

Joe, J. R., & Malach, R. S. (1992). Families with Native American roots. In E. W. Lynch & M. J. Hanson (Eds.), *Developing cross-cultural competence: A guide for working with young children and their families* (pp. 89–119). Baltimore, MD: Paul H. Brookes.

Omdahl, D. (1987, May). *Treatment strategies for Hispanic developmentally disabled clients.* Paper presented at the annual conference of the Children's Center, Detroit.

Peterson, N. L. (1987). *Early intervention for handicapped and at-risk children: An introduction to early childhood-special education.* Denver: Love.

Shu, K. E. (1989). *Professional perceptions of the differences in parental attitudes and behaviors and the behavioral manifestations of autism in Chinese and Caucasian children.* Unpublished doctoral dissertation, Teachers College, New York.

Shu-Minutoli, K. E. (1992, April). *Providing family support services to ethnically diverse families: Needs, challenges, & future directions.* Paper presented at the conference of the National Institute of Child Health & Human Development, Washington, DC.

Singer, G. H. S., & Irvin, L. K. (1989). Family caregiving, stress, and support. In G. H. S. Singer & L. K. Irvin (Eds.), *Support for caregiving families: Enabling positive adaptation to disability* (pp. 1–25). Baltimore, MD: Paul H. Brookes.

Taylor, R. J., Chatters, L. M., Tucker, M. B., & Lewis, E. (1990). Developments in research on black families: A decade review. *Journal of Marriage and the Family, 52,* 993–1014.

Traustadottir, R. (1988, August). *Family supports in the USA: Current trends in policy and practice.* Paper presented at the First International Conference on Family Support Related to Disability, Stockholm.

Turner, A. (1987, February). *Multicultural considerations: Working with families of developmentally disabled and high-risk children: The black perspective.* Paper presented at the conference of the National Center for Clinical Infant Programs, Los Angeles.

Willis, W. (1992). Families with African American roots. In E. W. Lynch & M. J. Hanson (Eds.), *Developing cross-cultural competence: A guide for working with young children and their families* (pp. 121–150). Baltimore, MD: Paul H. Brookes.

Yee, L. Y. (1988). Asian children. *Teaching Exceptional Children, 20*(4), 49–50.

Zuniga, M. E. (1992). Families with Latino roots. In E. W. Lynch & M. J. Hanson (Eds.), *Developing cross-cultural competence: A guide for working with young children and their families* (pp. 151–179). Baltimore, MD: Paul H. Brookes.

CHAPTER 9

Role of Parents in Responding to Issues of Linguistic and Cultural Diversity

Patricia A. Edwards, Kathleen L. Fear, and Margaret A. Gallego

Education is far too important to be left solely to professional educators. It is imperative that educators provide the framework for parental participation in the educational process so that more parents can avail themselves of this opportunity. . . . To promote positive parental involvement in education, educators must remove existing barriers.

(Lynch, 1992, p. 304)

While the authors of this chapter strongly agree with Lynch's statement, we feel that African American and Hispanic parents have had to fight to remove existing barriers in order to be heard by professional educators. Perhaps the reason African American and Hispanic parents have to fight to be heard may be found in the historical argument proposed by Ogbu (1992). Ogbu characterizes African Americans and Hispanics as involuntary minorities "who were originally brought into the United States or any other society against their will . . . [and] were often relegated to menial positions and denied true assimilation into the mainstream society" (p. 8). Ogbu notes that African American and Hispanic children "whose cultural frames of reference are oppositional to the cultural frame of reference of American mainstream culture have greater difficulty crossing cultural boundaries at school [in order] to learn" (p. 5).

We are fully aware that other groups of parents may have had struggles crossing cultural boundaries at school. However, these other groups, characterized as "immigrant or voluntary minorities," have different problems. According to Ogbu (1992):

Immigrant or voluntary minorities are people who have moved more or less voluntarily to the United States—or any other society—because they desire more economic well-being, better overall opportunities, and/or greater political freedom. Their expectations continue to influence the way they perceive and respond to events, including schooling, in the host society. Voluntary minorities usually experience initial problems in school due to cultural and language differences as well as lack of understanding of how the education system works. But they do not experience lingering, disproportionate school failure. The Chinese and Punjabi Indians are representative U.S. examples. (p. 8)

Over the years, African American and Hispanic parents have voiced their concerns, opinions, and fears about their children's educational development to professional educators. Unfortunately, their voices were not valued and often went unheard. According to Edwards (1990), African American and Hispanic parents have informed professional educators that "they want the educational system to reflect their values and way of life, and they feel they ought to influence and exercise control over their children's education" (p. 223). Despite the fact that African American and Hispanic parents made such appeals to professional educators, accomplishing this most important goal has not been an easy task. This chapter focuses on legal struggles that African American and Hispanic parents faced and redefinitions of the roles they play in the educational support of their children.

LEGAL STRUGGLES FOR EDUCATIONAL RIGHTS

Subordinate groups have fought legal battles to gain language rights and access to full participation in the dominant society. Hernandez-Chavez (1988) described an interesting notion about language policy and language rights when he said, "The concept of language rights, in its most general sense, refers to the right of a people to learn, to keep and to use its own language in all manner of public and private business. This is a human right. But it is not always a civil right" (p. 45).

African American and Hispanic parents, in particular, have fought hard to force school districts to provide their children with this civil right. In the 1978 case that has come to be known as the "black English case," *Martin Luther King Junior Elementary School Children* v. *Ann Arbor School District Board,* the parents of 11 black children charged school officials with denying their children equal educational opportunities by failing to help teachers overcome a language barrier. Cobb-Scott (1985a) reported, "the court found it appropriate to: require the defendant Board to take steps to help its teachers to recognize the home language of the students and to use that knowledge in their attempts to teach reading skills in standard English" (p. 63).

African American parents were aware that black English is a systematic rule-governed language. Although the black English controversy "was perceived as nonsense by some, as unimportant by others, as too obvious to be taken seriously by still others" (Cobb-Scott, 1985b, p. 9), African American parents realized the impact of black English on their children's access to school-based literacy instruction. These parents and the presiding judge, Charles W. Joiner, recognized that teacher attitudes toward black English were negative for the most part. Judge Joiner said:

> It is a straightforward effort to require the court to intervene on the children's behalf to require the defendant School District Board to take appropriate action to teach them to read in the standard English of the school, the commercial world, the arts, science and professions. This action is a cry for judicial help in opening the doors to the establishment. . . . It is an action to keep another generation from becoming functionally illiterate. (473 F. Supp. 1371, E. D. Mich. 1979)

In the Court Memorandum of *King,* Judge Joiner also referred specifically to nonacceptance attitudes.

> The research evidence supports the theory that the learning of reading can be hurt by teachers who reject students because of the "mistakes" or "errors" made in oral speech by black English speaking children who are learning standard English. This comes about because "black English" is commonly thought of as an inferior method of speech and those who use this system may be thought of as "dumb" or "inferior." (p. 18)

The evidence from the *King* case clearly reveals that African American children were denied access to school-based literacy. Consequently, the parents of these children had to force the school district to teach their children to read in standard English.

Similarly, Hispanic children were denied access to school-based literacy because they came to school speaking Spanish. The instruction they received in school was in English. Hispanic parents' legal struggles focused on helping their children receive language literacy instruction in their native language. Specifically, these parents put forth the argument that their children need to know English to succeed in school and to be competitive in the job market. Their point was that learning English is best accomplished by a strong foundation in a native language. In 1968, Congress recognized the special needs of these children when it passed the Bilingual Education Act. This mandates that initial school instruction should be provided in a learner's first language until a level of English proficiency is reached that will allow for success in classrooms where only English is used.

Unfortunately, the passing of the Bilingual Education Act did not automatically guarantee that language-minority students would receive appropriate language instruction. A series of lawsuits were filed before language-minority students received the assistance they rightfully deserved under the law. The major court decision on the rights of language-minority students, and the only such ruling by the U. S. Supreme Court, is *Lau* v. *Nichols*. The case originated in 1970, when a San Francisco poverty lawyer, Edward Steinman, learned that a client's child was failing in school because he could not understand the language of instruction. Steinman filed a class action suit on behalf of Kinney Lau and 1,789 other Chinese students in the same predicament. These children, he alleged, were being denied "education on equal terms" because of their limited English skills.

The 1974 decision of *Lau* v. *Nichols* required local school districts to develop approaches that would ensure that learners with limited English proficiency were not denied a meaningful education. The court argued that simply providing these learners with the same curriculum and texts as native speakers of English would not suffice. According to García (1990):

> After *Lau*, the domain of language-minority education lawsuits belonged almost exclusively to Hispanic litigants. Although some cases were litigated to ensure compliance with *Lau* requirements of some special assistance, most subsequent cases were about the issues left unanswered in *Lau:* Who are these students? and What form of additional educational services must be provided. (p. 57)

The lawsuits filed on behalf of Hispanic litigants included *Aspira of New York, Inc.* v. *Board of Education* (1975), *Otero* v. *Mesa County School District No. 51* (1977), *Guadalupe Organization, Inc.* v. *Tempe School District No. 3* (1978), *Castaneda* v. *Pickard* (1981), *U.S.* v. *Texas* (1981), and *Keyes* v. *School District No. 1, Denver* (1983). For a detailed summary of these cases see García (1990).

Hispanic parents played an active role in the case of *Los Padres para Mejorar Educacion Bilingue* (Parents for the Improvement of Bilingual Education) v. *Calistoga Joint Unified School District* (1979). Hispanic parents in one small school district in Northern California challenged the power of local policy makers to misinterpret, circumvent, and blatantly disregard both the letter and the intent of the law. These parents were well informed regarding legislative regulations. Curtis (1988) correctly points out that

> The role of parent involvement in educational programme planning and implementation carries with it a tremendous responsibility to become and to remain well-informed regarding the legislative regulations which bind the school district, the attitudes and positions of local policy makers, and the political activities of opposing community groups. With this information, a par-

ent advisory committee is in a good position to have impact on the planning and development of school programmes in their district. Without this information, no parent group can hope to have any meaningful influence on the instructional programmes in which their children are enrolled. (p. 278)

Los Padres para Mejorar Educacion Bilingue gathered evidence in support of their claim that the district was engaged in discriminatory educational practices. Beyond the obvious failure to provide bilingual instruction in accordance with state law, evidence against the district included a history of discriminatory hiring practices. Out of 17 teachers at the elementary school, 14 had been hired within a 2-year period. Of these 14, not one had any proficiency in the Spanish language or any training in bilingual-bicultural education at the time of hire. Other data compiled addressed the issue of academic failure at the secondary level among the Mexican American students. In November 1978, 82% of the Hispanic students received "cinch notices" warning parents of the likelihood that their child would fail one or more classes unless performance improved by the end of the term. By comparison, 50% of the non-Hispanic students received these notices.

On March 30, 1979, Los Padres para Mejorar Educacion Bilingue filed a formal complaint with the Office for Civil Rights (OCR) of the U. S. Department of Health, Education and Welfare, charging the Calistoga Joint Unified School District with discriminatory practices in violation of their children's rights to equal educational opportunity under the law. The OCR ruled in favor of Los Padres and ordered the school district to employ more teachers who had proficiency in the Spanish language. Further, the OCR ordered the school district to develop a training program for teachers in bilingual-bicultural education.

NEW STRUGGLES AFTER THE LEGAL BATTLES

The legal struggles of African American and Hispanic parents forced schools to be aware of excluding the language and culture of their children. However, when school districts finally decided that it was important to involve parents in issues of linguistic and cultural diversity, the school districts elected to use what Seeley (1989) calls "the delegation model." The model is one-directional because the school is the source of knowledge about the child and the curriculum. Seeley argues that "reliance on the delegation model in public education has created a fundamental gap between families and schools" (p. 46). This fundamental gap grew out of practices within schools that emphasized rational and technical research models that placed highest priority on quantified data, scientific theories, and transmission models of instruction. This paradigm set up a hierarchical structure, with researchers' definitions of theory and inquiry at the top, translators of theory in the middle, and practitioners at the bottom (Wood, 1992). Parents often were excluded from the hierarchy, silenced from discussions of their children's literacy development, and distanced from active involvement in school policy.

Perhaps school districts' unwillingness to relinquish control might be attributed to the fact that they felt that African American and Hispanic parents were not capable of serving as equal participants in the educational process and had to be told what to do. There are several examples of experiences that support this contention. Raim (1980) developed a reading club for low-income Hispanic parents. The purpose of the reading club was to show parents how to construct instructional devices appropriate for their children and to rehearse with these devices before using them with their children. Later, under the supervision of the reading teacher, the parents used the materials they had made with their children. In a small midwest community Grimmett and McCoy (1980) increased low-income families' participation in school by communicating with them about children's reading progress. Specifically, they explained to parents: (1) goals of the reading program; (2) terminology and definitions specific to reading (e.g., accountability and flexible grouping); (3) explanations of the diagnostic-prescriptive cycle; (4) instructional procedures; and (5) student profile components. The results suggested that parental involvement can influence children's reading when parents receive information about the reading program. It was noted that parents need ongoing communication with their children's reading teachers in order to increase the quality and quantity of their involvement in the reading program. Thomas (1985) described a plan to reduce the racial isolation of a Massachusetts school in a predominately Hispanic neighborhood. Specifically, the school involved different ethnic group parents as advisors and joint decision makers before and after their children arrived at school. To encourage more active participation of language-minority parents, the Oakland (California) Unified School District initiated a parent leadership institute called OPTIMUM (Gonzalez, 1986). This project helps parents establish cooperative school relationships, understand school organizations, upgrade their own education while helping their children, and capitalize on their linguistic and cultural resources. Wenn (1981) coordinates Tulane Follow Through, which serves an economically depressed, migrant, bilingual population. Its goals are, among others, to provide parents an opportunity to obtain skills and information related to parenting and to encourage parents, many with little previous decision-making experience, to assume roles as leaders and advocates.

The experiences parents encountered were similar to the literacy experiences their children encountered in the classroom. Complex tasks were analyzed and broken into component skills incrementally transmitted to students in a logical order determined by the teacher. Success based on mastery of language convention focused on the products' correct mechanical form. Such criteria excluded student life experiences, cultural values, and language diversity. Parents may have been informed of the literacy curriculum content, but continued to assume a passive role in curriculum development and in their children's literacy development.

NEW PERSPECTIVES: NEW PARENT ROLES

Over time, school districts finally recognized that African American and Hispanic parents' knowledge was valuable and that parents could play a critical role in mediating the curriculum. As a result, these parents started to enter the discussions by providing information about language, culture, and context. The purpose of these discussions was to inform teachers about how to better communicate and enhance the educational growth of African American and Hispanic children.

The work of Auerbach (1989) clearly shows that parent knowledge is valuable when constructing family literacy programs. For example, Auerbach and her colleagues at the UMass/Boston English Literacy Project reported that they did not go into their students' homes or communities to examine literacy uses and practices or to collect data, but they listened, read, and talked to students about literacy in their lives. From these interactions with their students, they were able to conclude that their students' homes did not lack literacy and that parents had local knowledge of their home situations.

Piper (1992) states that there may once have been a time when parents believed that the school was the proper place for children to learn to read and to learn the "basics" to prepare them for higher education or for the working world, without assistance from the home. If such a time existed, that time has become a passing memory. Parents are seeking more active roles and want to assume more responsibility for their children's education. However, the unidirectional approach of parent involvement in which teachers "instruct" parents on how to *prepare children for school*, with little attention to the *preparation of schools for children*, has proven to be of limited success.

New roles for parents, especially African American and Hispanic parents, have grown out of changes in research perspectives that identify local knowledge as legitimate. A movement away from an emphasis on decontextualized knowledge and transmission models as important sources of information for reforms grew out of critiques of traditional research models. Educational research that was "informed by a superficial comprehension of the contexts in which educational problems or phenomena arise" (Sarason, 1982, p. 129) was described as "wreaking havoc" on attempts to apply general research findings to specific sites (Huberman, 1987). In many instances conclusions were applied, knowledge delivered, and operations performed without looking beyond the surface conditions within specific schools. Consequently, criticisms were voiced because scientific research did not have a direct bearing on improving practices when compelling local issues were not taken into consideration (Goldenberg & Gallimore, 1991).

Educational researchers began to examine local needs and social constructivist assumptions about research and literacy. Bruffee (1986) explains these assumptions by describing writing as primarily a social act that originates in language communities. Social theories of language focus on exploring how students' social backgrounds affect their language in writing classrooms. Students from diverse backgrounds learn to differentiate expectations of different language communities. In social constructivist models parents and teachers play new roles. Parent knowledge is an important source of information for teachers when parents' conversations focus on students' intentions, purposes, and significant audiences. With teachers and students, parents generate an understanding of the purposes and uses of language within different communities. They grapple with the politics of language by examining the uses of different conventions and language patterns. When a fundamental change in perspective takes place, parents ask questions of teachers and cogenerate the literacy curriculum.

Shelton, as cited in Edwards (1990), describes a Family Involvement Communications System that increased communication between teachers and economically deprived parents. The program was based on the assumption that low-income parents could be trained to teach middle-class teachers to communicate effectively with parents and children living in low-income neighborhoods. Consequently, parents were informed about the school knowledge that students needed to be successful in the existing curriculum. In many cases, parents were involved as supporters, advisors, tutors, and workshop attendees. Information was exchanged so that parents played more active roles as they learned about constructing interpretations of children's literature as a means of helping their children to read and respond to texts.

The information provided by parents helped the school to transmit information to other parents and their children. Parents contributed knowledge about effective communication, approved final actions, participated in the classroom, or provided information about cultural differences that could present obstacles to assessment and achievement. Some models involved parents in discussions about school curriculum, and some focused on "home curriculum" (High, 1981), that is, information about drugs, single parenting, emerging adolescence, and parenting skills. Although the school retained primary responsibility for defining what constituted curriculum content, they did begin to recognize that parents and their local knowledge were valuable and could play a critical role in mediating the curriculum.

Analogous pedagogical changes that surfaced in classrooms prompted the abandonment of transmission models and the adoption of interactive and socioconstructivist approaches to teacher–student learning relationships. Teachers and scholars describe a movement toward an interest in the social and contextual functions of writing (Fox, 1990). Change in perspectives is apparent in literacy classrooms that have identified an emphasis on reading and writing process rather than on content and skill acquisition (Reyes, 1991). When the focus of instruction in the classroom is on meaning and the process of acquiring meaning, parents can expand their roles by contributing knowledge about the social functions of writing.

Social theories of language focus on exploring how students' social backgrounds affect language use in writing classrooms. All students learn to differentiate expectations of different language communities. When a fundamental change in perspective takes place, parents and teachers play new roles indicative of active stakeholders in school governance, curriculum development, and language policy. Within this perspective, parents provide teachers with information regarding their children's intentions, purposes, and significant audiences.

EXPANDING THE DEFINITION OF PARENT INVOLVEMENT: LEARNING FROM LINGUISTICALLY AND CULTURALLY DIVERSE PARENTS

Although parents and other family members are important to the success of children, most parents do not go to school unless called, do not attend meetings or volunteer in school activities, and generally are not members of parent organizations. For mainstream parents, obstacles such as work schedules, childcare needs, and other necessities keep them from being involved in their children's education. Negative school experiences and impersonal and unreceptive school bureaucracies have alienated linguistically and culturally diverse parents. Hispanic parents not only have had to deal with these constraints but have had to face language barriers.

Even though schools might not always recognize their involvement, these parents are indeed involved. The ways in which linguistically and culturally diverse families support and sustain children in their academic success are complex and sometimes not what one might expect or what is defined *by schools*. In fact, family cultural values often determine what students mean by success. When students talk about how their parents support them, involvement in school activities is rarely mentioned. What is mentioned is their parents' role in motivating them to stay in school, being communicative with them, providing an environment of high expectations and loving support, and making sacrifices to help their children (Nieto, 1992).

Although parents may lack formal education and have limited experience with the means for achieving academic success, they compensate by providing other critical support. Nieto (1992) outlines three factors that parents from linguistically and culturally diverse backgrounds use to support their children's academic success—maintenance of native language, maintenance of culture, and high expectations. Family members maintain language use in the home, in spite of conflicting messages received from school and society. Many schools, for example, send newsletters to the home encouraging parents to speak English rather than their native language. However, such advice from well-intended school personnel can have potentially disastrous results. In many cases, parents will use broken English or a mixture of their native language and English and spend less time interacting with their children because they are uncomfortable in using English (Cummins & Swain, 1986; Perez & Torres-Guzman, 1992). Resisting the advice of the school, some parents have *insisted* on native language use in the home as an important means of maintaining their culture and emotional attachment to their children through family values.

Maintenance of native language implies maintenance of culture. Hispanic families send the message that their culture is worthy of respect, as do families that are monolingual speakers of English. Culture is maintained not only through family rituals, traditions, and artifacts, but by underlying cultural values. One of the most consistent and least expected outcomes has been the resoluteness with which young people maintain pride and satisfaction in their culture and the strength they derive from it. A positive sense of cultural identification challenges the messages and models of an essentially assimilationist society, and it creates its own internal conflicts. Choosing between family and school may inevitably become a choice between belonging and succeeding. The costs of going through such an experience are high indeed, from becoming a "cultural schizophrenic" to developing doubts about one's self-worth and dignity (Nieto, 1992).

Another way in which linguistically and culturally diverse parents have demonstrated their support for academic success is through high expectations. Education is highly valued and sought after by parents, especially African American and Hispanic parents. In fact, in some instances working-class and poor parents place much hope in education (see Epstein, 1986). The ways in which culturally diverse families manifest high expectations, however, are sometimes indirect.

We contend that parent involvement, in whatever form it takes, affects student achievement. In an institution often far removed from its community, the entry of parents into the school means that their language and culture and the expectations they have for their children become a part of the dialogue and tension between school and home.

SUMMARY AND CONCLUSION

Traditionally the school's role has been to serve as an assimilating agent, often referred to as the great equalizer. The notion that equal education provides the same resources and opportunities for all students completely misses the point that education is a two-way process. Educational equity must involve the interaction of students with teachers and schools, not simply the action of teachers and schools on students.

Standard curriculum and pedagogy have kept the rich experiences of millions of linguistically and culturally diverse students absent and quiet. This absence of students' lives in the curriculum is a result of the silencing of cultural resources, as illustrated by the litigation described earlier in this chapter. Thus far, efforts at aligning home and school experiences have emphasized change in the *child* and the *parent* rather than change in the *school*.

What is needed are predictable structures that involve parents in their children's literacy growth. New structures also must develop more challenging and active roles for parents. Social constructivist models include parents as curriculum cogenerators who contribute knowledge about traditional and nontraditional uses of language. Within these new structures parents can be instrumental in rather than obstacles to effective policy outcomes. Parents enter the debate about what is and should be the nature of education and schools when discussions focus on "what" curriculum is important and "why" this curriculum is important. When this happens, parents become active participants in cogenerating curriculum rather than passive recipients of curriculum. As cited in Fox (1990), Pink and Nobilt describe what results from excluding parents: "Rather than rethinking the process and implementation of educational policy, policy makers resort to increased efforts at control, recreating the image of students, educators, and citizens as recalcitrants and resistents" (p. ix).

It has taken some time, but schools have come to accept Harrington's (1971) contention that "schools cannot and would not exist without parents. Parents supply the school with primary material—their children—around which the formal educational and organizational program for that school is constructed" (p. 49). African American and Hispanic parents' voices are finally being heard by school districts that recognize that those voices need to be heard. Not only have schools begun to hear African American and Hispanic parents' voices, but they have come to realize that these and all parents are important and reliable linguistic and cultural resources.

REFERENCES

Aspira of New York, Inc. v. *Board of Education*, 394 F. Supp. 1161 (S.D., N.Y. 1975).

Auerbach, E. R. (1989). Toward a socio-contextual approach to family literacy. *Harvard Educational Review*, 59, 165–181.

Bilingual Education Act. (1968). *United States Statutes at Large*, 81, 817.

Bruffee, K. (1986). Social construction, language, and the authority of knowledge. *College English*, 48, 773–790.

Castaneda v. *Pickard*, 648 F. Ed. 989, 1007 (1981).

Cobb-Scott, J. (1985a). The King case: Implications for educators. In C. K. Brooks (Ed.), *Tapping potential: English and language arts for the black learner* (pp. 63–71). Urbana, IL: National Council of Teachers of English.

Cobb-Scott, J. (1985b). Introduction: language and the teaching-learning process. In C. K. Brooks (Ed.), *Tapping potential: English and language arts for the black learner* (pp. 9–11). Urbana, IL: National Council of Teachers of English.

Cummins, J., & Swain, M. (1986). *Bilingualism in education*. White Plains, NY: Longman.

Curtis, J. (1988). Parents, schools and racism. In T. Skutnabb-Kangas & J. Cummins (Eds.), *Minority education: From shame to struggle* (pp. 278–298). Philadelphia: Multilingual Matters LTD.

Edwards, P. A. (1990). Strategies and techniques for establishing home–school partnerships with minority parents. In A. Barona & E. E. García (Eds.), *Children at risk: Poverty, minority status, and other issues in educational equity* (pp. 217–236). Washington, DC: National Association of School Psychologists.

Epstein, J. L. (1986). Parents' reactions to teacher practices of parent involvement. *Elementary School Journal, 86,* 277–294.

Fox, T. (1990). *The social uses of writing politics and pedagogy.* Norwood, NJ: Ablex.

García, E. E. (1990). Language-minority education litigation policy: "The law of the land." In A. Barona & E. E. García (Eds.), *Children at risk: Poverty, minority status, and other issues in educational equity* (pp. 53–63). Washington, DC: National Association of School Psychologists.

Goldenberg, C., & Gallimore, R. (1991). Local knowledge, research and educational change: A case study of early Spanish reading improvement. *Educational Researcher, 20*(8), 2–14.

Gonzalez, B. (1986). Schools and the language minority parents: An optimum solution. *Catalyst for Change, 16,* 14–17.

Grimmett, S. A., & McCoy, M. (1980). Effects of parental communication on reading performance of third grade children. *The Reading Teacher, 34,* 303–308.

Guadalupe Organization, Inc. v. *Tempe Elementary School District No. 3,* 587 F.2d 022 (1978).

Harrington, A. (1971). Teaching parents to help at home. In C. B. Smith (Ed.), *Parents and reading* (pp. 49–56). Newark, DE: International Reading Association.

Hernandez-Chavez, E. (1988). Language policy and language rights in the United States: Issues in bilingualism. In T. Skutnabb-Kangas & J. Cummins (Eds.), *Minority education: From shame to struggle* (pp. 45–56). Philadelphia: Multilingual Matters LTD.

High, V. (1981). Home curriculum program. In N. Cruz, Jr., N. J. Holland, & M. Garlington (Eds.), *A catalog of parent involvement projects—A collection of quality parent projects for assisting children in the achievement of basic skills* (p. 12). Rosslyn, VA: Inter-America Research Associates.

Huberman, M. (1987). How well does educational research really travel? *Educational Researcher, 16*(1), 5–13.

Keyes v. *School District No. 1,* Denver, Colorado, 423 U.S. 1066 (1983).

Lau v. *Nichols,* 414 U.S. 563 (1974).

Los Padres para Mejorar Educacion Bilingue v. *Calistoga Joint Unified School District* (a formal complaint filed with the Office for Civil Rights of the U. S. Department of Health, Education and Welfare, March 30, 1979).

Lynch, A. (1992). The importance of parental involvement. In L. Kaplan (Ed.), *Education and the family* (pp. 304–306). Boston: Allyn & Bacon.

Martin Luther King Junior Elementary School Children v. Ann Arbor School District Board, 473 F. Supp. 1371 (E. D. Mich. 1979).

Nieto, S. (1992). *Affirming diversity: The sociopolitical context of multicultural education.* White Plains, NY: Longman.

Ogbu, J. U. (1992). Understanding cultural diversity and learning. *Educational Researcher, 21*(8), 5–14.

Otero v. Mesa County School District No. 51, 568 F.2d 1312 (1977).

Perez, B., & Torres-Guzman, M. E. (1992). *Learning in two worlds: An integrated Spanish/English biliteracy approach.* White Plains, NY: Longman.

Piper, T. (1992). *Language for all our children.* New York: Macmillian.

Raim, J. (1980). Who learns when parents teach their children? *The Reading Teacher, 34*, 152–155.

Reyes, M. de la Luz. (1991). A process approach to literacy for Spanish speaking students: In search of a best fit. In E. H. Hiebert (Ed.), *Literacy for a diverse society: Perspectives, practices, and policies* (pp. 157–171). New York: Teachers College Press.

Sarason, S. B. (1982). *The culture of the school and the problem of change* (2nd ed.). Boston: Allyn & Bacon.

Seeley, D. S. (1989). A new paradigm for parent involvement. *Educational Leadership, 48*(2), 46–48.

Thomas, K. M. (1985). Parent involvement and Springfield's Chestnut Street Junior High School. *Equity and Choice, 1*, 44–46.

U. S. v. Texas, 680 F.2d 356 (1981).

Wenn, M. (1981). Tulane follow through. In N. Cruz, Jr., N. J. Holland, & M. Garlington (Eds.), *A catalog of parent involvement projects—A collection of quality parent projects for assisting children in the achievement of basis skills* (p. 25). Rosslyn, VA: Inter-America Research Associates.

Wood, D. R. (1992). Teaching narratives: A source for faculty development and evaluation. *Harvard Educational Review, 62*(4), 535–550.

CHAPTER 10

Preparing Teachers for Early Childhood Programs of Linguistic and Cultural Diversity

Olivia N. Saracho and Bernard Spodek

The number of educational programs available for young children has increased over the past 3 decades. With this increase has come an accompanying increase in the number of persons staffing them and programs to prepare those persons. For a number of years, the percentage of linguistically and culturally diverse (LCD) children also has been increasing in American public schools. Teachers in all grade levels face the challenge of responding to an increasingly diverse student population. This is particularly true of those teachers who are responsible for the second language learning and academic achievement of LCD students (TESOL, 1991). The increase in the LCD population's size and diversity as well as the limited number of qualified bilingual teachers prevent implementing bilingual programs for all LCD students (García, in press).

As teacher education programs have accepted the challenge of preparing increasing numbers of early childhood teachers, they also must assume the challenge of preparing teachers of young LCD children. Some of these programs are designed to prepare preservice teachers. Others are designed to extend the preparation of certified teachers who wish to work with LCD children. Teachers in these programs must possess the same knowledge, skills, and attitudes expected of all teachers of young children. Teachers of both LCD and regular classroom students need special skills that prepare them to cope with LCD students in an academic setting. This means that teacher preparation and training programs must develop or refine presently offered programs in order to become more responsive to the needs of professionals—specialists and nonspecialists—who will teach LCD students (TESOL, 1991). Saracho (1993b) has described the components of an early childhood teacher education program. They are recruitment and selection, general education, and professional knowledge, which includes foundational knowledge, instructional knowledge, and practical knowledge. These components, which can be found in programs preparing teachers to work with LCD children, will be discussed in the sections to follow.

RECRUITMENT AND SELECTION

Selection processes for teacher education programs attempt to identify those applicants who can successfully complete the program and who ultimately will become competent practitioners. When programs seek to enroll applicants other than those who apply for programs, they engage in recruitment practices. These may be designed to increase the number of teacher education applicants generally, or they may be designed to increase applicants with particular attributes, for example, members of ethnic groups or those who are academically successful.

One suggestion for selecting prospective teachers is to identify those individuals who have personal characteristics of good early childhood teachers. These teachers need to be patient, mature, energetic, responsible, and ingenious in providing teaching and play materials (Almy, 1975); they should also be flexible, warm, and able to enjoy and encourage children (Katz, 1974).

Additional criteria might be used to select potential teachers of LCD children. These teachers should

1. Believe that cultural diversity is a worthy goal
2. Respect the culture children bring to school
3. Believe that the children's culture is worth preserving and enriching
4. Appreciate cultural and linguistic differences as undeniable individual differences
5. Be willing to learn more about the education of LCD children
6. Have a positive self-concept
7. Enhance the children's self-image
8. Have confidence in the ability of LCD children to learn
9. Have a positive attitude toward all children of any ethnic group, regardless of socioeconomic status (Blanco, 1975; Casso & Gonzalez, 1974)

Some educators suggest that teachers of LCD children should be selected from the same ethnic group as the children being taught. Such teachers could provide positive role models, encourage children to perform better, and better understand and counsel children. However, teachers of the same ethnic group, but from a different socioeconomic background, may be less sensitive and more demanding of children, perceiving them as lacking in ability or motivation (Carter, 1971).

Programs for LCD children serve students from various languages and cultures. A teacher's attitudes, values, and competencies with respect to one language and culture may not necessarily transfer to others. Therefore, teachers need to be matched to a particular population. Also, language and cultural proficiency must be a selection criterion for teachers of LCD children if the program does not train staff in these areas (Saracho & Spodek, 1983). If supporting diversity in schools is a program priority, it should be reflected in the diversity of the individuals selected for the teacher education program. Teacher education programs also should provide knowledgeable role models from different ethnic groups for prospective teachers of LCD children.

Self-selection is the strongest factor in any occupational recruitment, but other factors in the recruitment process also need to be identified. Selection criteria might include (1) choosing teaching as the preferred career, (2) having prior experiences with young children, and (3) having a strong commitment to the education of LCD children (Saracho & Spodek, 1983).

Head Start programs, childcare centers, and nursery schools employ a number of people from diverse socioeconomic and cultural backgrounds who may have little formal teacher preparation but who have demonstrated success in working with young children and their parents. Generally, experienced mothers are most interested in early childhood (birth to 5 years of age). Both of these populations could be actively recruited. However, university requirements—prerequisites for admission, time commitments, daytime course schedules, cost, and academic standards—often screen these populations out. Nevertheless, many of these individuals have served successfully as aides and volunteers in Head Start programs and childcare centers (Haberman, 1988).

The recruitment and selection of prospective teachers should be done cautiously. Too stringent an application of any selection criteria might keep out large numbers of potentially good teachers who do not meet a particular set of requirements. Improvement in the recruitment and selection of teacher applicants will certainly result as teacher education programs change.

GENERAL EDUCATION

General education provides teachers with a well-rounded education. In a sense, it also represents the content of early childhood education. What we teach young children, even though it is quite different from what we teach college students, is a reflection of the various scholarly disciplines that are included in the general education requirements of most university programs (including language, social studies, mathematics, science, aesthetics, and humanities). The general education program ordinarily is taught in universities through separate courses. In the early childhood program, the content of these disciplines is simplified and integrated as they are applied to the study of the human environment and human condition.

Early childhood teachers may need to focus more on how discipline knowledge is applied to working with young children than on the traditional disciplines themselves. The National Association for the Education of Young Children (1982) recommends that general education account for at least 50% of an early childhood teacher education program. This may be low. The proportion of general education in teacher education programs has increased in many institutions as the result of pressure from reform groups to make teacher education more rigorous. Requirements related to special teaching fields have increased. For example, the National Association for Bilingual Education (NABE) and the Teachers of English Speakers of Other Languages (TESOL) have generated standards for preservice teacher education programs that build on general program standards, including those advocated by the National Council for Accreditation of Teacher Education (NCATE, 1994–1995) and the National Board for Professional Teaching Standards (NBPTS). NABE's (1992) program standards suggest an approach to enrich and improve prospective teachers' ability to satisfy increased educational standards in the schools. For example, prospective LCD teachers who experienced poor early educational opportunities may be encouraged to join the profession, but, unless they are helped, they may still suffer in their education from the consequences of their inadequate prior educational experiences. Program personnel should be knowledgeable about the distinctive educational barriers to success that LCD students may face and should provide prospective teachers with ongoing assessment and amelioration. Prospective LCD teachers must complete advanced coursework in at least two languages of instruction and demonstrate high levels of proficiency in both (a requirement often for English as a second language (ESL) teachers also) to ensure their familiarity with issues of second language acquisition and to expand their language repertoire (García, in press).

General education takes on added importance for teachers of young LCD children. They need to be well grounded in at least two languages and two cultures to be able to understand the meanings, traditions, and heritage of their future students and thus be better able to guide their learning. Productive instruction for LEP students (i.e., students who need to improve their proficiency in English) emphasizes intense use of their home language to conserve their improvement in overall language development, encourage proficiency in the core subjects, and develop a solid and broad foundation for learning English (García, 1994, in press; General Accounting Office [GAO], 1987; Lessow-Hurley, 1991; Nieto, 1992; Ramírez, Yuen, Ramey, & Pasta, 1991).

Language provides a means to understand and express a variety of experiences and represent the profundity and complexity of the world. Prospective teachers of LCD children can learn language and linguistics related to the target population. Literary language permits prospective teachers to express themselves aesthetically and appreciate the expressions of others in each language.

When prospective teachers learn a second language, they also may expand their insight into a second culture. Literature offers them information concerning traditions, values, customs, symbols, and history of the second culture. Although many consider the play of young children as universal, different cultures embrace different play forms and games that teachers of LCD children need to know.

This perspective integrates the understanding that (1) language, culture, and their accompanying values are learned in the home and community environment (Cummins, 1986; Goldman & Trueba, 1987); (2) children enter school with some knowledge about what language is, how it works, and what it is used for (Hall, 1987); (3) children develop cognitive and communicative skills as they engage in socially meaningful activities (Duran, 1986); and (4) children's development and learning interact with linguistic, sociocultural, and cognitive knowledge and experiences (Trueba, 1987). Learning is strengthened when it occurs within contexts that are both socioculturally and linguistically meaningful (Díaz, Moll, & Mehan, 1986; Heath, 1986).

Prospective teachers can learn to express themselves aesthetically through their own work and to appreciate both created and natural objects. Cultural groups differ in their aesthetic values and judgments. Literature, music, dance, and art forms vary in each culture. A classic interpretation in one culture may be unconventional to another. Teachers of LCD children must learn the aesthetic elements of the culture of the children whom they are preparing to teach.

Prospective teachers of LCD children need to know the history of the target cultural groups, their heroes, myths, and legacy to local, national, and world history. Frequently an ethnic group's contributions to the United States have been ignored or misrepresented in social studies textbooks. Prospective teachers of LCD children must learn the social sciences in such a way that the general concepts learned can be applied across many cultures. The focus, however, should be on the cultures in which prospective teachers of LCD children will be working and should include language, art, history, and music of those cultures, as well as social structure and relationships, values, religions, traditions, myths, heroes, and symbols (Saracho & Spodek, 1983).

Studies suggest the importance of general knowledge in preparing early childhood teachers. Some suggest, however, that information about children, how they learn, and how to teach them is more important. Implicit in this assumption is the belief that knowledge of "how to teach," or pedagogy, is more important than knowledge of the content of the liberal arts and sciences (Bowman, 1990). However, Berk (1985) compared early childhood practitioners who were high school graduates with those who were 2-year college graduates. She found that teachers with a minimum of 2 years of college show teaching behaviors that relate to increased outcomes of children's programs (e.g., more verbal interaction, indirect guidance, encouragement, and direction), thus suggesting "the relevance of broad higher educational foundations for the practical endeavor of providing developmentally stimulating caregiving experiences for young children and for fostering integration of caregiver child-oriented attitudes with behavior" (p. 127). Apparently, the teacher's general level of education relates to the quality of teaching.

PROFESSIONAL KNOWLEDGE

Professional knowledge represents that knowledge that is specific to the profession of teaching, including foundational knowledge, instructional knowledge, and practical knowledge.

Foundational Knowledge

Foundational knowledge reflects those facets of history, philosophy, sociology, economics, psychology, politics, linguistics, and anthropology that underlie education. This represents knowledge *about* education instead of knowledge of professional techniques and includes those theories that provide teachers with a basis for their decisions and actions.

Early childhood teachers of LCD children need a broad base of foundational knowledge, including (1) the history and traditions both of the education of LCD children and of LCD children, (2) principles of child growth and development, (3) learning theory, and (4) the cultural, social, and political contexts in which they will be working (Saracho & Spodek, 1983). They must have knowledge of at least two cultures and languages as well as the principles that underlie first and second language acquisition—knowledge gained through general education but placed in proper perspective through professional knowledge.

Teachers of LCD children need to be introduced to ethnic groups' movements to integrate school, college, and university curricula and to include ethnic content. An historical perspective that reflects on issues and concerns of LCD children presents prospective teachers with a context where they learn the contemporary progress and educational discourse for a productive reorganization of the schools, colleges, and universities (Banks, 1993). The intergroup education movement is an important antecedent of the current LCD movement but is not its actual roots, which Banks attributes to the early ethnic studies movement.

Understanding culturally diverse students requires knowledge of the interaction of the students' culture and the prevailing school culture (Tharp, 1989). Studies suggest that the educational failure of "diverse" student populations relates to a culture conflict between home and school for African American students (Boykin, 1986), poor white students (Heath, 1983), Hawaiian students (Wiesner, Gallimore, & Jordan, 1988), Navaho students (Vogt, Jordan, & Tharp, 1987), Mexican American students (García, 1988, 1991), and Puerto Rican students (Rodriguez, 1989). These researchers indicate that the contributions of the students' culture need to be addressed in order for the educational endeavors of students who have a unique cultural background to be successful. According to Sue and Padilla (1986), "The challenge for educators is to identify critical differences between and within ethnic minority groups and to incorporate this information into classroom practice" (p. 62).

Professional knowledge for teachers of LCD children has theoretical and philosophical bases in cultural and linguistic theories and in theories relating to the impact of culture on development. This should establish an understanding and appreciation of the richness of linguistic and cultural diversity and the process of cultural diversity and cultural diffusion.

The foundational knowledge component can offer a basic understanding of regional, social, and developmental differences in children's language and how culture is reflected in thinking styles, learning styles, and language development. The nature of bilingualism; the process of becoming bilingual; and the phonological, grammatical, and lexical elements of the two languages involved also need to be transmitted. An understanding of first language and second language acquisition theory, the effects of learning and speaking two languages on the developing child, and the cultural manifestations related to these language systems will help prospective teachers understand and appreciate the children they will teach. It also can assist prospective teachers to better understand and consider diverse alternative educational theories and methods (Saracho & Spodek, 1983).

Instructional Knowledge

Instructional knowledge refers to knowledge of teaching practice, planning, and evaluation. Prospective teachers learn to establish educational goals for children and to select and sequence instructional strategies to achieve these goals.

Sources of Teacher Knowledge. Prospective teachers acquire new knowledge, retrieve old knowledge, and integrate their new and old knowledge in their teacher education programs. Most beginning teachers have some knowledge of teaching before they enter a teacher education program. They need to place this knowledge in some theoretical framework.

The knowledge base of early childhood pedagogy suggests the importance of different realms of knowledge for beginning teachers. Teachers need to have knowledge of several disciplines from general education, such as social sciences, biological and physical sciences, mathematics, fine arts, and literature. They need to know what concepts, ideas, and principles of these disciplines are included in the early childhood curriculum. Teachers also must understand the interrelatedness of the disciplines and help young children to link the different kinds of knowledge (McCarthy, 1990). They need to teach the children in their class how knowledge is created and how it is affected by the racial, ethnic, and social class positions of individual groups (Banks, 1993).

Knowledge of Teachers' Roles. Knowledge that teachers require is related to the different roles that teachers play. Saracho (1984, 1993b) identified and validated six roles of the teacher, which are discussed later in relation to programs to prepare teachers of LCD children.

As *diagnosticians,* teachers use a range of methods (e.g., observation, informal and formal tests, anecdotal records, and collections of samples of children's work) to know children's needs and abilities and to develop an appropriate program for them (Saracho & Spodek, 1983; see also Chapter 4, this volume). Prospective teachers of LCD children need to learn about various formal and informal assessment techniques and understand the relationship of language and culture to the results they may get from applying these techniques. Instruments must match the children's language and culture as well as the program goals. Regardless of the diagnostic strategies teachers use, they must be careful that the information collected, even though it is only a limited sample of behavior, provides a symbolic picture of the child (Saracho & Spodek, 1983).

LCD children's home language often differs from the language of the school. They have achieved competence in a language with a complete sound system, grammar, and vocabulary (Saville & Troike, 1975). Teacher education students need to learn how to diagnose the language competency of each child and relate the child's knowledge to what is expected in school (Casso & Gonzalez, 1974; Saracho & Spodek, 1983).

As future *curriculum designers,* prospective teachers must learn the developmental levels of the children with whom they will be working, as well as the children's particular educational needs and strengths. They should understand the importance of working with parents to determine expectations for their children's learning and with the local community. They need to know and interpret research findings relevant to LCD children and their community, as well as to put aside all biases as they determine specific goals for the children (Saracho & Spodek, 1983).

It is important for teacher education programs to have as a goal designing curriculum to modify children's negative attitudes toward different races and cultures. Banks's (1993) review of the literature identified four types of modification studies: curricular intervention, reinforcement, perceptual, and cooperative learning. Although the studies have methodological problems, they still provide some directions for practice.

Many children enter school with misconceptions about outside ethnic groups and with a white bias. Racial attitudes can be modified to be more democratic. In fact, young children's racial attitudes are much more easily modified than older students' and adults' attitudes. Such modifications should begin early. Prospective teachers should learn to implement, beginning in kindergarten, a well-conceptualized and sequential curriculum that includes content, examples, and realistic images of diverse racial and ethnic groups (Banks, 1993).

The curriculum should reflect the similarities and differences among the cultural and linguistic groups, including differences in social structures, family organizations, patterns of authority, language patterns, knowledge forms, and art forms. Teacher education students need to be aware of the effects of socioeconomic factors and cultural factors on all children's learning. Such information is essential in determining a program's goals.

Preservice teachers must know how to determine which curriculum models, methods, and materials are appropriate for the LCD children in their classroom. As teachers select alternative strategies, they must know the relevant elements of the culture (e.g., language, music, and art) that are essential in the curriculum and the resources available in the community to strengthen educational activities related to the cultural elements in the classroom. Finally, teachers must know how to organize various resources, both within and outside the classroom, including, among others, educational resources, human resources, and cultural resources (Saracho & Spodek, 1983).

Prospective teachers need to learn both long-range and short-range planning so that they can be effective *organizers of instruction*. They must respect young children's interests, capacities, limitations, and aspirations in order to successfully arrange activity schedules, organize children into workable groups, and arrange classroom materials and equipment to make the best use of space.

The selection and integration of materials and resources that are relevant from both a language and a cultural point of view should be a high priority for programs designed to prepare teachers of LCD children. Learning to plan in advance assists teachers to better select materials and resources essential for instruction. Goals for each child and a variety of learning experiences to help children meet their needs within the program should be identified in advance (Saracho, 1984). If appropriate materials for LCD children are not accessible through traditional sources, teachers must use alternative sources, alter available materials, or create their own (Saracho & Spodek, 1983).

Usually teachers of LCD children feel that, while other parts of the program can be presented indirectly through activities, language instruction should be sequenced formally and presented directly (Saville & Troike, 1975). However, indirect instruction through play activities is more appropriate for teaching language to young children. Prospective teachers should understand that learning centers can be set up to permit children to move freely from one activity to another, and this freedom of movement could characterize language activities. Conceptually enriching activities that allow children to assimilate expressive and receptive language skills in a naturalistic fashion can be provided (Saracho, 1993a).

A wide range of first language and second language instructional strategies is available for early childhood education. Preservice teachers of LCD children should learn about these strategies to individualize their program using inquiry/discovery techniques and independent activities as well as direct instruction. Such strategies can be facilitated by learning to use audiovisual devices and organizing the classroom into learning centers (Saracho & Spodek, 1983).

Placing a group of 15, 20, or more children in a single classroom for many hours each day can generate problems unless the teacher is prepared to function as an effective *manager of instruction*. Children differ in their learning, competencies, cognitive styles, interests, and needs. If individual differences are ignored and teachers provide instruction only to the average, expecting other children to adjust to this situation, it creates educational disadvantages and chastises children for being different. Prescribed activities increase the conflict between individual and group needs. Therefore, individual and group conflict is reduced by offering children a broad variety of learning alternatives (Saracho, 1984).

Properly prepared as managers of learning, teachers can create an attractive educational classroom environment and organize educational and cultural experiences. Teachers need to know how to initiate work routines, introduce subject matter, and offer educational tools and classroom exhibits that are appropriate to the children's age level, interests, and culture (Saracho, 1984).

Management problems often occur during transition times, when students move from one place to another or from one activity to another. Children terminate their work at different rates. Those who finish first should not be expected to wait for the rest of the class. Problems usually arise due to boredom, an insistence on conformity, a failure to orient some children, unclearly defined tasks, and the fear of failure. Forcing children to clean up, line up, move from one area to another, or wait usually generates problems. Preservice teachers need to learn how to deal with these situations, knowing which children have difficulties and providing special support for them during transition. Anticipating transition problems and preparing for them can prevent unmanageable situations. During and after transition periods, teachers must use methods to re-situate a manageable situation in which children can continue with their educational work. Knowing how to use these approaches simplifies teaching performance (Saracho, 1984).

Teachers are responsible for aiding each child to acquire desirable behaviors, learn to cope with others, and endure with feelings. In this way, teachers serve as *counselors or advisors*. Teacher education students should understand that competent teachers become involved both personally and professionally in the educational process. They instruct, coach, and model to achieve these ends, continuously interacting with children during the day, providing caretaking, emotional support, guidance, and instruction. The classroom surroundings must create a sense of trust and security (Saracho, 1984). Children's strengths, needs, and weaknesses should be accepted and their sociocultural backgrounds respected (Saracho & Spodek, 1983).

Success in learning depends on children's motivation. A positive self-image and a sense of acceptance helps children become more willing to accept challenges, take risks in learning new things, and test themselves in new situations (Saracho, 1984). Preservice teachers need to realize that an important part of motivating children is being specifically sensitive to their culture and language. Language and culture are an integrated part of each individual. The values teachers place on language and culture indicate the values they place on their classroom children. Teachers must support the children's own life pursuits, nurturing their feelings of self-worth. Academic competence must never be achieved at the expense of a child's personal feeling of self-worth.

Young children can receive support as people if teachers stretch themselves by making contact with parents and community members, supporting the home and community in the school's programs, and supporting the school's activities relating to the home and community. In this manner teachers promote the child's development as an integrated person based on the experiences gained in two cultural contexts.

Prospective teachers of LCD children should learn that they must reinforce what has been taught in the home. For example, the Mexican American family fosters a sense of importance in young children, especially the youngest one in the family, which reinforces their self-concept and creates their trust in adults. Teachers have the responsibility to make these children feel important but at the same time teach them to make realistic judgments about their worth. Mexican American children are taught to have a deep consideration for others and to offer a great deal of warmth. Children who encounter a teacher who is cold and distant may experience culture shock (Saracho & Spodek, 1983).

The *decision maker* role of the teacher of LCD children parallels that of other teachers. However, the knowledge that these teachers need for making decisions is broader because of the communities in which they work, the wider range of goals instituted for the education of their LCD children, and the problems in locating appropriate curriculum models and materials. Curriculum models and materials need to be relevant to the children's language and culture. In decision making, teachers of LCD children must be certain that their decisions do not conflict with children's cultures (Saracho & Spodek, 1983).

Saracho's (1984, 1993b) descriptions of these different roles offer some insight into the theory, knowledge, and practice of teaching LCD children. Teachers assume the different roles for their professional practice. Some of the qualities for good early childhood teachers relate to their personal characteristics, which are as important as the knowledge and skills they need to work with young children.

Practical Knowledge

Practice assists prospective teachers to apply theory in real-life situations, with help and guidance from cooperating teachers and college supervisors. Intellectual methods are employed to understand and improve practice. The practice component usually consists of field experiences such as workshops, observations, simulations, and student teaching.

Field experiences integrate previous learning with emerging experiences and transform theoretical instruction into reality. An overemphasis on field experiences, at the expense of other program segments, may make teacher education a nonintellectual apprenticeship program. If only the practical is emphasized, basic theories and a unification of ideas with practice may be neglected or undervalued.

Workshops permit prospective teachers to demonstrate and practice teaching procedures with different kinds of materials and to study the effects of such procedures on children. A workshop usually involves the construction of children's equipment, introducing a movement and dance session, painting or sculpting, experimenting with science materials, designing and using puppets, or exploring new materials (Almy, 1975; Saracho & Spodek, 1983).

Classroom observation helps prospective teachers to relate practice to theory. Responsive observing permits prospective teachers to identify vital clues that lead to an understanding of events and permit inferences to be made on something more than intuition (Saracho & Spodek, 1983). Observation provides prospective teachers with concrete representations of the normative sequences of development. Systematic observation assists prospective teachers to relate their knowledge of normative developmental sequences and patterns and their understanding of the uniqueness of every child (Peters & Klinzing, 1990). Observation is typically directed, focused, and completely merged with the learning process (Saracho, 1993b).

In simulation, prospective teachers assume a hypothetical role in a simple and controlled situation. In micro-teaching, a model of simulation, prospective teachers teach a short activity to a small group of children; the activity is later viewed, analyzed, and evaluated. The interest or boredom of the children in the activity is examined, for example, as an indication of effectiveness (Almy, 1975; Saracho & Spodek, 1983).

Early field experiences can be merged with professional knowledge through activities such as visits to school board meetings, conferences with officials or teachers' unions, and meetings with parents and members of child advocacy groups. Early field experiences also help prospective teachers to develop greater responsibility and self-confidence.

Field experiences with LCD populations should be continual. Field placements can assist prospective teachers to acquire insights into the language and culture of the children they will teach. For teachers of LCD children, the practice element needs to embrace experiences beyond the school, in the homes and communities of the target culture (Saracho & Spodek, 1983). Experiences need to be in a variety of settings, and with a variety of children of different ages, reflecting the scope of the teachers' preparation; they must start with observation and increasingly assume more responsible roles, thereby developing the skills that will permit prospective teachers to assume full responsibility for instruction. Field experiences can be integrated into courses (e.g., parent involvement, curriculum, special needs) to help prospective teachers to develop the ability to assess, analyze, plan, manage, communicate, and evaluate. This is especially true when prospective teachers reflect in discourse that probes the premises of their actions (Freeland, 1988).

Student teaching is estimated to be the most important component in the preparation of teachers (Saracho & Spodek, 1983). Student teaching requires prospective teachers to organize their content and practice knowledge, draw upon their practical skills and teaching views, and develop a personal style of practice that is workable, defensible, and ethical.

CONCLUSION

Teaching is a complex process. Preparing students to become teachers is equally complex. Teacher education programs need to carefully plan experiences that bring together general studies, additional subject matter content, theories of child development, knowledge of teaching, and clinical experiences. Important strands of knowledge and skills need to be integrated throughout the program with increasing levels of sophistication.

Teachers have long-lasting effects on young children. Teacher proficiency is based on an understanding of children, their language, their culture, and their set of values. Teachers' responses to children determine the effects teachers will have on children. Therefore, all facets of teaching need to be considered in designing a teacher education program for early childhood teachers of young LCD children.

REFERENCES

Almy, M. (1975). *The early childhood educator at work.* New York: McGraw-Hill.

Banks, J. A. (1993). Multicultural education: Historical development, dimensions, and practice. In L. Darling-Hammond (Ed.), *Review of research in education* (pp. 3–98). Washington, DC: American Educational Research Association.

Berk, L. (1985). Relationship of education to child-oriented attitudes, job satisfaction, and behaviors toward children. *Child Care Quarterly, 14,* 103–129.

Blanco, G. M. (1975). La preparación de profesores bilingues [The preparation of bilingual teachers]. In R. C. Troike & N. Modiano (Eds.), *Proceedings of the First Inter-American Conference on Bilingual Education.* Reston, VA: Center for Applied Linguistics.

Bowman, B. (1990). Issues in the recruitment, selection, and retention of early childhood teachers. In B. Spodek & O. N. Saracho (Eds.), *Early childhood teacher preparation: Yearbook of early childhood education* (Vol. I, pp. 153–175). New York: Teachers College Press.

Boykin, A. (1986). The triple quandary and the schooling of Afro-American children. In U. Neisser (Ed.), *The school achievement of minority children* (pp. 57–92). New York: Perspectives.

Carter, T. P. (1971). Mexican-Americans in school: A history of educational neglect. In J. C. Stone & D. P. DeNevi (Eds.), *Teaching multicultural populations: Five heritages.* New York: Van Nostrand.

Casso, H., & Gonzalez, D. (1974). Bilingual bicultural education: a challenge to the open classroom unit. In *A manual prepared for the Teacher Training Institute* (pp. 17–29). Westport, CT: Mediax Associates.

Cummins, J. (1986). Empowering minority students: A framework for intervention. *Harvard Educational Review, 56*(1), 18–36.

Díaz, R. M., Moll, L. C., & Mehan, H. (1986). Sociocultural resources in instruction: A context-specific approach. In *Beyond language: Social and cultural factors in schooling language minority students* (pp. 197–230). Los Angeles: California State University, Evaluation, Dissemination and Assessment Center.

Duran, R. (1986). *Improving Hispanics' educational outcomes: Learning and instruction.* Unpublished manuscript, University of California, Graduate School of Education, Santa Barbara.

Freeland, K. (1988). A collaborative effort in field experiences. *The Teacher Educator, 24*(2), 22–26.

García, E. E. (1988). Effective schooling for Hispanics. *Urban Education Review, 67*(2), 462–473.

García, E. E. (1991). Bilingualism, second language acquisition in academic contexts. In A. M. Ambert (Ed.), *Bilingual education and English as a second language: A research annual* (pp. 181–217). New York: Garland.

García, E. E. (1994). *Understanding and meeting the challenge of student cultural diversity.* Boston: Houghton Mifflin.

García, E. E. (in press). Preparing instructional professionals for linguistically and culturally diverse students. In J. Sikula & E. Guypon (Eds.), *Handbook of research on teacher education.* Washington, DC: American Association of Colleges for Teacher Education.

General Accounting Office. (1987). *Research evidence on bilingual education* (GAO/PEMD–87-12BR). Washington, DC: Author.

Goldman, S., & Trueba, H. (Eds.). (1987). *Becoming literate in English as a second language: Advances in research and theory.* Norwood, NJ: Ablex.

Haberman, M. (1988). Proposals for recruiting minority teachers: Promising practices and attractive detours. (ERIC Document Reproduction Service No. ED 292 760)

Hall, N. (1987). *The emergence of literacy.* Portsmouth, NH: Heinemann.

Heath, S. B. (1983). *Ways with words: Language, life, and work in communities and classrooms.* Cambridge: Cambridge University Press.

Heath, S. B. (1986). Sociocultural contexts of language development. In *Beyond language: Social and cultural factors in schooling language minority students* (pp. 143–186). Los Angeles: California State University, Evaluation, Dissemination and Assessment Center.

Katz, L. G. (1974). Issues and problems in education. In B. Spodek (Ed.), *Teacher education: Of the teacher, by the teacher, for the child.* Washington, DC: National Association for the Education of Young Children.

Lessow-Hurley, J. (1991). *The foundations of dual language instruction.* White Plains, NY: Longman.

McCarthy, J. (1990). The content of early childhood teacher education programs: Pedagogy. In B. Spodek & O. N. Saracho (Eds.), *Early childhood teacher preparation: Yearbook of early childhood education* (Vol. 1, pp. 82–101). New York: Teachers College Press.

National Association for Bilingual Education. (1992). *Professional standards for the preparation of bilingual/multicultural teachers.* Washington, DC: Author.

National Association for the Education of Young Children. (1982). *Early childhood teacher education guidelines.* Washington, DC: Author.

National Clearing House for Bilingual Education. (1985). *Annual conference journal.* Washington, DC: Author.

National Council for Accreditation of Teacher Education. (1994–1995). *Standards, procedures, and policies for the accreditation of professional education units.* Washington, DC: Author.

Nieto, S. (1992). *Affirming diversity: The sociopolitical context of multicultural education.* White Plains, NY: Longman.

Peters, D. L., & Klinzing, D. G. (1990). The content of early childhood teacher education programs. In B. Spodek & O. N. Saracho (Eds.), *Early childhood teacher preparation: Yearbook of early childhood education* (Vol. 1, pp. 67–81). New York: Teachers College Press.

Ramírez, J. D., Yuen, S. D., Ramey, D. R., & Pasta, D. J. (1991). *Final report: Longitudinal study of immersion strategy, early-exit and late-exit transitional bilingual education programs for language-minority children.* San Mateo, CA: Aguire International.

Rodriguez, C. E. (1989). *Puerto Ricans born in the U. S. A.* Winchester, MA: Unwin Hyman.

Saracho, O. N. (1984). Perception of the teaching process in early childhood education through role analysis. *Journal of the Association for the Study of Perception, International, 19*(1), 26–29.

Saracho, O. N. (1993a). Literacy development: The whole language approach. In B. Spodek & O. N. Saracho (Eds.), *Early childhood language and literacy: Yearbook of early childhood education* (Vol. 4, pp. 42–59). New York: Teachers College Press.

Saracho, O. N. (1993b). The preparation of early childhood teachers. In B. Spodek (Ed.), *Handbook of research on the education of young children* (pp. 412–426). New York: Macmillan.

Saracho, O. N., & Spodek, B. (1983). The preparation of teachers for bilingual bicultural early childhood classes. In O. N. Saracho & B. Spodek (Eds.), *Understanding the multicultural experience in early childhood education* (pp. 125–146). Washington, DC: National Association for the Education of Young Children.

Saville, M. R., & Troike, R. C. (1975). *A handbook of bilingual education.* Washington, DC: Teachers of English to Speakers of Other Languages.

Sue, S., & Padilla, A. (1986). Ethnic minority issues in the United States: Challenges for the educational system. In *Beyond language: Social and cultural factors in schooling language minority students* (pp. 35–72). Los Angeles: California State University, Evaluation, Dissemination and Assessment Center.

Teachers of English to Speakers of Other Languages. (1991). *TESOL statement on the education of K–12 language minority students in the United States and TESOL statement on the preparation of primary and secondary teachers in the United States.* Alexandria, VA: Author.

Tharp, R. G. (1989). Psychocultural variables and K constants: Effects on teaching and learning in schools. *American Psychologist, 44,* 349–359.

Trueba, H. T. (1987). Success or failure? *Learning and the language minority student.* Scranton, PA: Harper & Row.

Vogt, L., Jordan, C., & Tharp, R. (1987). Explaining school failure, producing school success: Two cases. *Anthropology and Education Quarterly, 18*(4), 276–286.

Wiesner, T. S., Gallimore, R., & Jordan, C. (1988). Unpackaging cultural effects on classroom learning: Native Hawaiian peer assistance and child-generated activity. *Anthropology and Education Quarterly, 19*(4), 327–353.

CHAPTER 11

The Future Challenge of Linguistic and Cultural Diversity in the Schools

Olivia N. Saracho and Bernard Spodek

In America, education provides an entrance into the mainstream of American society, contributing to social mobility by extending opportunities. Supporting a democratic society based on equal opportunity, the schools have been the primary vehicle for conveying society's culture and values to the younger generation. The public schools have served this role since the establishment of the United States, educating generation after generation of children and serving the national need.

Young children's socialization into the larger society is an important and appropriate goal of early childhood education. While the family is the primary socializing agency in our society, the school serves to introduce children into the larger society outside the family, helping children learn social processes that may differ from those learned at home. Children learn about the roles and functions of individuals and of the interrelationships among them in our society outside the home. They learn to respond appropriately to others: to use language along with various behavioral repertoires to get along with others, and to acquire personal satisfaction in ways that are considered fitting (Saracho & Spodek, 1983).

Most children easily make the transition from home to school, easily adjusting to the new setting. The children learn the difference between situations inside and outside their home. The language of the school will be different from that of the home, as are the expectations, the required patterns of behavior, their own particular role, and the interactions in which they engage, but usually these differences are not great. They learn the new ways to function in the school. The children learn that the school's values are different from those of the home, and most of them learn to assimilate those values. While school is different from home, it is not alien to most children. What they have learned at home can be adapted to the school; generally, what is learned in one setting supports what is learned in the other. Especially in early childhood education, there is a sense of a partnership between the home and school that facilitates the transition from one social environment to another with little sense of displacement.

However, many children have trouble during the transition from home to school, especially when the language and cultural patterns of the school are significantly different from what they have experienced in the home. American schools serve children from many cultures, who speak many languages. Language patterns, social interactions, and the manifestations of values and culture may be totally unfamiliar to linguistically and culturally diverse (LCD) children. These children may need more than minor adjustments in their language and behavior to succeed in school. They may be forced to use a language that is both new and strange, and the social patterns and interactions expected of them may be equally unfamiliar. LCD children are required to learn their own family language and culture as well as learn to master an alien language and culture. Many may feel that they must reject the language and culture of their home in order to adopt those of the school. Such feelings may make LCD children feel bewilderment, rejection, and a loss of ethnic identity (Saracho, 1986).

In its struggles to fully assume the responsibility to educate all children, many American schools adopted educational plans that required children to surrender their cultural identity and ancestral language. Children in such circumstances have felt that in place of what they have learned in their family, they had to substitute the patterns of behavior and language of the middle-class, white, English-speaking society. This represented what it was believed all American children should be rather than what LCD children were. Too often these children became disoriented in school, and some rejected their personal and cultural identity while failing to adequately achieve a new identity. In the past, the spirit of the LCD children's life-styles, languages, and cultures were censured by the main institutions of a dominant society.

"Speak the way the teacher speaks, not the way we speak at home." "Learn to behave like a real American!" These were the warnings that these situations usually invoked in past generations. Those who grew up in a home with a language and culture that were strikingly different from the school's language and culture were strongly encouraged to disregard that culture. Success in the school requires LCD children to comply with the model that was provided by their "American" teacher. Everything else should be forgotten and repressed. Many of those who did succeed lost something in the process.

Recently, systematic research has failed to support the beliefs that LCD children's language and culture is degenerate and structurally underdeveloped. There is overwhelming evidence to demonstrate that when children, regardless of their native language, dialect, or ethnic background, first attend school at the age of 5 or 6, they completely control the grammatical system of their first language. The fact that their language system may differ from that of their teacher does not suggest that their speech is not rule governed.

Language characteristics which teachers perceive as different do not indicate failure to adjust to some universally accepted English norm. Such characteristics are a product of the LCD children's own dialect or language-specific syntactic rules, which are as complex as those of standard English. The linguistic differences reflect the systematic cultural differences that are found within our plural society. Each major ethnic group has its own heritage, body of traditions, values, and views about what is right and proper. Ethnic groups pass on their traditions from generation to generation as part of the informal family or peer group socialization process and are proclaimed in folk art and literature (oral or written).

When investigating this complicated structure, researchers need to examine more than grammatical analysis. They need to identify and describe its components, including ethnographic description of community and family, ethnohistory, and the study of folk art. The plurality of cultures affects the quality of individual lives. Ethnic groups in our society are integrated with the dominant group. When investigating the ethnic groups' way of life, their surroundings must be considered.

The fact that bilingual/bicultural programs have been developed in the public schools is a major step toward the acceptance and valuing of cultural and linguistic diversity in our society. Bilingual phenomena, primarily a linguistic term, refer to meaningful transformations in the verbal behavior of a unique population. Its usual linguistics characteristics may vary in social meaning, although to some degree social conditions influence verbal behavior. For example, studies show that behavior in a bilingual situation is not generalizable to another socially different one. Bilingual researchers have usually studied segregated middle class bilinguals living in monolingual neighborhoods, or immigrant farmers or their descendants. The relationship between how bilingual usage reflects the values of speakers and their social conditions needs to be examined. Bilinguals and bidialectals depend heavily on code switching as a verbal scheme. They are particularly susceptible to the relationship between language and context. Linguists also need to examine the code-switching paradigm in a variety of social situations, interaction sequences, speech events, and culture behaviors.

Language difference, which is influenced by culture, dominates in teachers' expectations and in learning environments. LCD children learn best under conditions of maximal contextual reinforcement. Exclusive concentration on the technical aspects of reading, grammar, and spelling can have a detrimental influence on the learning environment.

Instruction for LCD children needs more than superior teaching aids and improved textbooks. Teachers need to appreciate differences in communicative strategies. They should understand both the linguistic and ethnographic facets of speech behavior. They should know the code selection rules in formal and informal settings and the themes of folk literature and folk art that contribute to these rules.

The education of LCD children has come a long way, but it still has a long way to go. Researchers, educators, and child development specialists have gained insights concerning language and cultural values, especially the fact that each culture has contributed to our American heritage. Presently, language and culture are appreciated as the unique contributions of every group. Teachers are helping young children use their backgrounds as a basis for learning. Children are made to feel comfortable in more than one language and culture. They are helped to develop the flexibility and competence to function in both the home and school language and culture. These changes enrich the life of the child. With these understandings, a new role for early childhood educators has emerged for those who are working with LCD children. Socialization, for example, can take on new meaning in such a context.

In this volume, many early childhood researchers who study the many aspects of LCD children have come together from varied backgrounds with numerous concerns to share their views of research on language and culture and its educational implications. The implications of these studies can provide educators of young children with the basis for supporting cultural and linguistic flexibility in children.

REFERENCES

Saracho, O. N. (1986). Teaching second language literacy with computers. In D. Hainline (Ed.), *New developments in computer-assisted language learning* (pp. 53–68). London: Crown Helm.

Saracho, O. N., & Spodek, B. (1983). The preparation of teachers for bilingual bicultural early childhood classes. In O. N. Saracho & B. Spodek (Eds.) , *Understanding the multicultural experience in early childhood education.* (pp. 125–146). Washington, DC: National Association for the Education of Young Children.

About the Editors and Contributors

Martha E. Bernal was raised in El Paso, Texas, where she received a B.A. at the University of Texas at El Paso. Her M.A. degree was earned at Syracuse University and her Ph.D. in Clinical Psychology at Indiana University at Bloomington, Indiana. Her research interests are in two areas: the recruitment and training of ethnic minority psychologists, and the development, socialization, and mental health correlates of ethnic identity in Mexican American families. Recent publications include two edited volumes published in 1993: *Mexican American Identity*, co-edited with Phyllis Martinelli (Floricanto Press, 1993), and *Ethnic Identity: Formation and Transmission among Hispanics and Other Minorities*, co-edited with George P. Knight (SUNY Press, 1993). A recipient of numerous grants and fellowships, she served on the editorial boards of the *Journal of Social Issues*, the *Hispanic Journal of Behavioral Sciences*, *Behavioral Assessment, Behavioral Therapy*, and the *Journal of Applied Behavioral Analysis*. She is a past president of the National Hispanic Psychological Association, a 1994 recipient of the Lifetime Achievement Award bestowed by Division 45 of the American Psychological Association, and serves as an appointed member of the APA's Commission on Ethnic Minority Recruitment, Retention, and Training in Psychology. Currently she has a joint appointment as a professor in the Department of Psychology, and a research professor in the Hispanic Research Center, Arizona State University.

Margaret Borrego Brainard is an instructor in the Preservice Program in the Department of Curriculum and Teaching at Teachers College, Columbia University. After working as a classroom teacher, special educator, and administrator for 16 years, Margaret is currently working on her doctorate in teacher education. Her research interests include alternative assessment, the perceptions of beginning teachers, and inclusion of children with special needs in the regular classroom.

S. Jim Campos is an elementary school principal in the Carpinteria Unified School District in Carpinteria, California. He received his Ph.D. from the University of California, Santa Barbara. He is the founder of the Carpinteria Preschool program, which has been recognized for excellence by the California State Department of Education, and the National Association of Bilingual Education (NABE). He has devoted much of his school career to improving the schooling of limited English proficient students.

Gustavo Carlo received his Ph.D. in Developmental Psychology from Arizona State University in 1994. Currently he is an assistant professor of psychology at the University of Nebraska—Lincoln. His major interests include social and personality development, particularly prosocial and moral development. Much of his research has focused on the socialization of, and the relations among, moral cognitions, emotions, and behaviors. His publications have appeared in *Developmental Psychology, Child Development,* and *Journal of Personality and Social Psychology.*

Patricia A. Edwards is a professor of teacher education and a senior researcher in the National Center for Teacher Learning at Michigan State University. She has developed two nationally acclaimed family literacy programs: *Parents as Partners in Reading: A Family Literacy Training Program* and *Talking Your Way to Literacy: A Program to Help Nonreading Parents Prepare Their Children for Reading.* Her research focuses on issues related to families and children: parent involvement and teacher thinking, parent involvement in the reading/writing process, parent support of children's oral preparation for literacy, portfolio instructional conversations with parents during regularly scheduled parent–teacher conferences, and parents' stories of literacy and teachers' reactions to these stories. Recent publications include a book chapter "Responses of Teachers and African-American Mothers to a Book Reading Intervention Program" in D.K. Dickinson, *Bridges to Literacy: Children, Families, and Schools* (Blackwell, 1994), and an article, "Before and After School Desegregation: African-American Parents' Involvement in Schools in Educational Policy" (1993). Significant honors include being selected as a recipient of the International Reading Association's Elva Knight Research Award, a Spencer Foundation Research Grant, one of six recipients of the 1993–1994 Michigan State University Teacher Scholar Award, an invitation to serve on the 1994–1995 National Advisory Board for Sesame Street, and invited by the United Nations Educational, Scientific, and Cultural Organization (UNESCO) to participate in the First Work Symposium on Family Literacy in Paris, 1994.

Kathleen L. Fear is an assistant professor and Chair of the Education Department at Albion College, where she directs the elementary and secondary program and teaches a three-course literacy sequence. She works with her students and teachers as the director of two research projects, "Restructuring Teacher Education through Collaborative Partnerships," funded by the U.S. Department of Education's Fund for the Improvement of Postsecondary Education, and "Environmental Problem Solving in Lansing: Michigan Americorp," funded through the Michigan Service Commission. Her research in literacy instruction with researchers from Michigan State University was made possible by the Partnership for New Education and the National Center for Research on Teacher Learning.

Margaret A. Gallego is on leave from her position as an assistant professor of teacher education at Michigan State University. She is interested in how out-of-school learning can create better understanding and reform of in-school education. Her teaching focuses on community school connections, language diversity and literacy, and equity education. Her research has included the use of technology in preparing teachers and in teaching culturally and linguistically diverse children. Currently she is working on the Distributed Literacy Consortium at the University of San Diego as the projects' language and culture evaluation liaison. In this position Dr. Gallego is studying the effects of curriculum adaptation on children's literacy development across four research sites which vary in their approach to adaptation.

Dr. **Eugene E. García** is formerly the Director of the Office of Bilingual Education and Minority Languages Affairs of the U.S. Department of Education in Washington, DC. He is currently the Dean of the school of Education at the University of California at Berkeley. He earned his B.A. in Psychology from the University of Kansas. He has published extensively in the areas of language teaching and bilingual development authoring and/or co-authoring some 100 journal articles and book chapters along with seven book-length volumes. His most recent research is in the areas of language and education as they relate to linguistically and culturally diverse children and families.

Fred Genesee received his Ph.D. in Psychology at McGill University where he is currently a professor of psychology. He has conducted extensive research on alternative forms of bilingual education, including immersion, in Canada and the U.S. He is the author of *Learning Through Two Languages: Studies of Immersion and Bilingual Education* (Newbury House, 1987); *Educating Second Language Children* (Cambridge University Press, 1994); and *Classroom-Based Evaluation in Second Language Education* (Cambridge University Press, in press). His current research interests include simultaneous acquisition of two languages, learning to read a second language, and speech perception in bilingual children and adults.

Celia Genishi, a former secondary Spanish and preschool teacher, is Professor of Education in the Program in Early Childhood and Chairperson of the Department of Curriculum and Teaching at Teachers College, Columbia University. She is co-author (with Anne Haas Dyson) of *Language Assessment in the Early Years* (Ablex) and author of articles about children's language, observation, and assessment. She is interested in alternative assessment, childhood bilingualism, and language use in classrooms.

Rachel Grant is an assistant professor at the University of Maryland at College Park. She completed her Ph.D. and postdoctoral studies in curriculum and instruction, with a focus in reading and literacy education, at the University of Maryland. She has taught secondary classes in Washington, DC, and has served as an education specialist and curriculum coordinator for programs serving underprepared multicultural college students. Her current research is with the National Reading Research Center (NRRC) a consortium of the University of Georgia and the University of Maryland. Dr. Grant's work appears in the *Journal of Reading*, the *Reading Teacher*, and *Reading Research and Instruction*. She is the editor of a research highlights column for NRRC that appears in *Reading Today*.

Paul E. Heckman holds a doctorate in curriculum and the study of schooling from the University of California at Los Angeles. He is Associate Professor in Teaching and Teacher Education in the College of Education at the University of Arizona. He is also Principal Investigator of the Educational and Community Change Project, a foundation-funded effort to study conditions that enhance or deter the education of poor children of color whose first language is not English. His professional and research interests focus on schools and educational restructuring.

David R. Imig is a professor of family and child ecology at Michigan State University. He received his doctorate in child and family sciences in 1971, from Michigan State University, with a major in marriage and family therapy. Imig's research has focused on development, extension, and operationalization of family systems theory and unified family process theory, with particular emphasis on family paradigms. As a consequence of this interest, Imig has devoted time to developing an innovative methodology and instrument for assessing the diverse and complex paradigmatic configurations represented by contemporary family systems (the Family Regime Assessment Scale—FRAS). Imig is also the co-principle investigator of a project entitled Family's Strategies for Rural Children at Risk: Race and Community Comparisons. In addition to teaching graduate and undergraduate courses in family studies, Imig was the 1991 recipient of the Excellence in Teaching Award from the University of Missouri at Columbia.

George P. Knight completed his Ph.D. in Social/Developmental Psychology at the University of California at Riverside and then became an Assistant Professor at the University of Arizona. He is currently a Professor of Psychology and Director of the Graduate Program in Developmental Psychology at Arizona State University in Tempe. He is a member of the editorial boards for *Child Development* and the *Merrill-Palmer Quarterly*, and has been a member of the editorial boards for the *Personality and Social Psychology Bulletin* and Volume 15 (Social Development) of the *Review of Personality and Social Psychology*. He and Dr. Bernal have published two edited volumes—*Ethnic Identity: Formation and Transmission among Hispanics and Other Minorities* (SUNY Press, 1993) and *Ethnic Identity and Psychological Adaptation* (*Hispanic Journal of Behavioral Sciences*, special issue, 1991). His research interests encompass a broad range of topic within social development including the development and socialization of ethnic identity, crosscultural development, the development of prosocial and cooperative behavioral styles, developmental social cognition, and research and statistical methods.

Marjorie J. Kostelnik is a professor and chairperson of family and child ecology at Michigan State University. She received both her master's degree (1976) and doctorate (1978) in human development and family studies from the Pennsylvania State University. Specializing in children's social development and early childhood education, Dr. Kostelnik's background includes teaching, evaluating, and consulting experiences with a variety of elementary school, nursery school, child care, and government programs for children in the United States and abroad. She teaches graduate and undergraduate courses in child guidance, curriculum development, and program evaluation. Her scholarly activities center around writing textbooks and articles as well as developing training materials for professionals in the field. Dr. Kostelnik was recently elected vice-president of the National Association for the Education of Young Children. In 1993, she was chosen as the Michigan State University Senior Council Outstanding Faculty Member of the Year.

Barry McLaughlin obtained his Ph.D. from Harvard University and is Professor in the Program in Experimental Psychology at the University of California, Santa Cruz. His research interests include second language acquisition in adults and children. He has published *Second Language Acquisition in Childhood*, 2 volumes (Lawrence Erlbaum Associates, 1984–1985) and *Theories of Second Language Learning* (Arnold Publishers, 1987). He has also published numerous articles on second language learning and bilingualism and is currently Director of the National Center for Research on Cultural Diversity and Second Language Learning.

Elena Nicoladis is a doctoral student in the psychology department at McGill University.

Olivia N. Saracho is Professor of Education in the Department of Curriculum and Instruction at the University of Maryland. She completed her Ph.D. in early childhood education at the University of Illinois in 1978. Prior to that, she taught Head Start, preschool, kindergarten, and elementary classes in Brownsville, Texas, and was Director of the Child Development Associate Program at Pan American University. Her current research and writing are in the areas of cognitive style, academic learning, and teacher education in relation to early childhood education.

Dr. Saracho's most recent books are *Right From the Start* with Bernard Spodek (Allyn & Bacon, 1994); *Dealing with Individual Differences in the Early Childhood Classroom* with Bernard Spodek (Longman, 1994); *Early Childhood Teacher Education: An International Perspective*, edited with Roy Evans (Gordon & Breach); *Professionalism and the Early Childhood Practitioner*, edited with Bernard Spodek and Donald J. Peters (Teachers College Press, 1988); and *Foundations of Early Childhood Education* (Prentice-Hall, 1987, 1991) with Bernard Spodek and Michael J Davis. Dr. Saracho is co-editor of the *Yearbook in Early Childhood Education*.

Karen Shu-Minutoli is an international consultant and staff trainer in Latin America and the United States. She received her doctorate in special education from Teachers College, Columbia University. For 18 years, Dr. Shu-Minutoli has worked in special and regular education as a teacher, administrator, staff trainer, and consultant. She has worked with children and adults with all types of disabilities and within numerous settings. Dr. Shu-Minutoli's special interests include autism, severe disabilities, functional skills programming, vocational education, supportive employment, program design and development, family support, cultural diversity, and international special education. She is a senior program consultant for Sullivan Diagnostic Treatment Center in Harris, New York as well as several agencies in Latin America. In addition, Dr. Shu-Minutoli is an adjunct special education professor for Mount Saint Mary College in Newburgh, New York. She teaches a graduate course on working sensitively with culturally diverse families with disabled children. Dr. Shu-Minutoli currently resides in Santiago, Chile.

Howard L. Smith conducts research on issues of literacy in bilingual contexts. He directed the American School of Pachuca, Mexico, from 1986–1989. A translator and bilingual educator, he worked with the Educational and Community Change Project from 1990–1994. Presently, he is the editorial assistant for the *Bilingual Research Journal* of the National Association for Bilingual Educators, while completing his dissertation at the University of Arizona.

Bernard Spodek is Professor of Early Childhood Education at the University of Illinois. He received his doctorate in early childhood education from Teachers College, Columbia University, then joined the faculty of the University of Wisconsin at Milwaukee. He has taught nursery, kindergarten, and elementary classes. His research and scholarly interests are in the areas of curriculum, teaching, and teacher education in early childhood education.

Dr. Spodek has lectured extensively in the United States and abroad. He was President of the National Association for the Education of Young Children from 1976–1978, and chair of the Early Education and Child Development Special Interest Group of the American Educational Research Association from 1981–1983.

Dr. Spodek's most recent books are *Right From the Start* (Allyn & Bacon, 1994) and *Dealing with Individual Differences in the Early Childhood Classroom* (Longman, 1994), both with Olivia N. Saracho; *Foundations of Early Childhood Education* (Prentice-Hall, 1987, 1991) with Olivia N. Saracho and Michael J. Davis; *Today's Kindergarten: Exploring Its Knowledge Base, Expanding Its Curriculum* (Teachers College Press, 1986); and *Professionalism and the Early Childhood Practitioner,* edited with Olivia N. Saracho and Donald J. Peters (Teachers College Press, 1988).

Bernard Spodek is co-editor with Olivia N. Saracho of the Yearbook in Early Childhood Education. He is also editor of the *Handbook of Research on the Education of Young Children* (Macmillan, 1993).

Francisco A. Villarruel is an assistant professor of family and child ecology at Michigan State University. He received his master's degree in assisted computer learning and language in 1987 and his doctorate in child and family studies in 1990, both from the University of Wisconsin at Madison. Dr. Villarruel teaches graduate and undergraduate courses in human development and community services and conducts research about Hispanic adolescents and families. He has also been awarded a W. K. Kellogg Foundation National Fellowship to study community and economic development related to NAFTA, and a Lilly Fellowship to develop a paperless class. Villarruel is also an active volunteer with Lansing's Cristo Rey Community Center, serving as a tutor and consultant for an afterschool program. He is on the board of directors and leads the program committee for the Center.

Index

Acosta, A., 91
African Americans and African American students
and diverse families, 104–106, 112, 118–119, 127, 129
and family support, 127, 129
and parental roles, xxi, 141–143, 145–147, 150–151
stereotyping of, 112
and teacher education, 160
Allington, R. L., 107
Allison, K. W., 112
Almy, M., 55, 155, 165
Anderson, J. A., 107
Anderson, P., 34
Anderson, P. P., 126–130
Anderson, T. Z., 106
Anglin, J. M., 25
Anzaldúa, G., 72–73
Arnberg, L., 22
Asians, family support and, 126–127, 134
Aspira of New York, Inc. v. Board of Education, 144
Au, K. H., 10
Auerbach, E. R., 147

Baca Zinn, M., 112
Baker, K. A., 34
Bandura, A., 94, 96–97
Banks, J. A., 159, 161–162
Barbour, N. H., 107
Barrett, F. L., 15
Barrows-Chesterfield, K., 52
Basic interpersonal communicative skills (BICS), 7–8
Baumrind, D., 108
Bayard, M. P., 85, 89–91
Bell, D., xiv
Bell, D. C., 117
Ben-Zeev, S., 23
Bereavement, family structures and, 113–114
Bergman, C. R., 20
Berk, L., 158–159
Bernal, Martha E., xx–xxi, 85–102
Bernhardt, E. B., 2, 9

Berning, A. L., 87
Berns, R. M., 110
Berry, J. W., 93
Bialystok, E., 23
Bilingual Education Act, 4, 143–144
Bilingual education and bilingual education programs. *See also* Carpinteria Preschool program
and assessment of bilingual children, 50, 52, 59–61
and conflicts between Mexican American and English-dominant students, 72, 76–77, 79–81
and future challenge of linguistic and cultural diversity, 172–173
and meeting needs of SLLs, 4–5, 7–8, 15
and parental roles, 144–145
preparing teachers for, 145, 154–169
selected standardized tests used for placement in, 59–61
Bilingual school and preschool children, 58–59.
and Carpinteria Preschool program, xx, 34–36, 38–47
classroom implications of, 9–12, 29–30
code mixing in, 19–21, 25, 172
and cooperative learning, 13–14
and defining cultural contexts, xi–xii, xiv–xv
and demographic shifts, 1, 15
developmental milestones in, 21–24
dimensions of, 2–9
importance of, 15
and instructional practices, 12–15
and LEA, 14–15
and meeting challenge of linguistic and cultural diversity, xv–xix, xxii, 170–173
meeting needs of, xix, 1–17
overextensions of, 25
proficiency of, xix, 3–9, 18–33
and recognizing importance of culture, 9–10
situation-specific language preferences of, 24